JESUS' HEALING WORK
AND OURS

Ian Cowie

WILD GOOSE PUBLICATIONS

First published 2000 by

Wild Goose Publications
Unit 16, Six Harmony Row, Glasgow G51 3BA

Wild Goose Publications is the publishing division of the
Iona Community. Scottish Charity No. SCO03794.
Limited Company Reg. No. SCO96243.

ISBN 1 901557 27 8

Cover design © 2000 David Gregson
Photograph © 1995 PhotoDisk, Inc.

A catalogue record for this book is available from the British Library.

Distributed in Australia by Willow Connection Pty Ltd,

Unit 4A, 3-9 Kenneth Road, Manly Vale, NSW 2093, Australia.

Permission to reproduce any part of this work in Australia
or New Zealand should be sought from Willow Connection.

Printed by Bell & Bain, Thornliebank, Glasgow

ACKNOWLEDGEMENTS

Thanks to John McCall, the Rev. Irene and Duncan Gillespie, and the Rev.
Robin Anker-Peterson who read and commented on the first draft of this book.
Thanks also to John and Ann Sutherland at Straitway Computing for their help
in preparing the typescript.

CONTENTS

PREFACE

Three types of people might put this book down quickly, without bothering to see what is inside:

1. **Churchy folk** I can imagine them saying: 'Not those old stories! I've heard them all before. You've just got to have faith, haven't you? That's all there is to it.' Familiarity has bred contempt.

2. **Non-churchy people** They have heard about Jesus' miracles, but have always taken it for granted that these fitted in somewhere between Santa Claus and Peter Pan, perhaps with a touch of archaic Superman thrown in. They would certainly think that they had more to do than to read something about 'old legends' such as these.

3. **Rationalistic Christians** These are people who are sincere followers of Jesus but, in order to make the Gospel more acceptable to modern people, have tried to weed out the 'supernatural' element. It really is surprising how ingenious they are at explaining away the miracles. Yet all the time they are trying to point to Jesus. It is also surprising how hostile they become when somebody does take the healing miracles seriously. They cannot see the dark, mysterious and wonderfully beautiful depths of the wood for the intellectual trees.

Even if you do fall into one of these categories, you might be surprised. Give it a try!

The seekers

On the other hand there are people who are open-minded seekers, who do not begin with an axe to grind or a point to prove. These will probably find it best to plunge straight in. Never mind the rest of this Introduction for the moment, but take one account of a miracle at random further on in this book, see the sort of thing being said, and then decide whether or not it is worth your while to read through the whole book. If the story which you have read rings bells, then we will explore the whole topic together, and if it does not, then save time and money.

A confession

Let me say straight away that I too have been in the first category mentioned above. I know the feeling of boredom which descends when, for example, somebody in church reads out the story of Jairus' daughter yet again.

I, too, have been in the position of thinking that all this miracle stuff belonged to childhood and I had grown out of it, while still paying lip-service to Christian morality, saying: 'I believe in the Sermon on the Mount but not in all the miracles stuff.'

I, too, have read many books and heard many lectures that tried to explain away the 'supernatural' element in the Gospels in order to make them fit into the so-called 'scientific outlook'.

However, after forty-odd years of ministry, during which I was constantly brought face to face with human need and suffering, I found myself coming back to these accounts and seeing them in a new light. I still keep being surprised by new light and new truth breaking through when I read them in detail, looking at what the Gospel writers actually wrote instead of accepting the English versions.[1]

If after all this time I am still finding new treasure buried in familiar soil, perhaps you too can begin to dig in order to find some for yourself.

If you, too, are attracted by Jesus, however stumblingly you are following him, I am sure that you will find new light breaking in. He will show you new things as you think about his Word, just as he keeps showing me new things.

He may show you something quite different from what he has shown me, and your understanding of his works may turn out to be far better than mine. I would never argue my version against anybody else's, because we all see different things at different stages in our spiritual growth. All that I can do is to set out as clearly as possible whatever truth has been shown to me, allowing that others may see different aspects. Then we have to listen to each other carefully, and leave the issue to God.

Who is 'us'?

In the course of working this book out, I naturally refer to people who came to us. That usually refers to the Christian Fellowship of Healing in Edinburgh. We worked on a 'drop-in' basis, with prayer, fellowship and the sacraments available.

---

[1] In fact, even as I was writing this, I was thrilled at finding new treasure in one story which I had never previously explored.

INTRODUCTION

Wonders, works, signs

If you have whetted your appetite by sneaking an advance look at one or two of the stories, perhaps you can be patient enough to tackle one big problem. To sum it up let me ask you a riddle:

> *Q. When is a miracle not 'a miracle'?*
> *A. The answer: When the supernatural is natural.*

What is a miracle then?

In answering this question we shall have to look at what the Gospel writers actually wrote in the language they used: Greek.

It's a wonder! First of all they sometimes use a word *teras* which really means: 'Something that makes you wonder', which is to say 'a miracle'. Let us use the word 'wonder' instead of 'miracle', in order to get at the true meaning. This word, however, is not the only one used to describe Jesus' healings. It is certainly not the most usual word, for Jesus never healed in order to 'show off'. In fact in the story of his temptations we see that he was tempted to use wonders to gain power over people, but refused to do so. As we shall see, he met this temptation again and again when he was called on to heal.

Signs of life! The word that Jesus often uses himself is *semeion*, a sign, for each healing is a sign pointing to an important truth about God, and to an important lesson about the human condition. In fact we often find the words 'signs and wonders' together in the Gospels, stressing that the wonderful things were done as signs pointing beyond themselves. Jesus was never just a healer.

Reading this book will have been a waste of time if, having read it, you are merely convinced that Jesus did heal. In fact Jesus himself lamented that people did not 'see the signs', but just gawped at the wonders.[2] We, then, have to see beyond the wonders to understand what they are pointing to, so finding a new relationship with God and a new vision of what our own lives are about.

---

[2] In some translations, e.g. the New International, the word 'miraculous' is inserted wherever the word 'sign' comes in. This is just the translator's whim, and should be ignored. It misses the point.

The working man

Ergon is another Greek word which is often used, meaning *work*. This emphasises the fact that healing requires effort, struggle and skill. Too often, in a mistaken attempt to glorify Jesus, preachers have suggested that 'because he was God he could do whatever he liked'. A recent film on TV showed Jesus just reaching out with a touch and healing happening effortlessly.

Yet this quite undoes his true glory, which was that he became truly 'one of us', and in Philippians 2 Paul stresses that his true glory was in emptying himself of all that was not truly human, meeting us on our own level. His healings were *erga, works* – hard work!

Man or superman?

Or put it another way: I could admire, but not love and respect, a superman who could do what he liked effortlessly. However somebody who faces human suffering with the same equipment as I have, and yet who can heal at great cost to himself, wins my devotion.

Therefore it is important to see, as we study his healing work, that it was far more costly and complicated than we usually think. There was far more to it than a cursory reading would suggest, and certainly more than some of the film versions of the Gospel story portray. No wonder he usually used the word 'work', for that is what it was, often leaving him exhausted, so that on one occasion, for example, he fell asleep in the uncomfortable stern of a boat.

Giving us the works

As he was summing it all up at the Last Supper he said: 'The works that I do, you shall do also.' This underlines the fact that what he did, he did as a true human being, a true 'Son of Man', and therefore his healings were the sign of what is truly *natural* for the children of God. It is we who are sub-natural, not the miracles which are supernatural. He wanted us to share his true humanity, to discover our true heritage as the children of God. *Jesus fulfils the hidden potential in the universe, so that both the 'laws of nature' and 'human nature' reach their fulfilment.*

Laws of nature

Whatever popular ideas may suggest, there is no justification for saying that 'miracles' break the laws of nature. If you read John chapter 1 you will see that we live in a consistent universe, in which God cannot be inconsistent. Therefore we see Jesus' works as signs that hitherto-neglected resources are being called into action. The laws of nature or, to be more specific, God's designs for the universe are being fulfilled at last in Jesus, and it is to be hoped through his followers. *In Jesus we see WONDERS, because we see SIGNS of what should be natural WORK for God's children.* Now perhaps the riddle is clear?

Healing, salvation and therapy

As we go through we shall be noting that there are different words for healing. Those who are interested in the finer details may find it interesting to pause here to look at these words. Do not hesitate to skip this section if this sort of thing does not interest you.

Therapy

The Greek word *therapeuo* is the one most commonly used to refer to the activity of Jesus and of his disciples. It refers to the activity of a doctor or healer. It might be translated *treatment*, or just *therapy.* The verb would be *to treat.* I have used 'treat' where this verb is used.

Cure

Another word, *iama*, referred to a cure. The doctor *treats* so that the person is *cured.*

Made whole

We find the word *sozo* in two interesting places. To the woman who was *cured* of her haemorrhage, Jesus said, 'Your faith has *healed you.'* To the woman who had been a 'bad woman' but who washed his feet with her tears of penitence, Jesus said, 'Your faith has saved you.' But in the Greek he says the same to both women. *Saved/healed* are not two different things for the Gospel writers although they seem to be for us. We think of *saved* as being 'religious' and *healed* as being 'medical'. However, what we call 'salvation' and what we call 'health' were the same words in Jesus' language. Perhaps being 'made whole' would be the best translation (Chs. 4, 21). In fact, going back a step, in Hebrew the equivalent word is the basis for Jesus' Own Name, Ye-Shua (with the emphasis on the 'shu'), *God saves/heals.* There is much to think about there.

Some explanations

Before going further we must look at some of the terms which might puzzle those who are new to the Bible. Those familiar with the Bible may wish to skip this section. You have probably heard it all before. Many however have not.

The Christ

The Jews had expected *the King* (Christos in Greek, Messiah in Hebrew, both meaning 'anointed', i.e. to be king) to come to set them free, establishing the Kingdom of God upon earth, either like David, by force of arms, or else by superhuman means. They had expected that when this king-figure came, his first act would be to purge Israel of its 'rubbish', all those who had not kept the *Law of Moses* properly. Since most people thought that if you were ill it was because God was angry with you, the sick did not think they had much chance!

The great compassion of Jesus, reaching out to the sick and to the sinners, was therefore the very opposite of what people had expected. He was not calling the good, the fit, the clever, but was focusing on the very people who seemed like 'rubbish'. There is enough dynamite in this alone to blow up a lot of churchianity!

The Gospels

The stories about Jesus are to be found in four 'books'… they were once four separate scrolls. These were eventually brought together, selected from a number of other Jesus stories as the most reliable and tacked on to the Jewish Holy Books. Various other bits of Christian writing were selected and added, for instance St Paul's letters, and together, by about 150 AD, the selection we know came to be regarded as 'the Bible' by Christians.

How did it happen?

St Mark wrote his Gospel after Peter and Paul had been executed in 68 AD, putting down what Peter used to say. He had been Peter's secretary, and realised that there were by then few people who had been eyewitnesses. That was about thirty years after the Cross (as I write, 'the sixties' do not seem far away). Matthew and Luke followed up soon after that, and John wrote his about 90 AD. So the Gospels were circulating while people could remember Jesus.

Of course the stories had been passed around both in writing and orally before 'Mark and co' began to write them down. We have to remember that people who have not been subject to modern education have much better memories then we have, passing down stories and songs, word for word, over centuries, in a way we would find impossible.

Even today there are some people left in these islands, usually among gypsies and tinkers, who spend an evening listening to a story-teller chant a story lasting for hours. This has often been handed on, word for word, from the middle ages.

These four accounts, then, were copied out by hand century after century, sometimes with minor differences creeping in. When printing was invented 'chapters and verses' were included to help readers find their way.

Herodians

The Romans had set up puppet rulers whose family name was Herod, who had in turn developed courtiers, more Greek in culture than Hebrew. One can well imagine how people felt about these aristocrats who claimed to be fellow-countrymen, but whose real loyalty was to other aristocrats in the Empire. (The King Herod of Christmas fame was long since dead and his sons each had part of his kingdom during Jesus' adult life.)

Pharisees

As Jewish society became more and more exposed to Gentile ways of thinking, there was naturally a movement towards keeping their national life free from foreign taint. We see this in Islamic societies today. A strict observance of all the rules marked out a Jew as 'a person apart', and this movement for 'apartness' was called 'Pharisee', 'Apart-people'. They believed that the national life should be kept morally pure in order to be ready for the long-awaited Kingdom of God, and for the King who would introduce it. In many ways they were very fine people.

Priests

The Jewish priesthood was hereditary, and the high priestly families were aristocratic, compromising with the Romans, in order to be allowed to keep the Temple going. They dreaded the thought of an armed uprising, knowing that it would endanger the delicate balance which they had worked out with the Romans. These 'Sadducees' did not agree with much that the Pharisees taught.

Both Pharisees and Sadducees thought that they were leading people in God's Name, but as so often happens the rules, rituals and theologies which get such people excited mean nothing down at the grass-roots. They only make life more difficult by imposing an ever-growing list of 'thou shalts' and 'thou shalt nots'. Moral exhortations did nothing for the peasants, heavily taxed, crippled with debts to absentee landlords, many of whom were Pharisees. On top of all that, they had to cope with the fear of Zealots (see next paragraph) threatening them if they did not supply and hide them, and with the fear of what the Romans would do if they did.

Zealots

More extreme than the Pharisees were the Zealots, who had become terrorists, living in the hills, robbing travellers, blackmailing villagers, murdering any whom they thought were collaborating with the Romans. As with many terrorist/nationalist movements today, they were more of a problem to their own people than to the enemy.

The Sabbath

If, as you read on, you are puzzled as to why Jesus kept on getting into trouble with the Pharisees for healing on the Sabbath, the reason is that shut shops and resting farms marked out Jews from other nations. National pride and religious observance had become mixed up, and that is always disastrous.

Of course there is, in the Ten Commandments, the command to keep the Sabbath. But the religious experts had gone beyond the Bible and had books which they respected almost as much. These laid down in detail what 'keeping the Sabbath' meant, working out what you could and could not do. For instance, if someone was bleeding to death on the Sabbath, you were allowed to staunch the flow (that counted as saving life) but you must not do more, for that would be healing, and that was *work*. Religious pride and legalism had turned a day of rest into a burden, in spite of the protest in Isaiah 58.

A day's rest for all... great idea!

Let us look more closely at what had gone wrong. The command to have a day's rest a week is very much concerned with health and healing. In Deuteronomy it is set within the context: 'You Jews were once slaves in Egypt, being worked to death, seven days a week. You must never do that to anybody else.' In Exodus there is another slant: a day's rest a week is part of the basic pattern of Creation, and to ignore it is to get out of kilter with Creation.

Getting it wrong

How terrible that the beautiful healing compassion which had given rise to the Sabbath had been distorted by pride and legalism until it became a hindrance to healing. Nevertheless we must not forget that Exodus 31:14 lays down death by stoning for Sabbath-breakers.[3]

The structure of this book

Having settled what we mean by 'miracle' and sorted out some of the puzzling words which we will come across, let us get down to the process of looking at each of the stories about Jesus healing people. Each story is arranged so that:

The story is told

I have translated the stories from the Greek in which they were written down. I have tried to stick to translating the actual words, even if it does not read well in English. Sometimes the jerky style gets ironed out by translators, losing the freshness of the Gospels, but making it more acceptable to modern readers.

Where there are accounts of the same work in more than one Gospel, I use whichever account seems to me to be nearest to what actually happened, for instance choosing the one which gives the little details which tell us that the person who told the story was there. That is usually St Mark's account.

Notes

Next there are notes about the translation which are more technical. Skip these if you are not interested in that sort of thing. But if you wonder why I have put something different from what is in your Bible, then you can check it. For those who study more deeply, these notes are perhaps more important.

Then we come on to study the healing work itself, with a look at the *background* against which it took place, Then we look at the *initiative*. Was it the person who asked for healing or was it Jesus who chose to do it? *How Jesus set about it* then follows, noting the various things he did. We then ask *'And how about us?'* trying to see what the relevance is for our ministry today. Each story ends with a *conclusion* summing up the main points that have emerged in our study of that work.

The problem for ministers

Many ministers, in their training in Biblical Criticism, have been taught to see all sorts of problems in these stories of how Jesus healed. The result is that when they think and preach about them, about the last thing which comes through is that the healings actually happened.

Even the more conservative approach tends to see them only as illustrative

---

[3] Footnote For further information on life in Jesus' day, see *The Upside Down Kingdom*, Donald Kraybill, or the novel *the Shadow of the Galileean* (Theissen SCM Press)

material; for instance, when the Gospel speaks of how Jesus healed the blind man, the more conservative brethren are not interested in what he actually did and how he went about it, but rather they go on at length about how he 'opened our eyes to see the truth'. While the conservative commentaries then claim to believe it all literally, they actually fail to take the story seriously, using it only to boost some theological point.

My aim in all this, therefore, is

- *to break the familiarity-barrier of 'the faithful',*
- *to make the stories more credible to the newcomer,*
- *and to deepen the devotion of us all.*

What matters is THE STORY, and the person, Jesus, who 'comes alive' as we read that story.

Section One

Healing works in the Gospels

THE CALL

We begin by looking at an incident early in the story of Jesus and his disciples. The scene opens with a summary of what he had been doing in the early part of his ministry, and then we see how he began the business of delegating his work to ordinary humans – and eventually to *us*.

We see very clearly that Jesus never came to do a solo act, a 'look at me' show. He came in order to pass on what he was doing, to delegate his Authority to ordinary people.

This, of course, goes right back to the very first book in the Bible, in which God delegates his care for this planet to human beings (Genesis 1:26).

> *Delegation is the name of the game,*
> *from the very beginning.*
> *It still is.*

THE CALL (Matthew 9:35–10:1)

And Jesus did a tour of the villages and towns, teaching in their synagogues, and proclaiming the Good News of the Kingdom, and healing every illness and disease.

Seeing the crowds he was filled with compassion for them, because they were troubled and crushed, like sheep without a shepherd.

Then he said to the disciples: 'What a great harvest, but how few the harvesters! So pray to 'The Lord of the Harvest' for more workers to work his Harvest.'

Then calling out the twelve disciples, he gave them authority over unclean spirits, to expel them, and to heal every illness and disease.

Notes

Disciple
This word originally meant a trainee, somebody with L-plates. It certainly does not mean somebody extra-holy, who, so to speak, is a better driver than other people. Far from it. As the story unfolds that will become painfully obvious. Thank goodness!

For reasons which will become obvious as we go on through the book, notice that Jesus gave the disciples *exousia* (authority) to heal and exorcise, not *dunamis* (power).

Evangel
Evangel is a word which appears here, and I have translated it as *good news*. It is a word which had a very different meaning for people in those days. If some poor wretch had fallen out of favour with the Emperor he might be banished to some remote place, such as Scotland, or sent to the salt mines. However, if the Emperor relented, then he might send an *Evangelion*, giving the poor man permission to return home and resume his full citizenship.

It was this word that the Christians took over to summarise the message which they brought to the world. We translate it into English as *gospel* or *evangel*.

In modern speech, however, the words 'evangelistic' and 'Gospel' have taken on a very different meaning. We must get back to using them as they were meant to be used, to say: '*... free at last!*'

The Kingdom of Heaven/of God
The three first Gospels all sum up Jesus' mission as being to proclaim the arrival of the long-awaited Kingdom of God.

The term 'Kingdom of Heaven' does not mean what we normally mean by 'heaven'. Jesus speaks of it as being here, right now, on earth. So we look more carefully at this term.

The word translated as *kingdom* means *rule*. The Greek word does not mean a place, but *sovereignty*. We could express Jesus' message in graffiti-like style as: 'God rules OK.'

Kingdom?
Think of the situation in these islands about five hundred years ago. There was Queen Elizabeth I of England. There was Mary Queen of Scots. The English saw a kingdom as being an area. The Scots saw a kingdom as being people. Those are very different ideas about sovereignty, and it is the Scots one which comes nearest to the Biblical view, so the Kingdom of Heaven is not 'a place' but a people.

Of heaven?
Mark, Luke and John all refer to 'the Kingdom of God', while Matthew refers to 'the Kingdom of the skies'. We usually re-phrase that as 'the Kingdom of Heaven'. Why is Matthew different? Because Jews hold the Name of God in such awe that they avoid using it, even in worship, and Matthew's approach is very Jewish. So the terms Kingdom of God and Kingdom of Heaven both refer to the same thing, and neither is what we usually mean when we say

'heaven'. Jesus' parables try to explain what *he* meant by these terms. They enable us to see what Jesus means when he refers to healing as being a *sign* that the Kingdom is present in *him, here and now.*

That being so, *'Thy Kingdom come'* is not a pious hope for the future, but an invitation to God to come on in and reign in us now. The sign that *God rules* is that we do what he wants us to do. *'Thy will be done'* = *'Do what you want with us now, on earth.'* If we really meant what we said, we might see 'more signs of the Kingdom'!

Repent

As the result of this good news people were asked to repent. In some English versions it is expressed as 'repent of their sins'. The Greek word is *metanoia* which means to change your mind, to rethink. Most of Jesus' parables begin with the phrase 'The Kingdom of God is like…' That is because he was trying to get them to drop their idea of a nationalistic Empire, to be achieved through conquest, and see another picture altogether. He was not the sort of Christ who would bring in the sort of kingdom they were expecting and praying for. They were going to have to do a lot of rethinking.

All good news makes you rethink. If you win the lottery you have to do a lot of rethinking; in fact your whole life changes. If someone says, 'I love you,' or if a new baby comes along, you have to rethink. Rethinking in the light of such good news is a wonderful thing, very different from the usual idea of repentance. Equally, if you get the Good News that Jesus brought you will have to rethink your whole life. It is not a matter of delving into the past to dig up all the sordid details. That often becomes most unhealthy. Of course for some people discovering the Good News makes them realise how shabby their past lives have been. Yet for others, who have always assumed that they were nobodies and worthless failures, it means the very opposite.

Most of us have things in the past of which we are ashamed, things we regret. We can only face them truly when we know that God forgives and can redeem the situation and turn it to the good. Many preachers seem to think that you must 'repent' first and *then* hear the Good News. That is putting the cart before the horse. The Good News comes first. Then you can rethink what your life is about. Then you can work it out in practice.

Twelve

Now that we have gone into what some of the words actually mean, we can move on to the story itself. It seems that Jesus at one point gathered twelve of his followers and formed them into a special core group, which we know as 'the Twelve'. This was really the start of the Church.

He started the Church, then, because the needs of suffering humanity were too great even for him to cope with single-handed. What is more, it is clear that the whole healing ministry of Jesus springs from his compassion for the poor and the suffering. He passes on his Authority to the Twelve, and through them to all who will respond to his Word: us.

Authority

We have to be very clear that Jesus called the Church into being to meet the needs of the suffering masses, not to dominate them or to make money out of them. We have authority to heal, deliver and bless people, to spread the good news, not to boss them. (Sadly the Church has often forgotten that, becoming a power-seeking organisation. When she does so, she ceases to have Jesus' Authority to heal.)

Only those who are ruled by Christ's compassion can truly share his healing ministry. The moment we become power-seeking we have fallen.

The men with L-plates

He called people whose experience had come through sharing the life of the poor, through hard, dangerous work, like fishing, and through struggling with the problems of the market place. He did not choose people with academic qualifications, and his training of the Twelve from this point on was not academic. (See *The Twelve Together*, Ralph Morton, published by the Iona Community but now out of print.)

St John tells us in the first chapter of his Gospel that Jesus gathered the first four 'learners' at John the Baptiser's revival meetings in the south. Andrew and John seem to have been with John the Baptiser, and to have brought their brothers to meet Jesus. John and James were cousins of Jesus, their mother being his mother's sister (John19:25). Two more joined him on the long walk back to Galilee. They then returned to their jobs. Matthew, Mark and Luke tell us that some time later Jesus came back and called the first four from their boats to come with him on a tour of Galilee, picking up Matthew Levi at about the same time. The others seem to have gathered slowly. We know very little about them, although St John gives us one or two glimpses of Philip and Thomas.

The story we have just read tells of how Jesus took these 'followers' a step further, welding them into an actual team of 'disciples' sharing his work. It was, then, an important step which would have been a turning point, for the very fact of making a selection of twelve would tell any Jew who knew his Bible that Jesus meant business.

Motives

As we think of the call of those first 'learners' we naturally think about what we are being called to do today. There is a general interest in 'healing', and people think it would be wonderful to be 'a healer'. Yet Jesus did not offer to teach them how to be healers, but rather how to proclaim the Gospel of the Kingdom.

We shall see how he constantly drew back from 'being a healer'. His healing flowed from his response to the realities which he saw around him. It is his answer to 'the problem of suffering'. His main concern, however, was with the human sin which lay behind the whole problem of suffering humanity.

The problem of suffering

We today can take one of two lines in response to 'the problem of suffering':

1. *There is so much suffering in the world that I can't believe that God is love.*
2. *There is so much suffering in the world that, because God is love, nothing matters in life other than becoming a channel of God's healing, forgiving, redeeming Love.*

If you take the first line, you can give up the struggle, and you need do very little about the suffering in the world until it reaches *you*. If you take the second line, then you have to give up a lot of what society thinks of as 'success', and you have to take the Jesus road.

What if you do take the line of responding positively to Jesus?

You may, of course, find yourself becoming 'a healer', but you may equally find yourself, like Mother Teresa, doing the dirty work of caring for those who are discarded by society.

You may imagine yourself setting up a 'healing home' in a beautiful house in the country with people coming for healing and peace, but in fact you may find yourself in a housing scheme up to the eyes in protesting about what society is doing to the people there.

Jesus himself found that he was facing real temptation to misuse his powers, and anybody who starts on the same line will face the same temptations. There are many spiritual casualties among those who embark on 'healing' at any level, medical or spiritual. They tend to become 'little gods' instead of Christ-like people, 'playing at God' instead of being children of God. Or to put it another way: there is a world of difference, an eternity of difference, between *the person who wants to be a healer and the person who, following Jesus, has dedicated his/her life to focusing the Love of God on the sin and suffering of humanity in whatever way he/she seems called.*

The problem is that people in the first category probably *think* that they come into the second, and people who begin in the second can slip without noticing it into the first. Lord, have mercy on us all, mixed up folk that we are.

And as far as the Church is concerned, that first group of twelve was called into existence by Jesus to be the people through whom he could reach out to the mass of suffering humanity, and through whom he could make known the fact that there is forgiveness, cleansing and reconciliation for any who respond.

The Church today exists for the same purpose. As Archbishop William Temple pointed out, the Church is the only organisation which exists for the benefit of those who are *not* in it. Our function is to make it clear that our Father's 'Welcome home, child' awaits any who respond to the good news (Gospel) of God's love in Jesus. People may or may not find physical healing in the process. We hope and trust that they will, but healing remains a secondary concern. Where 'healing' moves up into top priority, trouble is never far away.

Introducing SIN AND SICKNESS

As a minister visits the sick, the dying and their families, no question comes up as often as this one:

> *What have I done to deserve this?*

The fact that people ask this so often shows that they have the feeling that the universe should be organised on a reward and punishment basis. Time and time again we find that life does not work out like that, but the feeling persists that it *ought* to run that way. It is just as well that it does not! (I am always uneasy about people who are sure that if life *did* work on a reward and punishment basis, they would come out on the profit side.)

Yet obviously there *is* some connection between sin and disease, and between right-living and health. In fact, modern medical research shows that there is a link between health and right attitudes, between sickness and stress.

We are therefore going to look at three of Jesus' healing works which raise the question of the connection between sin and disease.

1. The paralytic boy

Mark 2:1–12 (Matthew 9:1–8, Luke 5:17–26)

Coming into Capernaum again, after a day or two, word got round that he was at home.

In no time a crowd gathered. Indeed there were so many that there was no room to fit them all in, not even around the door. And he spoke the Word to them.

And so four men came, carrying a paralytic to him.

But because of the crowd they could not get near him, so they uncovered the roof over where he was, and, having broken through, they let down the bed-roll on which the paralytic was lying.

Seeing their faith, he said to the paralytic: 'Lad, your sins are forgiven.'

Now, some of the biblical scholars who were sitting there were reasoning to themselves: 'Who is he to speak like this? Blasphemy!' 'Who but God can forgive sins?'

Jesus knew perfectly well how their thoughts were running, and said to them:

'Why are you thinking like that? Which is it easier to say to the paralytic: 'Your sins are forgiven' or 'Get up, pick up your kip and walk'? To show you that the Son of Man does have Authority on earth to forgive sins'... He said to the paralytic: 'I say to you: Get up. Take your kip and away home with you.'

Immediately he got up, picked up his bed-roll and out he went before them all, to their astonishment. They glorified God saying, 'We've never seen the like.'

Notes

Kip

I have used a slang word for 'bed-roll' because St Mark does so.

Matt. 9:1–8 tells the same story, but without the detail about the roof. He too uses the word for a young man, but uses a polite word for the bed-roll.

In Luke 5:17–26 the story is the same. 'Tiles' are mentioned and the paralytic is just 'a man'. The polite word for bed-roll is used.

We wonder why Matthew and Luke use a polite word. Perhaps, even by the time Luke was writing, people did not quite like the idea of the Lord speaking slang.

We will, however, come across more evidence that Jesus spoke 'everyday' language, not formal Aramaic, far less formal Hebrew.

Modern films always have trouble here: Peter and the other disciples usually have 'accents', like real fishermen, but Jesus is always made to speak 'posh'.

At verse 17 Luke has the phrase 'and the power of the Lord was there to cure them'. This is one of the few times when the medical word for *cure* is used, not the usual word for 'heal'.

Then, too, it says 'to heal them' when no mention has been made of people present for healing, only of the theological critics. A number of English versions insert 'the sick' to make more sense of it, but those words are not there in the Greek

It is an intriguing phrase, for it comes before the man has been mentioned.

St Mark says that Jesus spoke *the Word* to them, using the same term as does St John in chapter 1 of his Gospel: *Logos*. It means not so much the sound you make with your mouth, but what you really mean deep down, as in 'I give you my word'.

Finally, a word on style: St Mark keeps using the word for *and*, like a breathless child telling a story. The other two Gospel writers tidy this up, and I have toned it down a bit. We will find this right through the book...it would not get good marks in an exam, but I have tried to keep the feel of what is there.

Background

Houses

As we read this story, and a number of others, we must not think of houses as being like ours. If you have been in the Mediterranean areas, off the tourist track, you will have seen them still today much as they were 2,000 years ago. A house begins like a shoe-box, made out of branches and sun-baked mud-bricks, perhaps seven or eight feet high. Over the front door there is usually a rough roof, often of bamboo, with a vine growing through it. This projects towards the street and it is under this that most of the family life takes place.

When a son gets married, a wing is added and the house becomes L-shaped. Then another wing is added, and it becomes U-shaped. At this point they often build a wall across, so that it encloses the yard, the patio. Meals and meetings usually take place in this patio under the roof with the vine.

So we can imagine such a yard, with Jesus and the elders under the sunroof. The boy would only be just out of reach when they began to lower him. It all seems so natural when you actually think of the houses of simple working folk in that area, although it seems fantastic to people who imagine it happening in a modern bungalow.

Now another point: If a holy man or some other itinerant had become a welcome guest, it was common to build a booth on the flat roof with stairs up to it, so that he could come and go at will. Getting on to the roof would therefore present little problem – the steps would be there already. It seems likely that either Simon Peter or the family of James and John had done this, for St Mark uses language that indicates that Jesus 'was at home' there. Matthew 4:13 is even more explicit.

The patient

We have already noted that it was a young man. Certainly his physical illness had a root in his feeling of guilt.

We need not assume that the boy had done something awful. We today often have to face people who have grown up under parents who were obsessively religious, and who gave their children the paralysing feeling that they could never do anything right, or live up to the high standards which they thought God required. This false guilt is very hard to tackle, and not many of us have been able to free somebody from such an upbringing as quickly as Jesus did, if, as I suspect, this was the case in this story.

The initiative

We do not know what the lad was thinking about all this, but the people who brought him and who were desperate enough to break in on such an occasion had the sort of faith which was the vital link. The initiative therefore lies with the friends or family who brought him.

How Jesus went about it 'no questions asked'

You will notice that Jesus does not ask the boy to confess, nor does he probe into his past.

By contrast, I remember one minister who said that he would never lay hands on anyone who had not first confessed and received absolution. I also remember a very distinguished preacher saying: 'Jesus always said, "Thy sins be forgiven thee," before he healed.'

Both were quite unscriptural. This the *only* occasion on which we are told that he began by facing guilt.

He healed this lad by his Word of Authority. There is no sign of touch or of any other physical action. As the lad makes his way home, the bed-roll over his shoulder, there is no suggestion in the text of a follow-up from Jesus.

And for us today?

On the strength of this story, we must not assume that, if a person comes for healing, we should always probe into the background in order to extract a confession.

CONCLUSIONS

- In some cases illness is indeed caused by feelings of guilt.
- This does not mean that the person has been particularly sinful.
- In some cases the assurance of forgiveness must precede healing.
- This is the *only* case recorded in which Jesus referred to forgiveness before he healed.
- Jesus did not lay hands on the boy.
- The faith of friends and family may play an important part in healing a person.

---

2. BLIND FROM BIRTH

John 9:1–38

*Passing by, he saw a man, blind from birth, and the disciples asked him:
'Rabbi, who sinned, this man or his parents, that he was born blind?'*

*Jesus answered: 'It is neither that this man sinned nor his parents. But in
order that the works of God may be revealed in him, we must get on with the
work of the One who sent me while it is daylight. Night is coming when nobody
can work. While in the world, I am the Light of the World.'*

*Having said this, he spat on the ground, making a paste with spittle, and
put it on the man's eyes, saying to him: 'Go and wash in the Pool of Siloam.'
(The name means* sent.)

He went and washed and came away seeing.

Notes

Now we are going to have to face some hard thinking about the Bible. All
translations known to me translate Jesus' response as being that the poor man
was born blind so that Jesus could do a miracle on him. Many of us find that
idea repulsive. So let us look at what St John actually wrote. I am going to put
the Greek words into English exactly as they stand: *Neither this man sinned
nor the parents of him but in order that be revealed the works of the God in
him we must to work the works of the one who sent me while the day it is.* You
will notice that there is no punctuation, because there was none when St John
wrote. It has been put in by translators comparatively recently. So conventional
scholars punctuate it like this: *Neither this man sinned nor the parents of him
(comma), but in order that be revealed the works of the God in him (full stop).
We must to work the works of the one who sent me while the day it is.* They
then make it into a more readable sentence, and some even add the words 'he
was born blind so that' before the comma, making it into: 'He was born blind
so that the works of God might be revealed in him.' In other words, so that
Jesus might do a miracle on him. But that is not 'what the Bible says' even if
some English versions say so.

So let us be clear that St John does not tell us that Jesus said that 'he was
born blind so that' he (Jesus) could do a miracle on him. The great Bible
scholar Campbell Morgan pointed out that you can punctuate it rather differently: *Neither this man sinned nor the parents his (full stop). But in order that*

be revealed the works of the God in him (comma), we must to work the works of the one who sent me while the day it is. It is this latter version that I have used in my telling of the story. It boils down to: 'Never mind the speculations as to who sinned – that is nothing to do with it. If the glory of God is to be seen in this situation I must get on with the work I have been given: *healing.*' Or, as they used to teach us in the army: 'Obey first, ask questions afterwards.'

Background

Begging was almost the only way the blind could earn a living, and we know from other sources that there were crowds of such blind crying out for alms.

The patient

The disciples see the man as a problem. They ask the usual *why?* Only too often we also are so taken up with wanting to know the reason why somebody is ill that we cannot get on with the practicalities.

I remember a much respected minister saying in a sermon: 'One of the things in my ministry which still pains me is the memory of a man who, I realised as he left the manse, had come to me for comfort, and I had tried to give him an explanation.'

Sometimes when we look back we do see reasons and understand why, but confronted with human suffering we have to put the questions aside and get down to the work of bringing as much of the love of God to bear on the situation as our measure of faith, hope and love will allow.

The initiative

It is Jesus himself who takes the initiative in this case. There is no indication that the man had faith or had heard Jesus preach. The disciples do not ask Jesus to heal him, only pose the question. So the initiative for the healing lies with Jesus.

How Jesus went about it

First, notice our Lord's thoughtfulness. To have given someone their sight in the full glare of the sunlight would have been cruel. The mud-packs he put on would have been protection for the new growth, and the long walk would give time in which the healing could 'take'. The Pool of Siloam is a dark grotto, an ideal place in which to begin to use the new eyes, especially on a quiet day such as the Sabbath.

The conventional Bible commentators tend to emphasise that there is a degree of suggestion in the making of the mud-packs, and that the long walk to the Pool was just 'a test of faith'. I do not believe for one moment that Jesus 'played games' with people in this way. There was a good reason for both the mud-packs and the grotto.

In this case there was no 'Word of Authority' such as 'Receive your sight' as there was with Bartimaeus (Ch. 22). Nor is the laying-on of hands mentioned, although it is mentioned in the story of the blind man in Bethsaida (Ch. 11).

Of course, Jesus must have touched him while putting on the mud-pack, and his spittle *was* in the mud, but still he did not apparently lay hands on the man.

The use of spittle is something we shall come across again later. It is not something that many of us are familiar with today.

Consequences

If we were making up a story, we would tell how amazed everybody was and how they all wanted to become disciples. Life is not like that! We have known many cases of people who were healed in a wonderful way, but when they went back to their congregations they were met with hostility, just as in the case we are looking at here. It is only too true to life.

Follow-up

We see an interesting detail here. This story tells us something never mentioned in the first three Gospels: Jesus follows up the healing.

There are only two other cases in which he is recorded as having done so: the paralysed man (Ch. 3) and Lazarus (Ch. 24), both these cases being in St John's Gospel.

The first three Gospels seem to suggest that each work was a one-off event. Yet in three out of the four healings in St John's Gospel we find Jesus in contact with the person later. As so often, St John puts in quietly what the others have left out. This is yet another pointer to the fact that his healing ministry was a lot more costly than might appear from the usual reading of the Gospels. We thought of this also when we looked at *erga – works.*

The Son of Man

Jesus here, as in the last healing we looked at, refers to himself as 'the Son of

Man', and that is puzzling to us, as it was to those concerned. It can mean just 'the human being', son of Adam...MacAdam. In the book of Ezekiel it is used to emphasise the frail mortality of the prophet. But it had also come to mean the heavenly representative of humanity, as in Daniel 7.

Jesus' use of this phrase has always puzzled people. It was, however, the way in which he tended to refer to himself in the context of healing, perhaps to emphasise that what he did, he did as a true human being, as we thought earlier when we looked at 'works'. Many of us were taught to see his healing as the sign of his Divinity. He saw it as the sign of his true humanity: *the* Son of Man!

We come back to the point that Jesus' life is a sign of the real potential in humanity, when that humanity is filled by the Holy Spirit. It is humanity as God meant us to be.

Reincarnation

One final point before we move on: Notice that one of the questions was whether the man had done something before he was born to merit punishment by blindness. Some people have suggested that one can sin in the womb...a bit far-fetched. But reincarnation was a common belief – even the great theologian Origen seems to have held it – and surely that was what was being referred to when the disciples asked if he was born blind because of some sin he had committed before birth. Jesus specifically denies its relevance in this case.

One final point: the man gets into trouble because it was the Sabbath. (Remember what we said in Explanations about the Sabbath.) The full story is well worth reading as the streetwise beggar ties the clever priests in knots, and the parents lie in their teeth to avoid trouble. It is very true to life.

CONCLUSIONS

- Jesus deliberately and specifically denies that the blindness is caused by the patient's sin, in this or in a previous life...
- We should never assume that we have to deal with sin *before* we deal with illness.
- If we are ministering to deaf or blind people, we have to be sure that they are in a quiet place or one with dim lighting. A public service is not a good place for such work.
- We must not wait until we understand the mystery of suffering before we get on with the work which God has given us to do.

3. 'SIN NO MORE'

St John 5:1–15

After this there was a Jewish Festival and Jesus went up to Jerusalem for it.
Now at Jerusalem there is a pool beside the Sheep Gate, called Bethesda in Hebrew, and it has five colonnades. In these there lay a great crowd of people with various troubles: blind, lame and withered.
There was one man there who had been ill for thirty-eight years.
Jesus saw him lying there, and knew how long he had been in that state. He said to him: 'Do you want to be whole?'
The invalid answered: 'Sir, I haven't anybody to put me in the water when it is troubled. Somebody else always gets there first.'
Jesus said to him: 'Get up. Pick up your kip and walk!'
The man immediately became whole, took up his bed-roll and walked off.
Now that day was the Sabbath, so the Jews said to the man who had been healed: 'It's the Sabbath! You're not allowed to carry your kip.'
He replied: 'But it was the man who healed me who told me "Pick up your kip and and walk".'
They asked him: 'Who said "Pick up your kip and and walk"?'
Now the man who had been healed did not know who it had been, for Jesus had slipped away, into the crowd that was there.
Later Jesus tracked him down in the Temple and said: 'Now look...you have been healed. Do not go on sinning, or else you will get worse again.'

Notes

When St John wrote his Gospel he gave no explanation of the troubling of the waters, but a later scholar made a note in the margin to explain it, and often this note crept into the text. It is there in the King James Version, for instance. However most modern translations rightly put it back as a footnote.

Kip Once again we find Jesus using the slang word just as in Mark (Ch. 1).

Background

The scene is easily identifiable and can be seen today. In the north-east corner of the old city is a deep glen, its sides lined with masses of ruined masonry. Looking down into it one can still see the two rectangular pools at a slight angle, end to end with each other.

The pool nearest the old Sheep Gate was the Sheep Pool at which they washed the sheep being brought in to be sacrificed at the Temple. The other pool is the one which concerns us. It had arcades round it, providing shade. St John mentions five arcades, and the old Bible commentators made much of this mystical number, but St John was only reporting a fact: there were arcades on four sides of the Pool of Bethesda, and another which looked on to the Sheep Pool.

The shrine

On one side of the pool you can see the ruins of a little church built by the Crusaders long ago. That is not surprising. However the archaeologists found beneath it the ruins of a shrine to Serapis, the Greek god of healing, dating back to the year which by our reckoning was 82 BC. This *is* surprising. One would never have expected a pagan shrine in the Holy City. But there it is. It all ties in with the facts which we read in the Gospel.

Healing pools

One thing is certain – we cannot use this story, as some do, to support the idea of 'healing wells' and the like. Indeed the whole point of the story is precisely that Jesus ignored the belief. It does, however, remind us that there were many healers and healing shrines in those days as in ours, and the examples of how they operated are in stark contrast to Jesus' simple commands and actions.

A puzzle

The fascinating question arises: What was Jesus doing at a heathen shrine on the Sabbath? One person in our party when we visited the site pointed out that it is in a line between the house of Anna, his grandmother, and the Temple. Could he have been 'visiting his grannie' and taking a short-cut to the Temple?

The initiative

There is no sign of faith or of expectancy in the man. It was Jesus who picked him out, and set about healing him.

The patient

This healing is distinctive. *The patient does not know who Jesus is, has never heard him preach the Gospel, and does not have faithful friends to bring him to Jesus.*

There is no way that we can say that he had 'faith' in any sense of the word. He was obviously a weak character, as we can see from his response to the challenge of the authorities. It contrasts very strongly with the response of the blind beggar about whom we read in the last section.

His obedient response to Jesus' commands was far short of the 'faith' we saw in the four men who brought their young friend to Jesus, and made sure that they reached him. This man was entirely passive. What is more, he must have known perfectly well that by 'informing' he was getting 'whoever it was' into serious trouble. Indeed 'whoever it was' was liable to be stoned. In fact he was getting Jesus into trouble in order to to divert the condemnation away from himself. This is typical of the neurotic who does not thank you for making him/her face the truth. (I have heard sermons saying that he was noble and brave bearing witness to Jesus. That, however, is not how I understand it. The reader must decide which way it was!)

'Records'

Like most long-term invalids, this man had developed a sort of set-piece about his plight – a 'record'. They tend to play it over and over to anybody who will listen. From painful experience we know how difficult it is to break through the 'Pity Poor Me!' record. We are not Jesus.

The trouble with a 'record' is that the person has said it so often to themselves and to others that it has built up an emotional armour-plate. It always hides the real cause of the trouble. Therefore the person who tries to be a sympathetic listener will probably finish up exhausted, having wasted hours and hours for nothing. The groove has only worn a bit deeper.

When people settle for asking for pity instead of love, they are very hard to heal. If you ask for pity, that is what you will get until people are bored with it and pity is worthless.

Seek to give and receive love and help, and there is hope. Ask for pity and you get less and less.

How Jesus went about it

Jesus begins by cutting through the man's 'record', and 'goes for the jugular' – *the will to live.* He puts this challenging question to the man. Sometimes we have to do the same. For instance a very charming young woman, diagnosed as having cancer, came for healing. She also told her story of a broken marriage. In the end we asked her: 'Do you actually want to live?' She thought hard and said, 'No.' Of course no one would want the unpleasant treatment or the pain, but she had not the will to live, so there was not much we could do other than hope that our prayers would help her through her illness. Perhaps if she had come back to share in the Bible study and fellowship, she could have found something new to live for, as many others had done, but she did not.

'Not wanting to be ill' is one thing. Wanting to be healthy, taking your place in society, facing your problems, accepting responsibility for yourself and for others is another question.

Once a person's illness has become his/her identity, and once seeking treatment has become a way of life, real healing is not easy to give. We may try shock tactics, as Jesus did in this case, but even if this succeeds we may find that the person does not thank us for having brought them face-to-face with reality.

The healing

Once more, there is no laying-on of hands or any other recognised healing act, just 'the Word of Authority', once more spoken in down-to-earth words: 'On your feet!' As in the first case we looked at, Jesus then uses the slang word for the bed-roll.

The follow-up

This is the other case of a 'follow-up visit' to which we referred when thinking about the healing of the blind man (Ch. 2). Both these cases are unusual in three ways:

1. Jesus seems to have been totally unknown to the two men concerned.
2. The initiative lay entirely with Jesus; neither they nor their friends had asked for healing.
3. Both were long-term cases involving a lot of adjustment, and both led to trouble with the authorities. These may be the reasons for the follow-up.

The follow-up had another purpose: the credulity of these two men had to be changed into faith, but that is jumping ahead to the chapter in which we look at the meaning of 'faith'. As far as I can understand, real faith *was* sparked off in the blind man, but it did not work that way with the paralytic.

Sin no more

We are left wondering about the actual words *sin no more*. That is the usual translation. The more accurate translation suggests that it was a continuing 'sinning'... 'do not go on sinning'. In the case of our invalid we have to take in the fact that by Jewish law he was certainly breaking the first of the Ten Commandments by going for healing to such a shrine. It may well have been this that our Lord told him not to continue, in which case the sin to which Jesus referred was idolatry. If this was the case, however, it was not this which was at the root of the illness. It was rather that the sin had come about through his illness. We may puzzle about it, but there is no set answer. All we can say is that it looks as if sin and the illness were indeed linked in some way, and that the man had to make some readjustments in his life as part of his healing.

We certainly conclude from this that it is not Jesus-like always to *begin* by suggesting that there must be an inner cause for the illness. In many cases it is the healing which leads people to see that they have been living selfishly and godlessly. That is where ongoing teaching is needed *after* the healing.

To end on a positive note, at least Jesus found the man *in the Temple*, so perhaps something did get through after all.

And for us...

This case underlines something which we are going to see over and over again. The Love of God, in certain cases, takes the initiative through those who minister in Jesus' Name.

It is not always right to wait until people ask or come to a healing service. It is *this loving initiative* which shows the person how wrongly they have been living, not lecturing them. In fact if people feel that they are being 'got at', as if we were taking advantage of their plight to get our point across, they just put up the shutters, while a loving act or loving words sometimes enables them to open up.

Finally, this is the third 'work' in the course of which Jesus mentions sin. *There are no other cases.*

CONCLUSIONS

- Every illness and every healing is a learning situation.
- But that does not mean that we have to teach the lesson *before* healing.
- There are times when it is right to try to understand what lies behind the illness.
- There may be sin and/or wrong living at the root of an illness, but sometimes it can only be faced in the light of an experience of the love of God.
- There are cases in which we must take trouble to follow up the healing, and then look at the root of the illness.

Summary SIN AND SICKNESS

We have looked then, at the only three incidents in which there is a reference to sin in the process of healing. We have seen how utterly different our Lord's approach was in each case:

In Chapter 1, Jesus deals first with the guilt.
In Chapter 2, Jesus denies that sin has anything to do with the blindness.
In Chapter 3, Jesus deals with the sin after the man has been healed.

Remember that in no other record of his healing is there reference to sin. What is more, in many cases, as in these three, the people Jesus healed had never heard him preaching. They had not heard the call to repent! Remember too what we said in the chapter on *The Call* about repentance and its real meaning.

I have often heard it said that the healing took place in the setting of his proclaiming the Good News, and that he dealt with sin in that. These three stories make it quite clear that this was not the case.

We underestimate the whole revolutionary impact of Jesus if we do not see how shocking his approach must have been to the religious people of his time. They had expected, as we have noted, the Christ to come and rally the fit, strong men into an army, to summon the people who had been carefully keeping the Law of God, and to lead them all to victory. They thought illness was inflicted on us by God as punishment, and therefore was to be borne humbly. How bewildering it must have been to see Jesus spending so much of his time healing the sick, without much reference to sin and punishment.

Disgustingly healthy?

How does all this fit in with something most of us have noticed: old reprobates who have broken all the Ten Commandments are often nevertheless disgustingly healthy while devout Christians who have never (apparently) put a foot wrong are quite the opposite.

To understand this it would be good to take a quick look through the Sermon on the Mount (Matthew 5, 6 & 7). Or even a quick flick through St Mark's Gospel. Make a note of the things which the Lord warns us against. You will find that he did not 'go on about sin' in the way so many of his followers have done over the ages. 'Wine, women and song' hardly get a mention.

But he does hit hard when it comes to the love of money and its resulting 'worry'. He hits hard when it comes to the failure to forgive others who have hurt you. Above all he was concerned that at the heart of life there should be that loving trust in God which we call faith.

Now if you read even the simplest articles on health from a medical point of view, you will discover that tension (worry) and suppressed anger (resentment) are behind a lot of ill-health. Or to put it another way...the 'man on the make' will be more likely to have a heart attack than the old reprobate. The 'Christian' fuming at the wicked all around, full of self-righteous anger, is more likely to get arthritis than the people he or she criticises.

The medical profession is continually dishing out expensive medication to people whose real problem is that they have no basic loving trust, and so are either desperately trying to convince themselves and others that they 'are somebody', or else are grieving that they seem to be nobodies.

In other words, the things against which the Lord warns us are the same as those which modern medicine recognises as lying behind a lot of disease.

Living in sin?

Most people do not think that the love of money, keeping up with the Joneses, looking after number one and so on are sins. In fact the very reverse. We would not say that those who are ruthlessly and successfully climbing up the social ladder are 'living in sin'. Yet they *are*, more so than the couple who love one another and are living together, and who are referred to as 'living in sin'.

Therefore when we ask questions about the connection between sin and disease, we must take in what Jesus taught about how we should live in loving trust, and ignore the popular ideas of sin.

CONCLUSIONS

- Some sins do sometimes lead to some illnesses.
- Yet we cannot read it back the other way, concluding that if someone has a certain illness, then they must have committed such and such a sin, and that we must make them face this before being healed.
- We must approach each sufferer with an open mind. Open to the sufferer, open to God's guidance.

An example to think about

Sandy dropped dead down the mine, and his widow asked angrily through her tears why God had taken such a good man. He did not go boozing like the others, he was a good father to his three children – it did not seem fair. Yet after the funeral one of the men he worked beside commented that he was a funny bloke: he had to have a big 'fry' for his breakfast, he came to work with his 'piece' oozing fat, he had to have another fry for his tea and would send out for fish and chips before bed time. On such a diet, in what sense can we say that 'God took him unfairly'?

Introducing FAITH AND HEALING

'You've just got to have faith.' This sentence has probably done more harm to the Church than any other.

Sincere seekers, agonising over truth, have been put off by some complacent cleric mouthing this phrase, and have never returned. These are the very people who should have been the Church's pioneers in the things of the Spirit. Instead, they have been diverted into exploring areas which are often dangerous and frequently futile.

A passive acceptance of authority never makes any spiritual progress. It is far from the biblical idea of faith. That is why we are going to look now at the place of faith in the Lord's healing work.

In two of the cases so far (the blind man and the man at the Pool), it cannot be said that the people concerned had faith before the Lord met them. *It was the Lord who aroused faith in them.*

In Chapter 1 it is obvious that a person in a neurotic state, paralysed by guilt, cannot have faith. To say to a person who is depressed, guilt-ridden, or self-hating, 'You must have faith before you can be healed,' is as cruel as to say to someone with broken legs: 'You must walk to hospital before we can treat you.' For the boy let down from the roof it was the faith of others which was the entry-point, and it was the impact of Jesus upon the lad which awoke faith in him at last.

For people with guilt and depression, finding faith *is* healing. To say, 'You must have faith,' as a condition for healing is to mock their condition.

We look now at two instances of faith, very different from each other and from the faith involved in the cases in the foregoing section.

We also look at the opposite of faith.

4. THE WOMAN WITH HAEMORRHAGE

Mark 5:25–34 (Matthew 9:20–22, Luke 8:43–48)

There was a woman (in the crowd) who had been haemorrhaging for twelve years.

She had suffered much at the hands of many doctors, and had spent everything she had, yet was not getting better in fact she was getting worse.

Hearing what people said about Jesus, and coming up behind him in the crowd, she touched his clothes, for she said to herself: 'If I just touch his clothes, I shall be healed.'

Immediately she felt that the flow of her blood had been dried up, and felt in her body that she was cured from this trouble.

And Jesus, knowing in himself that power had gone out of him, turned round in the crowd and asked: 'Who touched my clothes?'

The disciples said: 'Look at the crowd jostling you…How can you ask who touched me?'

But he kept looking round to see who it was that had done this.

And the woman, afraid and trembling, knowing what had happened to her, came and bowed before him, telling him the whole truth.

However he said to her: 'Daughter, it is your faith that has healed you. Go in peace. Be healed of what has troubled you.'

Notes

Luke has 'the fringe of his gown', presumably the blue tassel which Jews were supposed to wear.

Background

Here, for the first time in this book, we come across somebody who approaches Jesus with something like 'faith'. We will have, however, to look more closely at this.

Unclean?

If you read Leviticus 15 you will see that a woman in this condition was considered ceremonially unclean, unfit to take part in social or religious activity. Anybody she touched became unclean until sunset, when they had to wash themselves and their clothing. Jewish women have this dinned into them, and it cannot have been easy for her to break through this barrier. To understand this, perhaps you have known people from the Western Isles of Scotland, and you will know how difficult it is for them to 'break the Sabbath' by, for instance, washing up. It was like that for women each month in the orthodox Jewish tradition – to break through their upbringing was not easy.

The patient

No doubt, if she had gone to the rabbi at the local synagogue, she would have been dealt with, as we have already noted in Chapter 1, on the basis of 'you must have done something to deserve this' and therefore the rabbi would have told her to repent, to have faith in God, to obey the rules in the Bible and to wait upon the Lord for healing.

From that point of view, seeking healing from the various 'healers' was lack of faith. She should have trusted in God alone according to their teaching. They would certainly have advised her not to have anything to do with this Jesus of Nazareth. 'Faith' does not always mean believing what the clerics tell you. Sometimes it leads you to challenge them.

The will to get better

No doubt she had tied herself in knots trying to do what they said, obeying the rules of the Bible, but got no better. She had had enough of them!

The initiative

So she took the step which they would have said was 'lack of faith', and which broke the rules laid down in Leviticus. She must have had a very strong 'will to get better', and that is something very important, as we saw in Chapter 3. Therefore she made the effort.

In her own village, where everybody knew everybody, they would have known that she was 'unclean' and she would never have been allowed to be part of the crowd. Only in a strange town could she mingle as she did. It is probable, then, that she had made quite a journey. Imagine what a struggle it must have been for her to push her way through the crowd. After all those years of haemorrhaging she must have been very weak. God knows where she got the strength to do it (or maybe God *did* know).

How Jesus went about it

This is the reverse of healings two and three. Jesus seems entirely passive to begin with.

Suggestion and healing

The fact that Jesus felt the power go from him points to several things:

1. True healing is when there is an objective flow of his life-energy from the healer to the healed.
2. The power of suggestion (faith healing) was not enough. It needed (a) an actual discharge of healing power, and (b) that Jesus should make himself known to her.
3. The healing did not depend on his conscious mind contacting hers. Healing operated at a deeper level than that.
4. The healing flowed *before* she had told him the whole story; in fact it unlocked the gate which enabled her to tell her story.

A lot of people in the ministry of healing today need to ponder these points.

The objective element

The story of an electrician who came with us to Iona demonstrates the objective nature of healing power. He was mainly concerned with the rebuilding of Iona Abbey, but during the healing service he found himself carried forward to the front and sharing in the laying-on of hands. Afterwards he came to me saying: 'What's all this? When I laid my hands on that woman's head I felt electricity. I am an electrician, and I know electricity. I don't understand all this holy stuff.' We explained as best we could, and through this he came to be a man of real faith who leads a healing service in his parish church each week, conducting a quiet but effective lay ministry.

This example confirms the point made above, that healing is objective, it is not subjective. It is very dangerous to use 'suggestion' in order to achieve immediate results. There may be serious relapses afterwards when the atmosphere has evaporated. I remember one minister who gave his son the laying-on of hands for earache. The pain went; the infection did not. It was almost fatal. That is the danger of using 'suggestion'.

We have to be careful, then, to distinguish between those who have a genuine healing gift, transmitting an objective, almost physical, energy and those who work up such an atmosphere that people are made suggestible.

Using suggestion is not in line with Jesus' work, nor is an insistence on coun-selling prior to healing.

We also have to be careful to distinguish between those who 'believe in healing' and those who have a deep trust in God through Jesus.

Faith and credulity

To take this point further, put it his way: the faith which Jesus sought was not the belief that he *could* heal, but a loving trust which came from knowing *him*: (faith). That is very different from credulity – allowing oneself to be conned by a powerful personality.

Deep healing

As St Paul was to say later, 'In Christ God was reconciling us to himself,' and therefore Jesus was not just a healer whose concern was removing symptoms. He had come to establish a new relationship between humanity and God. He could not, then, be satisfied with an anonymous woman being healed by a healer whom she did not know. She had to come to know him personally – that is to say she had to find a loving trust in God through Jesus.

Finally note three things:

1. How graciously he gives *her* the credit for her healing, not 'chalking up another success' for himself. This must have come as a great surprise to the poor soul, who would have been expecting rebuke for having made him and many others 'unclean'.

2. *Jesus and the Law* People on the spot must have been shocked. He ignored the fact that according to Leviticus he was now unfit for any religious activ-ity, and continued on his way to Jairus' house. He should have stayed apart until sunset and then washed himself and his clothes. The laws and regu-lations of the Old Testament were laid down for the good of humanity. As he commented with regard to the Command to observe the Sabbath, it 'was made for humanity, not humanity for the Sabbath' (Mark 2:27). Jesus was responding to something higher than the Law of Moses, and so appeared to be in breach of that Law.

3. Jesus waited, urgent though his errand was, until the woman had faced him, shared with him, and could be sent on her way in peace. Without his assur-ance, she would probably have become ill again through guilt at having broken the biblical rules.

CONCLUSIONS

- It is not enough to believe that Jesus *can* heal. His concern is far deeper.
- There is an objective element in healing, independent of the emotional and intellectual aspects.
- We must be careful not to be bound by regulations in the Old Testament where they conflict with love and compassion.
- Sometimes the right time for speaking about Jesus and about the cause of the trouble is *after* the physical healing has taken place.
- Beware of healing services in which there is an emphasis on believing that healing is possible, i.e. on 'suggestion' (faith healing).

5. THE SERGEANT-MAJOR

Luke 7:2-10 (Matthew 8:5-13)

There was (in Capernaum) a centurion who had a servant who meant a lot to him and who was ill and dying. Hearing about Jesus he (the centurion) sent some of the Jewish elders asking him to come and heal the servant.

They duly came to Jesus and pleaded with him sincerely, saying: 'This man is worthy of being granted this request, for he loves our nation and has had a synagogue built for us.'

So Jesus went with them, but was not far from the house when the centurion sent friends saying: 'Sir, don't trouble yourself, for I am not fit for such as you to come under my roof. That is why I did not come to you in person. Just give the order and my servant will be healed.

'I myself am a man under authority, with soldiers under me. I say to one, "Go," and he goes, to another, "Come," and he comes. I say to my servant, "Do this," and he does it.'

Hearing this Jesus marvelled at him. He turned round and said to the people following him: 'I tell you...I have not found faith like that, not even in Israel.'

Then those who had been sent went back to the house and found that the servant was well.

Notes

I have taken the Luke version, since it contains matter that seems to come from direct memory. The beginning of the story in Luke is quite different from that in Matthew.

One of the differences between the two accounts is that Luke refers to 'the slave' whereas Matthew has *pais*, meaning 'boy'. This word is like the Gaelic *gille*, which means 'boy', but if you come to the Scottish Highlands to shoot or fish and ask for a *gillie* to help you, you may not find yourself with a boy! He may be older than you. Therefore in the story it could have been a boy or a slave-servant.

Matthew has Jesus' response as: 'Go! As you believe, so be it.' He makes a lot more of the lack of faith among the Jews.

Background

Remember that Palestine was an occupied country and that the Roman soldiers were the occupying army – the enemy. If you helped them you were a collaborator, liable to get a knife in your back.

The suppliant

This sergeant-major (that is what a centurion was – unlike the officers, he had risen through the ranks) must have weighed up Jesus carefully and formed his own opinion of him. It would be part of his job to know who might cause trouble locally, and possible 'messiahs' always caused trouble. We do not know whether he was going by intelligence reports or whether he had personally investigated Jesus.

We wonder whether having a synagogue built was just an astute move to 'win hearts and minds', or whether the man had come to admire the Jewish belief, as many in the Roman Empire did.

A man's faith

The centurion's faith is quite different from any we have seen so far. The nearest we have come to this is the faith of the men who let the lad down through the roof, but we know nothing about them.

The patient

As in that case there is no word of the sick person having faith. Indeed, if a person is delirious or semi-conscious, as seems to have been the case here, it is impossible to exercise conscious faith.

The initiative

Here it is quite clearly the Roman who took it on behalf of the 'boy'.

How Jesus went about it

He responded without hesitation, setting out for the house. That itself is a problem, for if the sergeant-major had lived in the town, the Zealots would have made short work of him. Married quarters maybe? Wherever it was, it was considered defiling for a Jew to enter a Gentile's house, since all Gentiles were considered 'unclean'. That is why the man did not expect Jesus to respond by coming to the house, and was taken aback when he seemed to be about to do so. As in the previous story, Jesus appears to disregard religious ideas about 'uncleanness'.

The healing

We note that, according to Matthew, once again it was Jesus' Word of Authority' which healed. There was no laying-on of hands, and there was none of the 'joukery pokery' which healers in those days usually employed. Jesus sends the messengers on their way, but his message is in the singular: 'as thou believest', making it clear that it is one man's faith which has counted.

Faith and consciousness

Note that we keep whatever level of 'faith, hope and love' we have *before* the brain mechanism is interfered with by illness. It is active beneath the confused ramblings or lapses of consciousness, and is responsive to prayer. Many who have regained consciousness have told us that they were aware of prayer when apparently unaware of anything else. Jesus' effect on the slave did not depend on consciousness.

In his own terms

The centurion expresses his faith in terms of his own job, not making any religious allusions. His was not the faith that Jesus was Son of God – the words 'son of a god' would have meant something very different to a man whose background was Greek-Roman religion. They had many stories, for instance, of sons begotten by Zeus from mortal women. These 'sons' were then pursued and hounded by the god's jealous wife.

Nor could he have had faith that Jesus was the Christ/Messiah, for if he had believed that Jesus was such, then the appropriate action would be to call out the troops. Faith for him was recognising true authority, a deep recognition of something which words could not convey. He saw beyond 'the carpenter of Nazareth' to the Authority.

We must not demand that people express their faith in *our* terms, and we must respond positively to people who cry out for help in surprising ways.

Checklist?

Jesus' response was immediate. Many people today in the healing ministry would have first submitted the poor man to a checklist to make sure that he did not have any idols in the house (one would expect such a man to have his 'household gods'), did not deal with astrology, etc. They would perhaps have queried his profession, since it involved sacrificing to the Emperor as a god. *There is no sign of any such probing on the part of Jesus.*

Finding faith in strange places

Many today, like the centurion, have a gut feeling about Jesus, but would not be happy expressing it in terms which conventional Christians would recognise. If those who claim to be Christian appear to be 'on guard' against them and are negative about their insights, then such seekers may never come nearer. If on the other hand we go out to meet them gladly, we may find that they teach us something. In fact we may find ourselves admiring the way they have come through some crisis, saying, 'I have not found such faith even among "Christians".' In point of fact, when we do take that line, they usually come to see what we mean by the more conventional terms. *Faith in Jesus does not necessarily begin by accepting 'received doctrine'. From whatever our starting point, we discover the faith while following Jesus.*

Asking for prayer on behalf of others

A genuine concern for another may justify our asking the Church or some group to pray for somebody, just as the sergeant-major asked the elders of the synagogue to approach Jesus. Nevertheless one has to beware of people who, 'at the drop of a hat', will ask for prayer for anybody they know who is ill. We must hesitate for three reasons, even though on this occasion Jesus did not:

1. Such requests are sometimes intrusive.
2. People and organisations with 'prayer lists' can be swamped with such requests.
3. Often putting somebody on a prayer list is an inadequate response to the sufferer's need and deeper spiritual treatment is needed.

CONCLUSIONS

- Faith is not the acceptance of doctrine but a response to the *person* of Jesus.
- Where we have a genuine concern, we may exercise faith on behalf of somebody who is not in a position to exercise their own faith.

May we be open enough to respond positively when we find surprising faith in surprising people.

6. Disbelief

Mark 6:1–6 (Matthew 13:55–58, Luke 4:16–30)

He came away from there and came to his own country, and the disciples with him. And on the Sabbath he began to teach in the synagogue. And many of those hearing were astonished, saying: 'Where does he get it from? What is this wisdom that is given to him? How come that such powerful acts come from him? Isn't he just the carpenter? The son of Mary and brother of Jacob and Joseph, Judah and Simon? And aren't his sisters here with us?'

So they were offended at him. So Jesus said: 'A prophet is not without honour except in his own country, among his own kith and kin.'

And he could not do any mighty works there, apart from laying hands on one or two sick people and healing them.

Notes

I have assumed, for the purposes of the story, that all three Gospels refer to the same visit. One cannot be sure whether this is so. Matthew's is obviously a shortened version, while Luke's gives us what may just be a longer version, including the text upon which Jesus' sermon was based, and the attempt to lynch him follows.

In St John's and in St Luke's versions the local people refer to him as 'son of Joseph the Carpenter', whereas in St Matthew's and St Mark's he is referred to as 'son of Mary'. It is unusual for a man to be referred to as son of his mother and we therefore assume that Joseph had died.

'Carpenter' is not a good translation of Jesus' trade. The old term 'wright' would suit better, but we no longer use it. Scholars still discuss what the term meant, but it does seem to suggest that in terms of social status he was not near the bottom of the ladder.

The last verse is literally 'not powered to do any...'.

Background

Family

Some Christians find it hard to believe that Mary and Joseph went on to have at least six more children. However, Matthew tells us that Joseph 'knew her not' until after Jesus had been born (1:25), which suggests that after his birth he *did* 'know her'. Moreover, he refers to Jesus as her *firstborn* which suggests that he was not the only child. Roman Catholics, however, find this unacceptable. They say that 'his brothers and sisters' were actually cousins, or Joseph's by a previous marriage. It is possible. One has to make up one's own mind.

Lack of faith?

Now we have the other side of faith: the neighbours and family knew very well that Jesus had performed miracles (John 7:2–5). In fact they challenged him to do among them the works that he had done in Capernaum (Luke 4:23). Yet it says that he *could not* do any great works there because of their unbelief. This is the 'other side' of what we noted when we looked at the woman with the haemorrhage: Faith is not just a case of believing that healing can happen, but it is a loving trust in the *person* of Jesus.

They *knew* that Jesus had performed miracles, but their *attitude* insulated them from his power.

Neighbours and family

The adverse comments of neighbours and family are scattered through the four Gospels. Apart from those mentioned at the head of this section, we find them also in John 6:42 and 7:15.

Such sneering dismissal of Jesus would not have been invented for propaganda purposes. After all, James, the Lord's brother, is referred to in Acts as the leader of the Church in Jerusalem. They would hardly have made up a story which shows him in such a bad light! We take it therefore that it actually happened like this.

It would also indicate that Jesus' life up to that point had not been anything out of the ordinary. He had begun by identifying himself with ordinary people, becoming truly 'one of us', the breadwinner for a large family in difficult times. The theories that he studied in Egypt, Tibet and Britain do not fit in with the rather unpleasant facts recorded here.

Could not?

Matthew and Mark both record that Jesus *could not* do any mighty works there. It was not that he needed a sympathetic atmosphere in which to work, for, as we shall see later, on occasions he healed people in the teeth of opposition. We wonder why, then, he could not do much.

Almighty?

This troubles people who want an 'almighty' God and an 'almighty' Jesus who can do anything. Yet the Gospels make it quite clear that the divine power is limited by human response, and in this case 'Almighty God' in Jesus could do little. I once asked a Hebrew-speaking minister what the words *Al Shaddai* really meant. This is the Name of God which is usually translated as *'The Almighty'*. His reply was: *'The God of Sufficient Strength'*. Very different! The idea of almightyness has to be rethought. There are situations in which God can do very little, *because God is Love.*

God's POWER is always subject to God's LOVE; therefore where the Love is rejected, the Power is limited.

How he went about it

The laying-on of hands Here, for the first time we find the laying-on of hands mentioned, although in a rather dismissive way. No details are given, so we cannot learn very much from this. We will, however, look at it again later. Matthew just has that 'he did not do many "powers" (*dynameis*) there'.

And for us?

Perhaps one can come nearer to understanding why Jesus could do little, if one realises that still today the most difficult setting in which to work is the 'churchy' atmosphere of those who think they know it all, and who resent any interruption of their routine. It is the very people who have grown up with Jesus, and have him safely pigeon-holed, who most resent anything which suggests that *here and now* a new understanding of the Bible and of the Church is called for *today, for them.*

In St Luke's version, that is just what Jesus did. He was not speaking about the heroes of old, nor of the dream of the future ideal world, which is what they would have expected. He spoke of the here and now, and of radical changes that were needed right then, on the spot. That was what led to the lynching.

Still today a lot of congregations prefer a God who is safely in the past, wrapped up in the 'old, old story', or safely in the future of the 'second coming', or in the next life.

Suggest that today something is happening *here and now* in your midst which is going to upset your routine, and there is trouble!

Real faith means always breaking new ground, leading us on to new things, and opening up new possibilities. This is set out wonderfully in Hebrews 11 – it leads Abraham out 'not knowing where he was going'; it leads Gideon and others to tackle impossible odds, and so on. What cuts off the divine power-supply is the superior 'we know it all' attitude. Real faith is always adventurous.

The opposite of faith, then, is not intellectual doubt as to whether God *can* heal physical illness; rather it is 'cutting God down to size' to fit our little ideas, accepting only what our little minds can understand, and resenting the Jesus who calls on us to change our ideas of Church life and to expand our consciousness.

CONCLUSIONS

- They knew that Jesus *could* heal, but their resistance to change insulated them from the healing that was there for them.
- The safety of well-established religious beliefs and practices may encourage complacency, not faith.
- We should never be concerned primarily with convincing people that healing in the Name of Jesus is possible.

Summary FAITH AND HEALING

What then is faith?

The instances at which we have looked so far have certainly made us question a lot of ideas about faith. It is clearly not just 'believing that Jesus can heal'.

In the cases of the blind man, the paralysed man at the pool, and the woman who touched him in the crowd, Jesus was careful to make sure that they did not just see him as a healer. In each case he spoke to them after the healing to make sure that their faith was not just in a 'man with a magic touch'.

In the first two cases, the men had no previous knowledge of Jesus as far as we can make out. Their faith grew out of his dealings with them.

By contrast the centurion, we assume, had observed Jesus carefully, while Jesus' neighbours knew him only too well.

We seek uniformity in vain. There is no one way to faith.

Real and artificial faith

It is, then, very important, especially for those responsible for healing services, to see the difference between the sort of faith which Jesus seeks and the mere belief that healings are possible. The telling of stories involving previous healings can increase the belief that the 'healer' concerned *can* heal: credulity. That, however, is not the point.

Once more we stress: *Creating an emotional atmosphere of suggestibility is not the same as awakening real faith.*

Real faith

Real faith is a response of loving trust to the Love of God in Jesus. It depends on the graciousness of God breaking through to contact the human soul. God is always the one to take the first step, even if we think that we have made the first move. The Church's function is so to re-tell the story that a clear picture of Jesus emerges, inspiring faith.

Having said that, perhaps it would be better for us to use the word *trust*, for that suggests a person-to-person relationship rather than intellectual acceptance.

We began this section by saying how wrong it is to say to a seeker: 'You ought to have faith.' Our function as a Church is to present the story in such a way that faith is kindled, not to demand it as a condition of healing. We have to build up a loving trust in Jesus.

And today?

In a previous age our forebears took it for granted that people knew the stories and that all they needed was the doctrine. This is no longer the case. We must tell the story in such a way that the grace may break through, then faith may be kindled.

Faith is always a mystery, like any aspect of human relationships. It cannot be forced, cannot be manipulated. It grows out of God's gracious self-disclosure to the soul.

The test of faith is whether it works out in adventurous, costly living. This brings us back to the passage referred to earlier: Hebrews 11. Faith is that which realises (makes real) the vision of truth you have glimpsed.

It is a call to adventure, like Abraham setting out not knowing where it will lead. It is the key to worthwhile living. It may mean challenging accepted morality and beliefs.

In fact to have found this loving trust in God is itself *healing* more than any physical cure.

CONCLUSIONS

- We should never tell people that they *ought* to have faith. It is our job to inspire it by presenting Jesus in the power of the Spirit.
- We have to be aware of the difference between an emotional atmosphere and a spiritual one. The emotional has its place, but merely working up suggestibility by the use of emotion may result in a negative reaction later, even if healings do take place.
- What hinders the work of healing is not so much the opposition of those who reject Jesus, but the complacency of those who claim to know him. God forgive us!

Introducing TOUCH

Whenever people speak of 'healing' they automatically think of 'the laying-on of hands'. This is natural, because in all cultures it is recognised that some people have a gift of healing in their hands.[4]

There were travelling healers in Jesus' time, and there were some very famous healing shrines with various religious connotations (we have already noted one such when discussing the Pool of Bethesda). So it was natural that when people heard that Jesus had been healing they thought of him as a travelling healer, and sought the laying-on of hands from him.

Touching

Let us look carefully, then, at what he actually *did* with his hands. When it comes to 'handwork' we find that there are four terms used in the New Testament:

- to touch lightly (*thigo*)
- to touch firmly, or even embrace (*haptomai*)
- to grab (*epilambanomai*),
- to lay on hands (*epitithomai*; noun: *epithesis*)

The first word is not often used with regard to healing. Jesus did not do things by halves! The other three words will be appearing as we go on through the book.

The surprising thing is that there are only two *individual* cases in which the word for 'laying-on hands' (*epithesis*) is used in connection with healing, although we saw that during Jesus' visit to Nazareth 'he laid his hands on a few sick folk and healed them'. We will come across it again when we look at the 'crowd scenes' later.

However, before we look at the two cases where *'epithesis'* is mentioned, we will look at cases in which, while he did in fact use his hands, the word *epithesis* is not used.

---

[4] See *Health and Healing,* John Wilkinson, Handsel Press, 1980, page 70.

7. PETER'S MOTHER-IN-LAW

Mark 1:29–31 (Luke 4:38–39, Matthew 8:14–15)

This story appears to have taken place on the Sabbath after Jesus had come to them while they were working with their nets, saying, 'Follow me.' The five of them had been to the synagogue together (see Ch. 13).

Leaving the synagogue they came to the house of Simon and Andrew, along with James and John.

Now Simon's mother-in-law had been stricken with a fever, and they told him about her.

And he came and gripped her hand, raising her up, and the fever left her, and she waited on them.

Notes

Typically, Matthew has Jesus *touching* her hand, while Mark has him *gripping* it. Dr Luke does not mention touch at all, but gives us the medical term for the illness: high fever. He mentions that Jesus 'stood over her', which is natural, seeing that she would be lying on a bed-roll on the floor. However, according to our English Bibles, he mentions rebuking the fever. This brings us to a word which is going to crop up several times:

Rebuking

The Greek word is *epitimao* and it means literally 'on-press'. It was used to mean 'exert authority', like an officer taking control of a badly disciplined squad.

On the basis of the translation of this word as *rebuke*, many people in the 'healing world' do a lot of shouting at diseases and demons. We have all had occasion in the course of everyday life to rebuke somebody, exerting authority over them in some capacity. However, we know that shouted rebukes are not always the best way of using our authority, whether we are officers, parents or managers. True spiritual authority does not call for shouting either. Indeed if a person is in a weakened state, somebody shouting the odds is *not* a good thing! The translation of *epitimao* as 'rebuke' has led to some unfortunate situations. A study of Jesus' use of authority would have avoided these.

We shall see the way Jesus exercises authority in other cases. In one

(Ch. 15) he says, 'It is I who command you'; in others he exerts his authority in a very low-key way, as with Jairus' daughter and with the blind man (Chs. 10 and 11).

Background

The background is interesting in several ways:

1. It is the only recorded healing in which Jesus deals with somebody actually connected with the Twelve. This is surprising. In most congregations where there is a healing ministry, a high proportion of the people who ask for ministry are 'home-grown'.
2. It is another reminder that after Jesus had called them from the fishing boats, saying, 'Follow me,' they still were living in Simon's house (Ch. 2) with his wife and mother-in-law, going to the synagogue together (Ch. 14) and having the equivalent of Sunday lunch at Simon's along with James and John. They did not head off into the blue, leaving everything behind, as some sermons and books suggest.

The patient

As noted already, having a high fever she would be delirious, but of course she knew Jesus reasonably well. We might assume that she had some sort of faith before she went down with the fever.

The initiative

We are not told who 'they' were, but it would seem that the family took the initiative in this case.

How Jesus went about it

Luke says that Jesus assumed authority over the fever, but does not tell us what words he used.

Notice that he does not 'cast out' the fever, as he would have done a demon. We cannot deduce from the word 'rebuke' that he thought that the fever was demonic, as is stated in some books. There is a distinction in the New Testament between the *sick* who are *healed* and the *demonised* who are delivered by '*throwing out*' (exorcising) the demon (see p. 90). Here, however, there is no sign of such a command, only bringing the body's disorder under control.

Once Jesus is in charge, the fever 'calms down' and Jesus stoops down to take her hand, lifting her to her feet. It is a very natural, gracious thing to do and we shall see that he did the same for Jairus' daughter (Ch. 10), who also was lying down.

Matthew and Mark do not give us nearly the same amount of detail, and if we had only their accounts we might have deduced that it was Jesus' taking her hand that was the decisive thing, whereas Luke gives a very different picture.

And for us

Healing does not require a 'theatrical' setting. It can happen in the kitchen, while food is being prepared, and with natural gestures, such giving a person a hand-up as in this case.

CONCLUSIONS

- Touch comes into the story, but only after the main work of healing has been done.
- In some cases healing is effected by speaking directly, with the Authority of Christ, to the disease or the physical organ which has gone out of control.

8. THE DEAF-MUTE

Mark 7:31–37

They brought him a man who was deaf and had speech difficulties, and they were pleading with him to lay hands on him.

And he, taking him aside from the crowd on his own, put his fingers into his ears, and spitting touched his tongue, and looking up to the sky grunted, and said, 'Eph-phatha (Be opened).'

And his ears were opened, and what tied his tongue was released, and he spoke clearly.

And he ordered them to tell nobody, but the more he told them not to, the more they did spread it about.

Notes

The verb *'they were pleading'* indicates something stronger than *'ask'*. It is as if Jesus had been hesitating.

Grunted The Greek word is given in the King James Version. as *'sighed'*. This is puzzling, for it refers to the sort of noise you make when you are making an effort. It is such a surprising word that it must come from a real memory.

Taking him aside The word here in Greek is the same as is used when Jesus grabbed Peter when he was sinking. It suggests something more forceful than 'Just come this way with me'.

Background

The people begin by asking Jesus specifically for the laying-on of hands, as if all that he had to do was to lay on hands and that would be it. It has not begun to dawn on them how disastrous it might be if Jesus did as they asked. To give someone their hearing in the midst of a noisy, excitable crowd would have been cruel.

The patient

Think for a moment about the man himself: he had never *heard* Jesus preaching. Nor had he heard people talking about Jesus. He can have had little idea as to why he was being led to this strange man. Being deaf cuts one off more than blindness.

The initiative

As in the last case we do not know who 'they' were, but it would seem that it was they who took the initiative, in fact a very determined initiative. The man appears to be passive.

How Jesus went about it

However, note what Jesus did. In the same way as he had sent the 'man born blind' (Ch. 2) to a shady place in which to begin to see, so now he takes the deaf mute 'away from the crowd on his own'. As already noted, the word for 'took him away' is the strong one, suggesting that he really got a hold of the man. As he did so, he began the difficult task of building up a relationship with him, for the man would be forced to look at Jesus, and there would be eye-contact. By the time they reached 'the quiet place' the man would have developed some sort of confidence in the stranger.

In Chapters 2 and 3 Jesus related to the people *after* healing them, while in this case he related to the man *before* healing him.

Not for him an uncomprehending patient.

The carers

Note furthermore that he took the man 'on his own', away from those who had brought him. Whereas the men who had brought the paralytic (Ch. 1) played an important part in the lad's healing, in this case Jesus leaves them out of it.

Signing

Most of what he then did is straightforward sign-language. He *uses* his hands, but in this case there is no laying-on of hands as such. The grunt, we have already noted, indicates effort.

Jesus at prayer

We get one glimpse of an important factor for Jesus: 'looking up to the sky'. That may have been just sign language to point the man to God, but on the other hand in a number of places we read: *He lifted up his face in prayer*. This seems to have been his prayerful attitude.

Too often we bow our heads like slaves before their master, when the Jesus-attitude is that of a child looking up to his father.

The Word
Mark lapses back into the Aramaic when he tells us what Jesus said. Once more, what he said was a simple word, with no religious phrases, but it carried his Authority. It is easily lip-read. We note again that Jesus was a man of few words when he was healing, unlike some of us.

Healing, not deliverance
We come back to a topic raised in the last story: the contrast between deliverance and healing. It is important to note that in this case it was straight 'healing', not deliverance. In the case noted in Matthew 9:32 the dumbness is attributed to demonic causes, and Jesus 'threw it out'. In the case of the 'epileptic boy' in Mark 9:14ff (Ch. 15) it is a 'deaf and dumb demon' which Jesus throws out. Yet in this case Jesus communicates by sign-language and then uses the Word of Authority to open the man's ears. It all goes to show once more that one must not generalise on the basis of reading one story and then assume that therefore anybody with similar symptoms must be treated in the same way.

Disobedience
The story ends with disobedience. The fact that the Gospel says that the more Jesus ordered them the more they spread it seems to indicate that he made several attempts to quieten things down.

'Keep it quiet'
Why in this case and in many others did Jesus stress that people who had been healed should not go telling everybody? For several reasons:

1. It is not good for them *physically*. The body needs quietness and peace in which to readjust.
2. It is not good for them *emotionally*. Only too easily the fact of having been healed can become an obsession, and the story becomes a bore to all concerned.
3. It is not good for them *socially*. We have known a number of people who have gone back to their churches full of wonder at what has happened, only to be met with cold hostility, as happened with the blind man we considered previously.

In other words, Jesus is trying to save the man from the emotionalism which is often connected with 'healing', and he is concerned that by the time the healed person does 'come out', he has been able to readjust at all the above levels.

4.   Finally there is another reason. Jesus did not want publicity as just another healer.

It brings us back to the difference we saw earlier between 'a wonder' and 'a sign'. The newly healed person can be so excited by 'the wonder' that 'the sign' is missed.

Only some time later would the man understand what it had really been about. *Then* his witness would be valuable. Much harm can be done by getting 'the healed' to talk about their experience prematurely.

And for us

Sometimes we too have to rescue a patient from the smothering concern of those who have brought him or her to us, thus making sure that we are relating direct to the person to be healed.

We too must learn sensitivity about the setting:

Sometimes we must take the person aside, either with or without the friends or relatives.

Sometimes we must involve those who brought the person; sometimes we must separate them.

Sometimes it is right to heal in a service in full view of people, and sometimes that would be harmful.

We must never go along with the popular idea that the laying-on of hands is what is needed.

It is not for those seeking healing to decide the form of treatment we give, saying, for instance: 'I want the laying-on of hands.'

CONCLUSIONS

- Sometimes healing involves far more costly involvement than just giving the laying-on of hands.
- Touch did play an important part in this work, but it was to communicate rather than to heal. It was the Word of Authority once again that healed.
- People with similar symptoms may require to be treated in quite different ways.

9. TWO BLIND MEN

Matthew 9:27–31

As Jesus was passing by, there were two blind men following, crying out and saying: 'Be kind to us, Son of David.'

When he got home the two blind men came up to him, and Jesus said to them: 'Do you believe that I have the power to do this?'

'Yes, sir,' they replied.

Then he touched their eyes saying: 'If that's what you believe, that's it.'

And their eyes were opened, and Jesus snorted at them saying: 'See that nobody knows about it!'

But when they left, they spread his reputation all over the country.

Notes

'Have mercy' is a phrase which is usually used here as the beggar's cry, and it comes into the Gospels often. We still use the same Greek word today when we say, *'Kyrie eleison.'*

Kyrie
In our Bibles this is translated as Lord, as if the blind men were acknowledging the Lordship of Jesus. However still today in Greece it is the normal polite way of addressing a man. It seems more likely that they were doing just that, and I have translated it as 'Sir'. (There is the same problem in German where 'Der Herr' means 'the Lord', but we address a man as Herr Schmidt.)

Eleison
The verb from which we get 'eleison' originally meant 'to oil'. Before the days of showers (and still today in places where there are no showers), when weary, sweaty travellers arrived, they were greeted with sweet-smelling oil. So when we sing *'Kyrie eleison'* we are asking the Lord to oil us. However, the people in the New Testament stories were not using it literally. It had come to mean 'Be kind to us' because anointing is a welcoming, soothing act. The English 'Have mercy' does not quite get the meaning.

When he got into the house
I have put it as 'when he got home'. It might just have been the house in which

they were staying, but it could also mean the house which was 'home'. (Compare the French 'à la maison' at the house = at home.) Most translations prefer 'house', but it is a matter of opinion.

The puzzling word is the one translated in all versions as 'commanded them' or some such. Prof. A.M. Hunter used to say that it was the word used to describe 'snorting, as with war horses'. We will come across it again at Chapter 20 (The leper) and yet again when we come to Lazarus. It is a stage stronger than the word we translated as 'grunt' in the last case.

Oddly enough it also comes in when the disciples object to the waste of money involved in pouring all that expensive perfumed oil over Jesus' feet. Most versions have that they grumbled, but something more explosive is suggested – 'harrumphing'?

In the meantime let us just note that his reaction was rather explosive!

It is strange that translators go for 'commanded'. Are they afraid of portraying a Jesus who showed real emotion and had deep feelings?

Background

It seems to have been a chance encounter.

The patients

This story is very puzzling in two ways. It is quite clear in the Greek that they were following him through the streets and were crying out repeatedly.

1. It is puzzling because one wonders how two blind men could follow Jesus through the crowded streets. There might have been somebody with them to guide them, or perhaps one of them had some vision. We do not know.
2. It is also puzzling because it seems so out of character for Jesus not to have responded at once, but to have walked on until he reached the house. They seem to have come into the house uninvited, but remember what we said about houses in the first story. It would probably be the patio they came into.

The initiative

There is no doubt about this. But we do not know whether it came about just because somebody had told them about Jesus or because they had heard Jesus preach and had been there when others had been healed. Once again we ask why might Jesus have hesitated. Perhaps there is a clue in one incident in my own ministry.

I remember a man who came in asking for healing. As we began to minister to him, he objected: 'I went to a spiritualist healer, I paid my ten bob, got my healing and went out. There wasn't all *this* business.' (The 'business' he was referring to was our focusing on Jesus.)

Sometimes people do take healing for granted, unaware of the cost to those ministering, both at the spiritual and the financial level. Sometimes all they want is to be able to continue with their self-centred lives, thinking that just a touch will do the trick.

On the other hand Jesus may simply have delayed until they got into the shade of the house before restoring sight (compare with Ch. 2).

Jesus' question

A distinctive feature in this story is that Jesus asks them if they believe that he has the *dunamis*, the power, to do this. (The word used is stronger than just asking if he *could* do this.) This is the only case in which he *begins* by asking if the person has faith. Jesus usually decided that for himself. Of course this account, like all the others, is very whittled down to bare essentials, and there might have been a lot more to it than just this question and answer, but that can lead to dangerous guesswork.

Faith and healing

Jesus' comment, 'If that's what you believe, that's it,' leaves us with a lot of questions. For them it was the right starting point.

Yet some of the most spectacular healings happen to people who seem to have little mature faith, while deeply committed Christians often do not receive physical healing. We cannot conclude, therefore, that because Jesus said it to these two it applies to everybody in every situation.

This comes back to what we said in Chapter 4 about faith and credulity. The two stories make an interesting contrast.

I have heard sermons which did imply that if we *believed* enough we would all be perfectly healthy. As we shall see later, St Paul himself would have failed that test! Such talk leads to people going away in a worse state than when they came, questioning the little faith they did have, whereas Jesus said that we only need a mustard-seed of faith.

The touch

After their assurance, Jesus touches their eyes. The word used is that which refers to a firm touch, but not *epithesis*, the laying-on of hands. Perhaps, being blind and therefore unable to see that Jesus had responded to them, they needed assurance that something was happening. Perhaps, as in the previous story, it was sign-language rather than therapy.

Whatever it was, he follows it up by speaking his Word of Authority and they see.

They too are told to keep quiet, and of course they do not.

CONCLUSIONS

- Touch plays an important part in this story, even though it is not the 'laying-on of hands'.
- Once again, we must not allow ourselves to be manipulated by those who seek healing.

Summary TOUCH

Looking back on the cases which we have studied so far we have seen that Jesus used his hands in many ways:

- To make paste to put on the blind man's eyes (Ch. 2)
- To help people to their feet once healed (Chs. 7 and 10)
- As sign-language (Chs. 8 and 9)
- In one case the patient touched him (Ch. 4)
- In many cases no touch seems to have been involved (Chs. 1, 3, 5).

It seems clear that 'the Word through whom all things were made' (John 1) speaks creatively again and it is this which heals in most cases, although given physical expression by actions. This is what we have been calling 'the Word of Authority'. (There is an extra chapter at the end of the book which deals in more detail with this subject.) There are, of course, many gestures and actions that also express this Word, and we shall come across others as we go on, but they are all secondary to the Word of Authority.

It becomes obvious that the Church's Ministry of Healing must be a contact-ministry, while avoiding the idea that the laying-on of hands is the appropriate treatment in every case.

CONCLUSIONS

- The Church's Ministry of Christian Healing takes place when we are so 'tuned in' to God's creative Word that we can speak it in Jesus' Name (i.e. as his representatives).
- We must be ready to give physical expression to the Word in many ways.
- Jesus discouraged people from spreading the news that he was a 'healer', and we must ensure that any healing we do is incidental to the preaching of the Gospel.

Introducing THE LAYING-ON OF HANDS

We come now to those stories in which the laying-on of hands (*epithesis*) is mentioned. In Chapter 6 we noted a fleeting reference to it. Of course the term for laying-on of hands is used in other contexts too: 'Jesus took children in his arms, *laid hands* on them and blessed them.' The emphasis there was in blessing, not healing.

Paul writes to Timothy about the 'gifts of the Spirit which were his through the *laying-on of hands'*. This seems more like ordination.

The laying-on of hands, then, is when there is an objective transfer of energy from one person to another through the hands.

For Christian healing, this, of course, is the life of Christ flowing through us in the power of the Holy Spirit. (What that means we will explore in the section on healing in Acts.)

In non-Christian laying-on of hands there is the big question as to where the power comes from. There have been people with undoubted healing powers, but whom I for one would not allow anywhere near me.

In contrast to the loving touch, the actual laying-on of hands for healing is usually given to the afflicted part – not always, but usually. Such is our experience.

In most cases one waits until the power flows, and one keeps hands on until it ceases. This may be for minutes or even for hours.

In many cases I have known, there has been an accurate diagnosis because, when the ministrant's hands reached the appropriate place, the power began to flow (remember the electrician in Chapter 4). I have known cases in which both the ministrant and the patient knew at exactly the same moment that the flow had stopped.

Lest, however, we become dogmatic, I have known several ministers and others who have reached out to give a loving friendly touch and have found that something almost physical has flowed into the sufferer through that touch. They came into the healing ministry after that!

We now look, therefore, at one case in which the laying-on of hands was specifically asked for and then at the two cases in which it is definitely stated that Jesus did give the *epithesis*.

10. JAIRUS' DAUGHTER

Mark 5:21 (Luke 8:40–56, Matthew 9:18–26)

The president of the synagogue, Jairus by name, came and, seeing him, fell at his feet, and pled with him: 'My daughter is dying. Come and lay hands on her that she may be healed and live.'

And he went with him, and a great crowd followed him, jostling him. (Then follows the story we looked at in Chapter 4 – the healing of the haemorrhaging woman.)

While he was speaking to her a message came from the president of the synagogue's house saying: 'Your daughter has died. Why trouble the teacher further?'

But Jesus, overhearing the message to the president, said: 'Don't be afraid, just have faith.'

And he would not allow anybody to come with him except Peter, James and John, James's brother.

And they came to the president's house and he saw a great uproar, much weeping and wailing.

And when he came into the house, he asked: 'Why all this fuss? She's not dead, she's asleep.'

They laughed at him. but putting them all out he took the girl's father and mother, with his companions, and went in where the child was.

And taking the child's hand, he said to her: 'Talitha cumi' (which means: 'Up you get, lassie').

And immediately the girl got up and walked. She was about twelve years old. And they were absolutely astonished.

And he ordered that nobody should know and that she should be given something to eat.

Notes

'Talitha cumi' is Aramaic, meaning as above. It is what any Galileean mother might say to her daughter any morning. So why revert to the original language here?

Those who are native Scots or Gaelic speakers will recognise the problem. There are things you can say in Scots or Gaelic which do not seem the same when you put them in 'proper' English. So no wonder that when Mark retold the story as Peter used to tell it, he records that Peter slipped back into his mother tongue at this point. Such homely words were lost when put into Greek – and when translated into English as 'Damsel, I say unto thee arise' (KJV).

Background

The president of the synagogue was an important person in the community. The synagogue had elders, and one of them was the president. He would preside at worship, and also when people were summoned before the elders for breaking some religious or moral law.

Rabbi

The official teachers of the Law employed by the synagogue were called rabbis, but of course Jesus was not one. This is plain when we look at the criticisms people made of Jesus, e.g. Mark 6:2.

The patient

Some scholars make much of the fact that the woman had suffered for twelve years and that the girl was twelve years old. In this book we are only concerned with the healing itself, so we leave such points on one side.

Was she dead?

Some take the Lord's words literally, suggesting that she was in a coma. Others, wanting to maximise the miraculous element, think he was speaking figuratively. However, she would have been dead if they had buried her, so why argue?

The initiative

It is clearly the father who takes the initiative, even to setting out the request to 'lay hands' on his daughter.

How Jesus set about it

We have already noted when looking at the story of the woman who touched him (Ch. 4) that Jesus continued to Jairus' house even though she had technically rendered him 'unclean' and therefore unfit to do God's work in orthodox Jewish eyes.

The power to heal

Jesus kept going in spite of the news that she had died. I would imagine, from experience in lesser cases, that it would have been because he would have felt in himself that God was already giving him the power to do the work. People today who have a healing ministry involving touch know when the necessary power has been given. It is perhaps dangerous to infer from our experience in this way, yet if he was truly 'Son of Man', born human, working as one of us, then we are entitled to recognise where our experience explains something in the Gospels.

The mourners

It is usual in hot countries for the body to be buried the same day. So when somebody was very ill, the professional 'mourners', mostly poor widows, would gather and wait for the death. They would be expected to raise that terrible keen-ing sound which sometimes we hear on TV news reports from Palestine.

One can hardly blame them for being indignant when Jesus said she was not dead, for mourning a death was one of the few ways that they could earn a handful of coppers and share in a meal. He was depriving them of that! No wonder they were angry.

The laying-on of hands

Now we come to the real point at issue: the fact that Jairus specifically asks for the laying-on of hands. Why?

As we have seen, that is what is generally expected of healers. Yet Jesus *does not do as requested.* Nor does he do anything spectacular as, for instance, Elisha did for the widow's son. Jesus acts naturally, almost casually.

Touch does come into it, of course, as with Simon Peter's mother-in-law. Like her, the girl would have been lying on a bed mat on the floor. So it would be natural to stoop down and take her hand to help her to her feet as she woke up. It was indeed a natural, homely gesture, not a 'religious' one.

Talitha cumi

It is this Word of Authority which wakes the girl up...yes, but remember it is spoken in such homely terms that it is hard to think of it that way. His Author-ity does not require bluster and raised voices. Jesus' actions are so low-key that they leave us gasping once we have realised what has actually happened. It is the utter simplicity of walking in and waking her up as a natural thing which was so astonishing. Matthew and Luke include the story but leave out this homely bit. Commentators miss the point when they speak of these Aramaic words being quoted to deepen the sense of 'mystification'.

Then notice that Jesus immediately takes steps to keep the emotional temperature low by telling them to keep quiet about it – some hope! Also 'he told them to give her something to eat'...rather as we, on occasions when something needs to be done to lower the emotional tone, would say to some overwrought person: 'How about a cup of tea?' Giving people something to do like that helps them to keep a hold of themselves.

A question of atmosphere

That brings us on to another point. Some writers make much of the fact that the Lord put out all those 'thinking negatively', keeping with him only those thinking positively. Yet in other instances he healed in front of hostile crowds.

However, as far as the girl is concerned, a highly emotional atmosphere would be very harmful for her as she recovered. Imagine how these mourner-women would have reacted as the lassie came round. They would have been hysterical! Imagine the effect on the girl. She would need peace to reorientate and to come to terms with what had happened.

As Jesus had considered the light when healing the man born blind and the noise with the deaf-mute, here he considers the need for quietness when the girl comes round.

And for us

Emotionalism is bad practice in healing, even when a certain amount of emotion is in place.

We have to consider the needs of the person when the healing becomes effective.

CONCLUSIONS

- In this case Jairus expects the laying-on of hands, but the Lord does not do so.
- Once more we note that we must not allow ourselves to be put in the position of having to lay hands on somebody when that is not the right thing to do for that person.
- As with all true authority, there is no need for outwardly impressive words and actions. Even less is there a need for emotionalism.
- It is Jesus' Authority as Lord of Life which counts in all truly Christian healing, rather than some magic touch or ritual.
- Once more we note that touch may well be involved as a natural expression of love, human and divine, but it takes second place to the Word of Authority.

11. THE BLIND MAN OF BETHSAIDA

Mark 8:22–26

And they come to Bethsaida, and they bring him a blind man, and pleaded with him to touch him. And, grabbing him by the hand, he led him away out the village, and, spitting in his eyes, he lays hands on him.

He asked him: 'Do you see anything?'

And, looking up, he said: 'I see the men like trees...look, they're walking!'

Then once more he placed his hands on the man's eyes.

And he looked steadily, and it was restored, and he saw everything clearly.

Notes

This story must have about the highest density of 'ands'.

Pleaded It is a strong word, and the versions that translate it as 'asked' miss a point. Again there seems to be some suggestion that Jesus did not react at once.

'Grabbing him'? Yes, it is the violent word we came across in Chapter 8, not just 'taking him' as in most English versions. It is used of a violent arrest in Acts. We would expect Jesus to take the man gently and kindly by the hand. But no...

Touch Here at last we come to a case of *epithesis*, 'the laying-on of hands'.

The Gospel says that sight was *restored* so that we know he was not born blind.

Background

They are back on their home base, Bethsaida being the fishing village most of the disciples came from.

The expectation

Once more we see that people imagined that all that Jesus needed to do was to *touch* the man, but we also see once again that much more was needed.

The initiative

As with the story of the boy let down through the roof (Ch. 1), the initiative seems to be with those who brought the man. This explains one or two of the details of the story. For instance, it might explain why, as we shall see later, Jesus healed blind Bartimaeus on the spot, yet he did not do so here. After all, Bartimaeus had taken the initiative himself, while this man seems to have been passive.

How Jesus went about it

The first striking thing about this story is that, as in Chapter 8, Jesus seems to have hesitated. A possible reason may become apparent as we go on through the story.

The grab

The second striking thing is the violent verb used, as noted above: grab. It is the action of an angry man. He may well have been annoyed by the attitude of those who had brought the man. It is the sort of surprising little detail which reminds us that it is an eye-witness account.

Separating

In the previous case we thought about getting the patient away from smothering 'love'. Now let us take a step further: Any of us who have a physical handicap will tell you how annoying it is when well-meaning friends do business over our heads, when we know that we are quite capable of doing it ourselves. Jesus was right in 'doing business' with the man himself, not with his 'carers'.

There is another possibility. We have known people who brought somebody for healing with the glib assurance that 'the wee magic touch' would solve all their problems, but often with a lack of real compassion for the patient, only a desire to be rid of the bother which a sick or blind person causes.

One can imagine them saying, for instance: 'I'm fed up with this. He can't do anything, and he's an extra mouth to feed. We'll see if that miracle-worker Jesus can do anything.' That is not faith! (Compare with the folk of Nazareth, Ch. 6)

When people have come in that sort of spirit, it becomes obvious that, while they say all the right things, their attitude is basically wrong. In such cases we too have to separate the sufferer from those who brought him/her, and then relate to the sufferer directly. Sometimes this means leaving aside some indignant people who were looking forward to being in on a miracle. That might explain why Jesus took the man away from them. It is only a guess, however.

Building up faith

Then Jesus led him away, out of the village. Allowing yourself to be blind-folded and guided by somebody else is a quick way of building up a relation-ship, as many of us have found in parties or encounter groups. In the same way, by the time they had found the right place, Jesus and the man would have been relating to each other man to man.

Those who had brought him had known that Jesus *could* heal, but now *he* knew Jesus for himself. We are back at the contrast we looked at in the section on faith.

Eventually they reached a place outside the village, but obviously still within sight of people walking about. I assume that Jesus would pick a shady place, just as we saw he chose the Pool of Siloam as a place of healing for the man born blind (Ch. 2).

Two-stage healing

Now we watch Jesus at work, 'spitting in the man's eyes'. One wonders how the Lord did that! It is not a method which many of us have tried. Perhaps he spat on his thumb and then dabbed the man's eyes. The use of spittle was not so surprising in the east. It was seen as 'the essence of me'. Therefore it would be seen as Jesus' self-giving. All healing is in some sense self-giving. Spittle is also an antiseptic, as we know from the fact that licking a wound is a natu-ral reaction in animals…and in humans.

The laying-on of hands

It is after this healing act, a sort of anointing by spit, that Jesus lays hands on the man, on his eyes. After finding that the healing was only partial, Jesus gives the laying-on of hands again, this time completing the work.

This is the only occasion in the Gospels in which healing does not take place fully at the first attempt, apart from the Gadarene demoniac. We will look at that later.

Like trees?

It is interesting to try to work out what the man saw. Was it that he was still only seeing people as moving blurs when he described them as 'trees walk-ing'? An eye specialist came up with another idea: he had inverted vision, seeing people upside down, their legs waving like the branches of trees.

We note the strong instruction not to go into the village and to keep quiet about his healing, as with the deaf-mute (Ch. 8).

CONCLUSIONS

- Taking the man away on his own began the treatment.
- Anointing the man's eyes with his spit was the next stage.
- The laying-on of hands was given, in this case in two stages.
- The laying-on of hands was only part of the treatment.
- Once more Jesus took far more trouble than the people had expected.

---

12. THE WOMAN IN THE SYNAGOGUE

Luke 13:10–17

And he was teaching in one of the synagogues on the Sabbath, and look! There was a woman who had had a spirit of weakness for eighteen years, and was bent double, unable to straighten herself completely upright. But seeing her, Jesus summoned her, and said: 'Woman, you are released from your weakness.'

And he laid hands on her, and at once she was straightened up, and glorified God.

Notes

There follows a very lively encounter between Jesus and the president of this synagogue. Jesus pulled no punches.

The word I have translated 'summoned' implies not that he shouted across the synagogue to her, but that he called her to him. In some versions it suggests only that he called to her. But then, since he later laid hands on her, it is clear that he did summon her right up to where he was.

Background

One aspect of this story which might escape even an informed reader is that in synagogues the women were separated from the men, usually behind a screen. To summon the woman into the men's part of the building, right up to the teaching platform, would have been something utterly shocking. Probably no woman had ever stood there before. And as for her praising God at the end, this would have been even worse – a woman daring to open her mouth in the synagogue during worship!

Another point would have antagonised them: No doubt there were *men* in the congregation who needed healing, and he could have picked on one of them, but he *chose* a woman. That was no accident.

The initiative

Jesus takes it – and how!

No doubt it would have been simple to have found her the next day and to have healed her then, but he chose to do it on the Sabbath day as in Chapters 2, 3, 7, 13, 17, 19, and as part of the worship, as in Chapter 13.

He was quite deliberately breaking rules and conventions right, left and centre, in order to teach what God really wants. Not least, he was saying that healing was one of the activities which were indeed what God meant to happen on the Sabbath in worship. He was refuting the accepted ruling that, since healing was work, it should not be done on the Sabbath.

In this case he goes out of his way to pick his subject. There is no indication that she had asked for healing. His healing here is 'a visual aid' to his sermon, and is carefully chosen to make the points mentioned above.

The woman herself

Now let us look at this woman. We note three things:

She was there in the synagogue in spite of her disability, a fact which shows that she was 'a good Jewess'. At least on that occasion, she had heard Jesus preaching the Gospel of the Kingdom. Jesus refers to her as the woman 'whom Satan had bound for 18 years'. It does not say that she had a demon, nor does it say that Jesus 'threw out a demon'. It says 'she had a spirit of weakness'. Now the word 'spirit' could refer to her own spirit, and it can just be a Hebrew way of saying that she was spiritually weak.[5] To understand that we must ask what it means to be spiritually strong:

The spiritually strong have:

1. A deep trust in God: faith.
2. A strong sense of purpose in life: hope.
3. A self-forgetting love for God, for people and for God's Creation: i.e. love.

Without these one is spiritually weak, and a sitting target for the old enemy.

Obviously, lacking these he had her tied in knots when she developed back trouble. Those who are spiritually strong are 'more than conquerors in all these things' (Romans 8:37) overcoming their disabilities. However, self-pity soon allows a bondage to form and one is tied into the trouble, as it become one's way of life.

Bondage

The use of the word bondage may be puzzling. To work out what it means, here is a rough guide:

[5] *Health and Healing*, John Wilkinson, Handsel Press, 1980, p. 77.

- A physical handicap may develop into a bondage through self-pity or resentment.
- Relationships with the living or the dead can develop into a bondage through resentment or possessive love.
- Pleasures can develop into a bondage through being enjoyed in selfish isolation or as escapism.
- Religion can develop into a bondage through authoritarianism or through the abuse of fear.
- Interest in the supernatural and the occult can develop into a bondage if we depend on such things for guidance or for 'good luck'.

Over-dramatising

Of course it can work the other way. We all have our particular temptations with which we struggle. We fall at times, but confession and perhaps a bit of counselling can set us back on the right path. We must not over-dramatise our resident temptations by calling them a bondage, allowing the enemy to tie us in knots that way. No matter how we have grown spiritually, each of us has some temptations which are liable to trip us up.

How Jesus set about it

Now to come back to the woman. Once his Authority released her from her bondage, Jesus went on to lay hands on her. As we noted earlier, when *epithesis* is involved, it is the affected part that is touched, therefore one assumes that he would have touched her back.

It is important to note that he laid hands only after he had freed her to respond to his healing, just as in the previous 'work' we noted that he only laid hands after building up a relationship with the man and spitting in his eyes.

This is the second individual case in which we are told that Jesus laid hands on a person. *There are no further individual cases.*

CONCLUSIONS

- A wrong spiritual state, such as self-pity, can lay us open to influence from outside ourselves. In some cases this may lead only to emotional un-health, which can be dealt with by counselling, but there is the danger of 'outside interference' leading to bondage.
- A bondage is 'broken' by the Word; it is not exorcised.
- Where there is a bondage, it must be broken before the laying-on of hands is given for physical healing.
- The laying-on of hands, in this story once again, is only part of a process, and the process is different from that in the previous story.
- Healing is an appropriate activity on the Sabbath (or for us, on Sunday) in worship, but the initiative should be with the person conducting worship. The sick should not be allowed to take over the service.

Summary THE LAYING-ON OF HANDS

Having looked at the two cases in which Jesus is recorded as having given the laying-on of hands (*epithesis*), and at ten cases in which he did not, we are ready for some conclusions.

Expectations

The expectation that the Lord will give the laying-on of hands is there in three cases (Chs. 8, 10, 11). In the case of Jairus and in the case of the deaf mute (Ch. 8) the request is specifically for him to lay hands, but the Lord did not use this method.

In the case of the blind man (Ch. 11) he did eventually do as requested, but only after he had taken a lot more trouble than expected.

We do not know what the woman in the synagogue was expecting (Ch. 12).

Yet again, beware of falling into the trap set by the expectations of others, and by our own expectations for ourselves.

We noted in the summary of the previous section that there are many ways of expressing the healing love of God, and we note now that even in these two cases in which he did lay on hands, there are diversities. Let us note them:

- People bring the blind man to him, but on the other hand he takes the initiative with the woman.
- He takes care to get to know the blind man first, but by contrast he moves straight into a form of deliverance ministry for the woman.
- He seeks privacy for the blind man, whereas with the woman he deliberately heals her in front of the congregation.

The only thing the two cases have in common is that the *epithesis* is only part of the treatment, not the whole. Also we note that he lays hands on the affected part in the case of the blind man; we only guess that he did so with the woman.

As we have looked at these cases the differences underline the fact that each healing was 'tailor-made to fit'. There was no uniform pattern. There should not be for us either. Because, for instance, *epithesis* worked in one case, it does not mean that it will work in similar ones.

When there has been a subtle switch to trust in the procedure rather than in the Word, superstition is not far away. Therefore the popular idea that Jesus went about healing people with a mere touch is far off the mark. He shows far more costly concern and deeper insight than that. *(People are always surprised when it is pointed out that there are only two individual cases in which the laying-on of hands is mentioned. I have known many ministers who have tried to read* epithesis *into passages where it is not used.)*

And for us

What do we conclude for ourselves in our ministry? For us too this healing ministry is a touching ministry. Sporty people talk about 'contact games' – well, it is a contact ministry.

Reviewing what we have been studying:
There are four main ways of contact, although like the colours of the rainbow they merge into each other.

1. There is touch used as a form of communication, when perhaps words are of limited use, for instance if the patient is deaf or blind.
2. There is touch expressing compassion and understanding.
3. There is touch when we bless somebody in the Name of God.
4. There is touch when we lay hands on the affected part to transmit God's healing power.

Is it a special gift?

Let us turn aside for a moment to look at this question. It does, in practice, seem that there are people with special gifts in their hands, both Christian and non-Christian. St Paul in 1 Corinthians 12 refers to *'Gifts of cures'* (not 'the gift of healing', although most English Bibles do have 'healing' – we looked at the difference on p. 11). The way St Paul puts it in that passage underlines the fact that nobody has the gift of healing for everybody and for every disease. Each 'cure' is a fresh gift, when God's chosen vessel does what God wants ('God's will').

Christian healing and psychic healing

Since others, apart from Christians, lay hands on people, we have to think in more detail about the relationship between Christian healing and other 'healing'.

In Christian healing that energy transfer is from 'Christ-in-us to Christ-in-you'. In non-Christian healers the source of the power is questionable, although they are always sure that it is good. There are real dangers here. For instance, a bondage may develop.

Having said that, we have to be clear that even Christian healers and Christian healing groups can slip. People who begin healing full of the Holy Spirit can slip, only too easily, from being an instrument of God's healing to channelling energies from psychic sources (see Ch. 33, 'The Other Simon'). We may begin in all sincerity to serve the Lord and to respond to the suffering of people. Then gradually it becomes an ego-trip, and we slip downwards imperceptibly. Work at this lower level may still achieve short-term healing but will leave long-term uncleanness and confusion.

A health warning

Those with such a gift must, then, be lovingly shielded from the temptations which arise from such a ministry. The discipline of corporate prayer and Bible study is essential. Once such a gift becomes central to the individual's life, or to the life of the community of which they are a part, then trouble is not far away. It is the Gospel which is central, not any specific gift.

This means that 'healing' will involve not just the person with a gift in his or her hands, but also others in the Christian community. It is the work of the whole Christian community, not of just one person.

Those with pastoral and teaching gifts rather than healing in their hands may in some cases open the way for the healing to flow, while in other cases they may follow up. There is no set order. Or, to put it another way: in some cases witness to Jesus may *lead into* the laying-on of hands, in others it may *flow from it.*

Blessing

While *epithesis* is usually effective when done by those who have been gifted to do it, *blessing* is the work of the Church as a whole and of ministers in particular. To conclude any service, we give God's blessing to all present and it is up to each person in the congregation to be open to God's gift.

There is no reason why we should not take that a step further and offer a blessing to any individual who comes seeking it. In that case the hands are usually placed on the head. This does not require a special Gift, but in a public setting it is usually those who are authorised to do so by the Church who impart the Blessing. Even then its effectiveness depends much on the spiritual depth of those who share in imparting it.

Such a Blessing may be all the healing needed. Many have been healed through this alone.

An assumption not to make

If a minister finds that he or she has no contact gift, it should not be assumed that the ministry of healing is 'out'. There will be people in the congregation who have been given the gift, and whose gifts should be encouraged.

Furthermore, there are other aspects of the ministry in which each one of us can share, especially the Blessing, as we have seen.

Touch and the laying-on of hands

Finally, let us stress again that one cannot draw a clear distinction between the friendly touch, the blessing and the laying-on of hands. This brings us to something which is fundamental to our outlook:

The sacramental principle

God often takes ordinary things, such as the friendly touch, water, bread or wine, to convey something far more than can be accounted for in purely physical terms. As we respond to the cry of the suffering, we will naturally begin to use all these means. We may then find that on occasion there is a real power flow, and we have to develop the vital sensitivity to God in order to use it rightly.

CONCLUSIONS

- In most cases healing will include a loving, friendly touch or a blessing rather than the laying-on of hands.
- We must not allow ourselves to be pressured into laying-on hands by the expectation of patients or of those bringing them.
- The laying-on of hands is to be given at times, but only as part of the healing process, under the guidance of the Holy Spirit, by those anointed by the Spirit for it, as Jesus was.
- We expect to lay hands on the affected part, and to keep them there, possibly for some considerable time, until the power switches off.
- While the laying-on of hands may be an essential part of the treatment in some cases, it is never the whole treatment.
- The sort of healing service in which the laying-on of hands is offered to all and sundry is not in line with what we know of our Lord's practice. On the other hand the blessing can usually be offered to any who wish it.

For further teaching on these topics see my books: *Prayers and Ideas for Healing Services,* Wild Goose Publications, 1995. *Across the Spectrum,* Handsel Press, 1993.

Note: As I write there is publicity surrounding Brendan Nolan from Ireland, a 'seventh son of a seventh son' who is well known as a healer. (There is a Celtic belief that the seventh son of a seventh son has 'the gift'. It was taken for granted that he had it, and it seems to work.) However, we have to note that he is not in the same class as those who have become so Christ-like in character that they have become Christ-like in healing. Such healing gifts are no more and no less 'from God' than gifts of music or physical strength. It all depends on how we use them.

Introducing EXORCISM

The aspect of our Lord's ministry which poses most problems for modern people is that of his dealings with those who are 'possessed'. We have already touched on this when considering the bent woman (Ch. 12).

Like most people I grew up to think that 'possession' was just a quaint way of speaking of mental illness. However, in the last few decades, when so many people have been dabbling in the occult and even in Satanism, we have found out that there is a real difference between those who need treatment in a mental hospital and those who need what we now refer to as 'the ministry of deliverance'.

Experience has taught us that:

- There are people who seem sane, but who need deliverance.
- There are people who claim to hear 'demonic' voices but who are in fact mentally ill.
- Telling the difference is the function of someone with the gift of discernment.
- You can do terrible damage to the emotionally disturbed or the mentally ill by introducing such a topic.

BUT
Counselling will make no progress if deliverance is needed; on the other hand counselling will be needed once the person is freed.

Possession?

Many church people get very upset when possession is mentioned. It implies a world-view very different from the conventional 'scientific' one, and therefore most people feel threatened by the subject. It upsets their tidy universe. It may also remind people of terrible mediaeval practices which still surface occasionally. So let us face this.

Who said 'possession'?

Our first step must be to get rid of the very idea of *possession*. It is a frightening concept and it is not biblical, even though it appears in most English translations of the Bible. So I put in nice big letters: THERE IS NO SUCH THING AS 'POSSESSION' IN THE BIBLE. Let us look at what is really there in the Greek. Two words are used, often translated as 'devil', 'spirit' or 'demon'. There is no official distinction, so in what follows I use the following translations:

Spirit when the Greek uses *pneuma* (it can also be translated as *breath, wind, life*, as in John 3:5–8). (Remember the bent woman and the *pneuma* of weakness in Chapter 12?)

Demon when it uses *daimon*. This Greek word did not necessarily refer to something evil. In those days they would have found nothing sinister about having a 'gift' (*daimon*) for poetry or music. Hence in the New Testament they usually refer to 'an *unclean* demon/spirit', to explain why it needed to be thrown out.

The following terms are used when diagnosing cases:

- *A spirit of uncleanness* Mark 1:23 ('in a spirit'), Mark 5:2, Mk.7:25, Luke 4:36 (plural), Luke 6:18, Luke 11:24.
- *Demonised,* i.e. affected by demons in the same way as others are referred to as affected by the moon, i.e. moon-ised (see below): Mk.1:32 and 5:32, Matt. 8:28, 9:32.
- *Having a dumb spirit* Mark 9:17
- *Having a spirit of an unclean demon* Luke 4:33
- *Having an evil spirit* Luke 7:24, Luke 8:27 (plural)
- *Having a spirit of weakness* Luke 13:11
- *Having evil spirits* Acts 19:12
- *Moonstruck* comes into St Matthew's Gospel, firstly in 4:24 as one of the categories with which Jesus deals, apparently not the same as 'demonised', but in Matt. 17:15 the epileptic boy is said to be 'moonstruck', while the other Gospels refer to him as 'having a dumb spirit'.

Another example of different words for the same case is that St Mark tells us that the Syro-Phoenician woman (Ch. 18) said to Jesus that her daughter 'had an unclean spirit', while St Matthew says that her daughter was badly demonised. All of which makes it hard to draw any conclusion other than that the terms were not neatly differentiated.

Nowhere does the Bible say that somebody has a *diabolos*, a devil, although some translations put it this way. It does refer to the Devil, but not to people having devils. It is therefore a pity when people use this phrase.

So we have four main terms: 'having a spirit', 'in a spirit', 'having a demon', 'being demonised'.

Nowhere is there the reverse, the demon *possessing,* or *having,* the person. People may have demons, but demons do not have people. The term 'demon-possession', therefore, is unbiblical and should not be used. It creates fear and one could say that it is propaganda for 'the other side'. The truth is that we can be affected by demons/spirits, but they cannot *possess* us. I prefer to refer to 'psychic infection' and I regard these entities as psychic viruses. If we catch such an infection, we know how to get rid of it, and there is nothing to be frightened of except fear itself.

Understanding

How can 20th-century people understand demons and suchlike? Perhaps you too have known people who are very sensitive to atmosphere (not what the astronomers mean by that word). For instance, there are those who can go into a room and say that it has a happy feel about it, or the opposite. I have even known people who could go into a room and say rightly: 'Somebody has been angry in this room,' or, 'Somebody has been having sex here.'

If such a sensitive person is 'run down' *spiritually,* then they might 'catch' that anger or lust, just as, if they were run down *physically,* they might catch a cold in a room where somebody had been sneezing.

Long ago Leslie Weatherhead suggested that the Gadarene demoniac may have witnessed a scene such as happened at Sephoris, when a Roman legion marched in and destroyed it, with its inhabitants. The fear, anger, hatred and cruelty of such a scene might well have left a surviving child with the legion marching round and round in his head, doing terrible things. This is how psychotherapy would understand it. Some of us, however, have come to the conclusion that in *some* cases there is a more objective reality to be dealt with. Hence my reference to a 'psychic virus' rather than the word 'demon' with all its associations.

Deliverance and healing – getting our words right

The Greek word which we translate 'exorcise' literally means *throw out,* so, to get our terms right, *you deliver a person, you throw out a demon.* (You do not exorcise people unless they get unruly in the pub!).

One may read in some books that the Jews saw all illness as demonic but this is obviously wrong. Wherever lists are given of what Jesus and his disciples did, throwing out demons is quite clearly separate from healing the sick (e.g. Matt. 10:8).

If we look at the way in which Jesus dealt with the various illnesses in this book so far (Ch. 7 especially) we can see the difference between exorcism and healing. To put it yet another way: you *heal* a disease, you *throw out* a demon.

Of course, all illness was seen as in some way the work of the devil 'under licence' from God, so to speak, as we see in the book of Job for instance. That, however, is not to say that every sick person has a demon.

The rituals

We will be better able to understand why people were so shocked by Jesus' way of dealing with demons if we know something of the elaborate rituals of exorcism, both Jewish and pagan. They are reasonably well known to scholars. To put it briefly, and rather crudely, if it was a corporal in the demonic army that was causing the trouble, then the exorcist had to find the name of a sergeant in the angelic army and use the sergeant's authority to chuck the corporal out. The higher up through the angelic ranks one climbed, the more care you had to take with spiritual insulation in case you got a shock, to mix the metaphors a bit.

They would have believed that only God could assume power over all demonic and diabolic influences without calling on angels, saints, etc. Therefore when Jesus did just that, he was assuming an Authority which no human should assume. No wonder that people were amazed, and asked, 'Who does he think he is?'

And for us...

For us today, there is a tendency to over-dramatise this side of ministry. Some of the reports on TV and in the papers show us how it goes wrong. This tendency to over-excitement is fear-creating rather than liberating, and it is contrary to what we read in the Gospels. As Francis McNutt put it: *'The better the diver, the smaller the splash.'*

So let us examine the cases of exorcism in the Gospels, without fear.

13. THE MAN IN THE SYNAGOGUE

Mark 1:21–28 (Luke 4:31–37, Matthew 7:28–29)

This story follows the account of how Jesus had returned to call Simon Peter, Andrew, James and John to follow him. After the incident at which we now look they went on to have a meal at Simon's house (Ch. 7).

And they went into Capernaum and immediately on the Sabbath, entering into the synagogue, he taught.

And people were astounded at his teaching, for he was teaching as one who had authority, not like the scribes.

And immediately there was in their synagogue a man in an unclean spirit, and he yelled, saying: 'What are you to us, Jesus of Nazareth? Have you come to destroy us? I know who you are! The Holy One of God.'

And Jesus rebuked him: 'Shut up, and get out!'

And convulsing him, the unclean spirit came out, shouting in a loud voice.

And everybody was amazed, so that they were discussing among themselves: 'What's this?' 'A new authoritative teaching?' 'And he commands the spirits and they obey!'

Notes

Mark says he is 'in an unclean spirit' while Luke says the man has 'the spirit of an unclean demon'. Luke says that it 'throws him in the midst...not hurting him', whereas Mark has a slightly puzzling word, 'tearing him up', which I have translated 'convulsed', although it could refer to gashing himself, as sometimes happens in serious cases, and in some forms of mental illness. The word remains a puzzle. Luke says that he was not harmed, so he could not have gashed himself.

Matthew does not mention the demoniac, only the impression Jesus had made.

We notice how many words such as 'at once' and 'immediately' occur here. One gets the feeling of urgency and authority running through the whole account.

Background

First let us notice that the demoniac is in the congregation. Jesus is preaching the Word.

The patient

If he had been obviously 'possessed', as people imagine it, he would never have been allowed in. This reinforces the point made already that there are quite sane people who have a nasty psychic infection that poisons relationships but does not get them labelled 'mad'.

The initiative

It is the presence of Jesus and his Authority which brings the hidden poison to the surface, and this is still the way today. General religious talk about God and the like may not ruffle the surface. Yet when the presence of Jesus starts to become real, things explode.

So in one way it was the demon who took the initiative.

How Jesus went about it

The short, sharp command, and that was it.

And for us

In one such case a person came for help, and at first we talked and prayed in general terms with regard to 'God'. During this the patient behaved quite normally. However, when I began to pray in terms of the presence of Christ, I was aware of movement and, looking up, saw the person standing over me with a large crystal vase ready to smash down on me. I bound the demon, ordered it out and that was that.

Later I found that a similar thing had happened when this person had gone to the chaplain in the mental hospital. It had taken four male nurses to get the patient back to the ward – the chaplain did not know about deliverance!

The difference

Those who are emotionally disturbed or mentally ill find Christ's presence soothing and helpful, while those who are infected psychically react violently. (The only exception is people who have had an unfortunate experience of

'Christians', for instance those who grew up with very narrow, fear-filled 'Christian' parents. Another exception is the attention seeker who has read a book such as this, and who acts up accordingly).

I know who you are!

Again it is still true that those with demonic infection know who they are dealing with. They can tell real Christians from non-Christians and they react to them with hatred and fear, just as the man in the synagogue did (or rather the demon in him did) towards Jesus.

How Jesus went about it: exorcism

Now look at what Jesus did. He said three words. The first means literally 'be muzzled'. That was the 'rebuke', claiming authority over it (see comment on *epitimao,* Ch. 7). It is the equivalent of 'Shut up.' Then comes the exorcism: 'Get out.' The two words are linked by 'and'. That is why I have put: 'Shut up, and get out!' As we have already seen, Jesus was a man of few, earthy words when healing.

No hands

Notice that he does not lay hands on this or any other case where the demonic is involved. It is his Word of Authority that sets this man free. The laying-on of hands is for physical illness.

The response

The violent response is quite usual when dealing with such cases. It is important for the people ministering not to be alarmed, but to keep all under control by the Authority of Jesus. On one occasion when a patient went into convulsions as part of deliverance we had a doctor present who confirmed that this was not a medical condition.

The Authority of Jesus

We come back to the fact that the way in which Jesus assumed authority cut through all the 'usual channels', which was truly amazing to people who were used to thinking in terms of the rituals we have referred to. It must have been terrifying for those present when they realised that Jesus was assuming the Authority of God. Only God could speak like that to demons and be obeyed without question. Who was Jesus indeed? The demon knew.

And for us

If we are preaching the Gospel effectively, with the Authority of Jesus, such happenings will occur; it is a good sign. *However, such an outburst can be upsetting for onlookers who are not prepared for this sort of thing. That is why we should not normally exercise this ministry in public.* People who are already upset and seeking healing can be badly damaged by such a scene. Of course, if it happens in public, as in the synagogue, one has to deal with it as quickly and in as low a key as possible, as Jesus did. Once you start 'playing to the gallery', you have had it.

CONCLUSIONS

- The presence of Christ brings the demonic to a head.
- It is very often this that shows us that perhaps we are dealing with the demonic rather than mental illness.
- It is dealt with by the Word of Authority, not by ritual or by the laying-on of hands.
- We must not be surprised if there is a violent reaction.
- Where possible such ministry should take place in private.

---

14. The Gadarene demoniac

Mark 5:1–20 (Matt. 8:28–34, Luke 8:26–39)

And they came across the sea to the country of the Gadarenes. And coming out of the boat there immediately met him, out of the tombs, a man in an unclean spirit, and nobody was able to bind him with chains any more, because when he had been bound with chains, he had just burst them off, and nobody could subdue him.

And he was crying out by day and by night among the tombs, gashing himself with stones.

And seeing Jesus from afar, he ran and bowed before him and yelled with a loud voice: 'What are you to me, Jesus Son of the Most High? In the Name of God I charge you not to torment me.'

For he was saying to him: 'Come out of the man, unclean spirit.'

And he asked him: 'What is your name?'

'Legion is my name, for there are many of us.'

And he besought him not to send them away out of the country.

Now there was a great herd of pigs feeding near that mountain, and they besought him saying: 'Send us to the pigs that we may go into them.'

And he allowed them. And coming out, the unclean spirits entered into the pigs, and the herd rushed down the steep slope (there were about two thousand of them) and were drowned in the sea.

And the swineherds fled and told the people in town and country, and these came to see what had happened.

And they come to Jesus to find the demonised man who had had 'the legion' sitting clothed and in his right mind. And they were afraid. And the witnesses told of what had happened to the demonised man and to the pigs, and they began to plead with him to leave their district.

On getting to the boat, the man who had been demonised pled to be allowed to come with him. And he did not allow it, but said to him: 'Go home, and tell your people what the Lord has done for you, and how he had mercy on you.'

Notes

The name of the place is doubtful – Matthew has Gadarene while Mark and Luke have Gerasene. I have kept Gadarene for convenience. It was obviously non-Jewish territory on the east bank of the lake. Matthew has *two* demoniacs. He uses the term 'demonised'. Luke has 'having demons', 'the one who had demons', and says that the man was naked.

A legion was a unit in the Roman army roughly equivalent to a brigade in ours.

Background

In St Mark's Gospel it is quite clear that this story is part of a sequence of events which begins in the late afternoon (Mark 4:34), probably about 5 o'clock, and ends in daylight as the people from the town come out. We are dealing, then, with an all-night session. This is not clear in the other two versions.

We begin by following the story from the above verse. First of all we notice that even Jesus needed to get away from it all at times, and St Mark's phrase 'they took him just as he was' gives us some idea of their haste to get away. Even Jesus could be so drained by the work that he needed a break and could fall asleep in that way. He was truly human.

The storm

Such storms as this are common on the 'Sea of Galilee', which is really quite a shallow lake. The cold mountain air is funnelled down the glens, and the shallow water is soon whipped up (Mark 4:37). Jesus speaks to the natural forces as if they were naughty children, and throughout the Bible nature is seen as being responsive, not just as dead 'scenery'. We are back at the word *epitimao*, exerting authority, translated wrongly as 'rebuke'. His words are summed up in two phrases: the first means to be quiet, the second, as we saw in the last case, is literally 'be muzzled'. Perhaps: 'Calm down. Shut up.' Some books confuse this with exorcism, but it is quite different.

The patient

The description of the demoniac is striking, but people who know these parts of the world tell us that such cases are still known. This case is the best illustration of what people think of as 'possession' but, remember, the Greek word 'possession' is not used in any version.

The initiative

Note that the man is sufficiently in control to come to Jesus for help, even while the demons in him complain. His body-language says, 'Help,' while the voice cries out in protest. He is therefore not completely under the control of the demons. They do not possess him. It is interesting that the demons can claim to speak 'in the Name of God'. As pointed out earlier, it is Jesus whom they find unbearable.

How Jesus set about it

There is a clue which is easy to miss, indicating that this was a case for prolonged treatment. It is in the verb in verse 8, which is in the imperfect tense, implying that 'Jesus was saying repeatedly', not 'Jesus had said' as in some English versions. To have cast them all out at once would have been too much for the man's constitution, so they had to be dealt with one at a time with a period of rest and in-filling between each. It is the same today.

'Legion'

This is the only instance of our Lord naming the demon. This was the usual practice in his day among exorcists, and is often part of modern exorcism. Normally, however, it is important that we should 'know the Name of Jesus', not just in a superficial way, but in a deep sense. We should concentrate on Jesus, not on the demons. There is a real danger of over-emphasis on the demonic side. However on some occasions it does seem to be necessary to command the demons out by name.

The pigs

It is the pigs which are the puzzling feature in this story. Yet it has the ring of truth, for it is not the sort of incident that would be made up for propaganda purposes. If it had not really happened, who would have made up the story and why? Perhaps we sympathise with the local folk who asked Jesus to go away after causing such trouble, no doubt having given them considerable financial problems! Two thousand pigs equals a lot of money.

As a starting point to understanding this part of the story, I remember that during one Bible-study on this passage a man who had kept pigs gave us examples of how psychically sensitive and inquisitive pigs are. He found the behaviour of the pigs quite understandable. Inquisitive beasts that they are, they would come snuffling round in the dawn light. The psychically terrifying atmosphere would send them into a panic, and they would bolt.

No return

Another point is that when dealing with such a case, one finds that there is a real fear that 'they' will come back. How often one has heard the cry: 'What will I do if they come back?' It must have been in the man's mind, even if the Gospel writers did not mention the question. A further point, which I cannot verify from experience, is the idea that somehow demons and water do not mix (cf. *Tam O'Shanter* by Burns, in which the witches cannot cross running water and so Tam escapes). As the pigs plunged over the cliff and into the water the man would have a visual aid to tell him that they would never return.

Having said all that, we are left with a number of questions to which there are no definitive answers. We may interpret them in various ways, but we are left with mystery. That is the way it was. We must take it or leave it.

The sequel

The sad reaction of the locals is only too predictable. These people are obviously not Jews, for Jews do not keep pigs. In Decapolis, the region in which presumably this place was found, they were a Greek-speaking people with no ideas about the coming of a Messiah. They would interpret the incident quite differently from the way in which a Jew would, which is possibly the clue as to why Jesus charged the man to tell people about it, whereas in his own country he usually told people to keep quiet. So they set sail for Galilee again, where more trouble awaited as we have seen in Chapters 4 and 10.

And for us?

We are not likely to come across such extreme cases, but if we do we must be ready to spend a lot of time on the process. However, it is still the Word that delivers the person, while the sort of practices about which we read in the papers from time to time are not scriptural.

Animals

We should note that one should never do exorcisms when there are animals about. A lot of animals, apart from pigs, are very sensitive psychically, and there are many examples of self-destructive behaviour in animals that have been in the house when exorcisms have taken place.

CONCLUSIONS

- There are cases of multiple infection in which one has to tackle one demon at a time.
- In some cases one needs to name the demon.
- Keep animals out of the way.
- Note the costly care of Jesus: he came to this place for peace yet spent the night struggling with darkness in this man.

---

15. 'Why could we not?'

Mark 9:14–29 (Luke 9:37–43, Matthew 17:14–21)

The story begins after Jesus had led Simon Peter, James and John up a mountain, presumably Mount Tabor, and had become radiant while praying: Mark 9:1–13.

Coming to the disciples, they saw a great crowd gathered around them. And immediately, on seeing him, the people in the crowd were astonished, and ran to him to greet him.

He asked them: 'What are you discussing with them?'

One of the crowd answered him: 'Master, I brought this my son to you. He has a dumb spirit. And whenever it seizes him, it throws him, and he foams and grinds his teeth, and he is wasting away. And I told your disciples, so that they might throw it out, and they were not able to.'

And he replied: 'What a faithless lot! How long shall I be with you? How long must I put up with you? Bring him to me.'

And seeing him the spirit immediately threw him down, and falling to the ground he thrashed around.

And he asked the father: 'How long has he had this?'

And he said: 'From infancy. And it has often thrown him in both fire and water, to destroy him. But if you can, help us, have pity on us.'

And Jesus said to him: 'IF YOU CAN? Everything is possible for one who trusts.'

At once the child's father cried out: 'I trust! Help my lack of trust!'

So, seeing the crowd gathering, he assumed authority over the unclean spirit, saying:

'Dumb and deaf spirit, it is I who command you. Come on out of him and never go back.'

And, yelling and convulsing him severely, it came out.

And he appeared dead, so that many said: 'He has died.'

But Jesus, taking him by the hand, lifted him, and he stood up.

And, once in the house, the disciples questioned him: 'Why could we not throw it out?'

And he said: 'Nothing gets this kind out except prayer.'

Notes

The words describing the boy's symptoms mean 'throw' and 'tear'. We came across the 'tear' word earlier when it said specifically that the patient was not hurt, so at that point we decided that it did not mean 'gash' physically. The words obviously refer to convulsions, and I have translated it in terms of what I have seen in these cases.

The father's cry

I have put 'trust' rather than the familiar 'believe' and 'faith'. For people today, these words have become associated with accepting stated doctrines. That is *not* what was happening here. It was a person-to-person encounter.

Rebuke?

The Greek verb here is *epitimao* once again. It describes precisely what Jesus did, saying: '*It is I* who command you.' It does not mean that he gave the demon a telling off!

Prayer

In the final answer, Jesus says 'except by prayer'. Some versions have added 'fasting'. For Jews the two words 'prayer and fasting' normally went together, and most scholars seem to think that the original is just 'prayer' but that the two words had crept in together from habit.

Background

We have a 'crowd scene', with Jesus having gone up the mountain, while the remaining disciples were healing in Jesus' Name (i.e. as his representatives). Then this father and son arrive. The disciples' later bewilderment that they were unable to heal this case suggests that they were succeeding in others.

Let us begin by being clear about one thing:

Epilepsy

While this boy had symptoms which we would call epilepsy, and it was a case for exorcism, that does not mean that epileptics need exorcism. There are physical reasons, such as brain damage, for this condition too, and one may do a lot of harm if one tries exorcism on a person whose convulsions have a physical basis. They need 'healing'.

As mentioned earlier, a doctor or nurse can tell whether or not the convulsions have a medical base and constitute an epileptic fit.

The initiative

The initiative in this case lay with the father, obviously, but we do not know what the boy thought in his lucid periods.

How Jesus set about it

He begins by speaking to the father. There is no other case in which we find Jesus asking about the history of the trouble. This delay makes the father wonder if it is going to prove too much even for Jesus. His desperate cry for help is one with which we can well sympathise. His faith is at very low ebb.

Jesus replies by echoing that poor man's '*if...*' He emphasises that any hindrance to healing lies on the human side, not on the divine. However the father's honest confession of a lack of trust (the Greek has 'help my no-trust') is enough for Jesus to work on. There is no point in trying to kid God and oneself that one believes if one does not. Being honest is the first step of real faith.

Deliverance

His command has an emphatic '*I*', which is why I have put it as: '*It is I who command you.*' The implication is: 'You are dealing with me now, so no nonsense.' (Remember the point about the rebuke in the Notes.) As with the man in the synagogue (Ch. 13), there is a violent response and then a deep sleep-like state. We normally would be praying for in-filling by the Holy Spirit at this stage. We do not know how long Jesus let him rest, but eventually he took the boy's hand to help him to his feet. Again we note that he did not 'lay hands' on the boy, although he helped him to his feet, as with Simon's mother-in-law and Jairus' daughter.

The question

The big question is faced when they get back to the house: 'Why could we not cast it out?' It is one which all of us in this ministry of healing find ourselves asking. Time and time again we find that we have prayed for somebody, or even laid hands on a person, and there has been no healing. Sometimes we find that we have been able to help but not to heal someone. This is where we face disappointment, and it may lead to disillusionment in all concerned.

The crunch

Of course, we may blame 'The will of God' in such circumstances, or we may say: 'God hasn't answered my prayers.' We may even say: 'The answer was no.' Or we may just give up. Such responses to our failure let us off the hook nicely. That was not how Jesus answered the question about why it hadn't worked. But we look at that again when we come to the case of the leper (Ch. 20).

Failure?

If, in a 'failure' situation, we have only a shallow 'interest in healing', then we will probably give up or resort to self-deception. Hurt pride is the danger here. If, however, we are truly motivated by love for God and love for people we will have to go on and listen to the answer which Jesus gave.

Jesus' answer

In the notes on this chapter we considered the two versions of Jesus' reply. Matthew gives Jesus' answer as being 'lack of faith', Mark gives 'lack of prayer'. However both versions of his answer stress that the reason that nothing had happened when they prayed was a lack in the disciples. Yet they must have been thinking: 'But we were praying hard…and the boy only got worse.' However, the men who had been up the hill with Jesus had seen him in such deep communion with the Father that his body glowed. They knew that if *that* was prayer, then they had not started! In giving this answer, Jesus puts the ball back in *our* court.

When it looks as if we have failed

We may blame the patient, saying that he/she has not got enough faith. If we do, the state of the person may be worse than before they came to us. We may give up – feeling that it is too painful to get involved in this sort of situation. Or we may find it an incentive to learn to pray together more deeply. However we can be sure that if we have acted in love for God and in love for the person, some good will come out of it in God's long run.

Getting sidetracked

There is a real danger that, when we find that we have too shallow a prayer-life to be effective in healing, and are lacking in faith, we will try to develop other techniques to fill in for where we fall short, e.g 'suggestion' or amateur psychology.

Now of course there are people who are called to heal at the physical and psychological levels: doctors, nurses, counsellors and so on. It is right for them to develop their techniques. However those of us who are giving the Church's Ministry of Healing must never lose sight of our main priority, which is: *so to grow in faith and prayer that we become more and more able to heal as Jesus did. As we grow more Christ-like in character, we shall grow more Christ-like in our work of healing.*

Of course we shall do what we can to express the love of God, even at the humblest, most earthy level – first aid, for example. But we must never lose sight of that aim.

Doing his work

Or look at it from another point of view. As we saw right at the beginning of this book, healing is *work*. It is part of the *work* that we have been told to do: 'The works that I do shall you do also' (John 14:12). Our function as a church is to express the love of God, not just in words but in power, and that includes healing.

Part of the reason for what appears to us as unanswered prayer is that we have been asking God to do for us something that he has delegated to the Church. (You do not ask the teacher to do your homework for you.) If the body of believers is lacking in *faith*, in *hope*, or in *love*, it cannot do the *work*, and then not much healing will result from its prayers. *God does not do for us that which we are supposed to do for God: heal.*

Nowhere is this more vital than in the business of 'deliverance ministry', for there is no treatment for demonic infection at the medical level. Counselling and psychotherapy on their own are insufficient. There is only the Authority of Jesus of Nazareth. If the Church is too weak in authority to do it, as those disciples were that day, nobody else will. *'If the salt has lost its saltiness, how can the world be preserved from rottenness?'* (Matt. 5:13) If even the Church cannot do the Lord's work, what hope have the poor victims of the evil in the world?

Urgency

We draw this to a close, then, with a real sense of urgency. Our faith must be deepened, and our prayer life must take on a new vitality – not just for our own sakes, but for the sake of those who are sick and suffering in the world around us. And this, of course, is not just for us as individuals, but for the

Christian community, the Church, or whatever you call it.

Re-making

We often sing a chorus in which we say to God: 'Break me, melt me, mould me, fill me.' That is a painful process, as we know well in the healing ministry. We are broken over and over again, having to ask, '*Why* could we not heal?' And then we have to face the Lord's answer. Especially in those Last Supper chapters in St John's Gospel with which our study of the Gospels concludes, Jesus stresses over and over again that it as we obey his commands, his commands to love one another, that prayer will be effective.

If we are one, if we are like branches in a vine, all intertwined in love, then we will bear fruit, and do the works that Jesus did. Our growth in faith and in prayer is never a solo performance, though each individual has a part to play.

We grow *together* in love and in faith. As we do so, we grow in the ability to carry on Jesus' healing work.

Conclusion

• God help me, I've a long way to go! Help my lack of faith, hope and love.

Summary EXORCISM

We have now looked at the three main accounts of deliverance, leaving one to be tackled in the next chapter, i.e. the daughter of the Syro-Phoenician woman (Ch. 15). We have also looked at a case in which a form of deliverance led into healing, although it was not actually exorcism: the bent woman in the synagogue (Ch. 12). There are two further cases of demonisation: Matthew 9:32–33 and 12:22 and Luke 11:14. They are both very short and are given with no real context. They therefore do not lend themselves to the treatment we have given the others. The best we can do is to look at what they *do* say and leave it at that.

Symptoms

In both cases the word used is *demonise*. In the first case the trouble is dumbness, and in the second it is blindness and dumbness. What we are not told is whether there were symptoms other than these, or whether the behaviour of the men concerned indicated demonisation. In both cases we note that we have come across cases who appear to have the same symptoms, but of whom it was *not* said that they were demonised (Chs. 8, 9, 11, 22). It is worth stressing this again: *In the Gospels there are cases of blindness and of dumbness which are not attributed to demons.* We cannot conclude on the basis of those two miracles, as some people do, that therefore all cases of blindness and dumbness are demonic.

This brings us yet again to face the fact that people with the same symptoms may need very different treatment. Once more we stress that each case must be approached with an open mind, open to God and open to the person.

Jesus' response

In neither of these cases are we told what Jesus did. In the first case it just says, 'The demon having been cast out, he spoke.' In the second, Matthew rather surprisingly says that Jesus *healed* him, using the word *therapeuo*. In no other case is this verb used of exorcism. Some do need healing as well as deliverance.

On the other hand Luke, in reporting what we assume to have been the same incident, says that Jesus 'was *casting out* a demon'. This is the more usual term, but it is used in such a way as to suggest it was something Jesus 'was doing' not something 'he did'. This links up with the story of the Gadarene demoniac (Ch. 14), where a longer procedure seems to have been involved. It is interesting to note how different are the accounts of what appears to be the same incident.

There is clearly not enough detail for us to draw any conclusions from these two cases, beyond what we have seen already in the previous ones.

Mary of Magdala

Another case referred to in the Gospels is that of Mary of Magdala 'out of whom He had cast seven demons', but no account is given. It was probably so well known at the time that they did not bother to write it down.

The initiative

In examining these cases it seems that the initiative comes in various ways: the father of the boy (Ch. 15) and, as we will see, the mother of the girl (Ch. 18) both come to Jesus asking for healing for their children, one bringing his child, the other on behalf of hers. The man in the synagogue did not begin by seeking healing.

The Gadarene demoniac seems to have come to Jesus in spite of his demon. In both the latter cases it is the presence of Jesus which provokes the crisis, so in a way one could say that he took the initiative. Certainly today one of the ways in which the demonisation becomes apparent is that a crisis is provoked when, in the worship of a Christian community, the presence of Christ becomes strong.

Jesus' response

Jesus' response is more or less uniform: the command *'Come out'*. Apart from the incident of the pigs, he does not tell the demons where to go.

In the synagogue he began by saying, 'Be muzzled,' and in the case of the boy whom the disciples could not heal he begins by 'taking authority over' the demon. There seems to be no equivalent to 'binding' the demon as many do today.

He does not lay hands on people for exorcism.

In the case of the Syro-Phoenician woman's daughter (Ch. 18), we shall see that we do not know what he actually did.

Aftercare

One further point is that Jesus stressed the need for aftercare, so that the 'newly cleaned house' would be firmly occupied, but we have no examples of how he went about this. Of course, one might see the fact that Mary of Magdala (Luke 8:2) became part of the inner circle in this light (Matt. 12:43ff and Luke 11:24ff).

Worried?

No doubt there will be readers who have been upset by our taking the idea of demons literally. This may be because they have seen the dangers in this ministry, or it may be just that it upsets their whole view of the world in which we live.

However the concern of this book is not to convince people that there are such infections, but rather that the Name of Jesus is the effective cure.

There is no doubt that the popular idea of 'possession' is fear-creating, false and counterproductive. It is based on horror films and novels. We have to play it down and keep our eyes on Jesus in faith and love. Remember: 'Perfect love casts out fear.'

The real battle

Let us conclude this section by coming back to the all-important point: Jesus cast out many demons, yet by the time he went to the cross he was still struggling with the human sin in those closest to him. It is human sin which is the real enemy, not demons. We tend to over-dramatise the demonic element, and miss the real need to bring the Gospel to bear on human lives and human situations. It is far easier to deal with a demon or two than with human selfishness, or with mental illness for that matter. Admittedly it is sin which lays us open to the demonic, but you cannot blame demons for everything that is sinful.

Therefore we find destructive, even criminal, people who are not demonised, and respectable, well-meaning people who are.

We deal with our sins by bringing them into the light of the forgiveness of God, facing them in the light of the cross, and being renewed by the Holy Spirit.

Getting priorities right

This leads us to look at one last aspect of deliverance before moving on – Luke 10:17. It seems that Jesus had sent out 72 followers on a rapid tour of the area, probably to publicise his coming. This is the result: *The seventy-two returned with joy saying: 'Lord, even the demons submit to us!' And he said: 'I saw the Satan falling from heaven like lightning. Look! I give you authority to tread on snakes and scorpions and all the power of the enemy and there is no way that any of this can harm you. But all the same, do not rejoice that the spirits obey you, but rather that your names are written in heaven.'*

Jesus' reaction is twofold:

1. He sees profound, cosmic significance in the fact that simple people now had authority over evil. He knew that the 'tide of war' had turned, just as we knew, in World War II, that once the Falaise Gap had been closed the war was as good as won, while there would be a lot of bitter fighting yet. He sees that we have an importance far greater than we realise.
2. But he warns them not to get carried away just because they could 'mop up' a few demons. The important thing is our relationship to God.

We have seen, to our cost, how easy it is for Christian groups to get over-excited and fascinated by the fact that they are chucking out demons and so on. It then becomes a colossal ego-trip, involving feelings of power. As a result, such people become very unhealthy spiritually.

The important thing for us, and for those to whom we carry the Gospel, is not deliverance or miracles, but a new relationship of love with God, and with other people. The first activity of the Holy Spirit is not to produce in us 'tongues', 'deliverance' or 'healing', but to seal in our hearts the fact that, to us also, God says, 'You are my beloved son/daughter in whom I delight.' Get that right and the more psychic aspects of the Christian life – tongues, healing, deliverance, etc. – will fall into place and be kept healthy.

Further reading

The best teaching I have come across is in the novels by Susan Howatch, *Glittering Images,* etc. These explore the relationship between the psychic and the spiritual (commonly confused), between the medical, psychiatric approach and the ministry of deliverance. They also show where the ministry of deliverance can go badly wrong. Incidentally, they are good novels as well, the sort it is hard to put down.

Conclusions

- Demonisation is a reality, not just a name for psychosis or neurosis, although it may be a contributory factor in both. It may also be present without either.
- The appropriate treatment is the Word spoken by one who has the Authority of Jesus by the Power of the Holy Spirit.
- It is human sin, not necessarily in the victim, which leads to infection, not infection which leads to sin. Sin is the greater problem.
- There are cases in which prolonged treatment is needed, with one infection at a time being dealt with.
- Elaborate rituals have no biblical authority.
- Aftercare is needed.
- There is nothing to fear except fear itself.
- We have to be careful to distinguish between:
  - the highly charged *spiritual* atmosphere which is vital for deliverance, and
  - the highly charged *emotional* atmosphere which may result in damaging those who seek help.
- To quote Francis McNutt again: 'The better the diver, the less the splash.'

An example

A young woman had had a bad fright on her holiday. The next year she found she was terrified of going on holiday with her husband and three children. She went to her doctor for a sedative, but the doctor knew that travelling with three children one needs to be 'on the ball', not sedated!

So the doctor brought her to the Christian Fellowship of Healing hoping that we could inspire some faith in the woman. However, when we began to pray with her we found through the gift of discernment that there was something demonic. Silently we told it to go. Then I said out loud a short prayer on the theme 'perfect love casts out fear'.

When I had finished, the woman looked up and handed the valium back to the doctor. She knew she no longer needed it. If we had told her that she had had a demon, she would have been terrified, and we would have had a much tougher job getting her over that real fear than getting rid of a demon. She thought it was the spoken prayer that had solved the problem.

Introducing OUT OF CHARACTER

There are some instances of situations in which Jesus seems to act 'out of character'. We now turn to look at three examples of this. Reading these stories one may get quite a surprise.

This is perhaps because for generations children were introduced to Jesus by the hymn 'Gentle Jesus meek and mild', and *this* is the picture which sticks in the mind, so that when we read a story in which he is not meek and mild, in fact when he is quite aggressive, we are taken aback.

Yet it is the 'meek and mild' picture that causes real problems for many people. Having served in three industrial parishes, I know that down the pit, on the factory floor, in the workshop, men who are meek and mild will not last long. If the picture of what it means to be a Christian is somebody 'meek and mild', then it is no wonder that there are not many industrial men in the Church.

Yet the word 'meek' does comes into our Bibles, and it is there in the Beatitudes (Matthew 5:5). However the Greek word translated as 'meek' describes a well-trained horse, a horse which is responsive to the guidance of the rider. People who are responsive to God are formidable people.

Our next three stories show us a Jesus who could get tough with people, who could be angry, and who would not be shoved around by 'the authorities'. This is a side of his character we need to know, even if it is not often presented to us. Without it we cannot understand a lot of what happens in the world, for God is not an indulgent uncle, but a Heavenly Father, and this 'tough' Jesus is *the visible expression of the invisible God'* (Colossians 1:15, Phillips' Translation). Having quoted that verse, perhaps we should pause to 'unpack it'. The Greek actually says that Jesus is the *ikon* of God. For us *ikon* means a holy painting, but in those days it referred to a tablet which was given to somebody going on an errand representing an important person. It described the bearer so that there could be no doubt that he or she was the right person, authorised to do business on behalf of the sender. So now let us come to terms with the tough Jesus, the ikon of God.

16. THE HEALING OF THE NOBLE'S SON

John 4:46–54

He came, then, to Cana in Galilee, where he had made the water into wine, and there was a nobleman whose son was ill in Capernaum.

This man, when he heard that Jesus had left Judea and had arrived in Galilee, came to him, and asked him to come down and heal his son, who was dying.

Jesus said to him: 'Unless you people see signs and wonders, you will just not believe.'

The nobleman says to him: 'Sir, come on down before my child dies.'

Jesus says to him: 'Go! Your child lives.'

The man took Jesus at his word, and off he went.

As he was going down the road, his slaves met him saying that the boy was living.

He enquired from them as to the time of day at which he had got better.

They said to him: 'Yesterday, at about one o'clock the fever left him.'

The father knew that it was the very time at which Jesus had said, 'Your son lives.'

He and his household became believers.

Notes

Jesus expression of exasperation is puzzling. 'Jesus said to him: "…you people…"' It is a bit confusing. The 'you' is plural.

Background

Cana is a hill village not far from Nazareth, and the account of the wedding feast in John 2 makes it plain that Jesus' mother was a person of some importance there, and therefore he himself was known. In a small village like that everybody knows everybody.

This is one of the occasions when John actually indicates the time of day – the healing took place at about one o'clock. If you are familiar with the Middle East at all, you will know that not very much happens at that time of day.

The patient

This nobleman was presumably an official at the court of the puppet king set up by the Romans. An 'important' man such as this must have been really desperate before he could bring himself to come as a suppliant to Jesus.

In order to get to Cana by one o'clock, a journey of twenty uphill miles from the lakeside town, he must have begun early. We note that it was 'the next day' before he met his slaves on the road, and this indicates that the journey was a long one. No doubt he had with him a train of servants, for travelling was dangerous for the rich in those bandit-ridden hills. The whole village would come awake when such a party arrived.

The initiative

The man's concern for his son and his determination to reach Jesus are an important factor in this case.

How Jesus went about it

Jesus begins with an expression of frustration. This is surprising. It seems so out of character. Taking account of what we said in the Note, it would seem that he was speaking to all those who had gathered, not just to the nobleman.

Consider now why he might have been frustrated and angry. Remembering that the last time he had come to the village he had turned 120 gallons of water into wine – and good wine at that! – what do you think would have been uppermost in the minds of the folk in the village?

Imagine their excitement when he arrived on his way home to Nazareth! As he tried to speak of the Kingdom of God to them, imagine the glazed looks, the murmurings: 'Why doesn't he get on with it?' 'How about a wee miracle, Jesus?' As the morning wore on and the hour of siesta approached, might not the good Lord have felt some frustration building up?

No wonder Jesus' response begins with an expression of frustration and anger. As noted, the 'you' is plural, so it is the crowd he is addressing, not the father. The fact that the nobleman breaks in impatiently suggests that the speech was longer than we are told. With all respect, it would seem to me that Jesus would have to get this frustration off his chest before he could deal with the poor father. The attitude of the village folk we saw in Nazareth had prevented any 'works' there, and it could have hindered the work here.

Love and anger

We often dehumanise Jesus, when God took such care to become human in Jesus. The picture of God we get in Jesus is not of a serene, placid, unmoved Being; rather we see a real love – love that is deeply wounded, love that is angry and frustrated at the selfish obtuseness of us humans.

Remember some of his cries: 'Unless you see miracles, you lot will never believe.' 'Have I been all this time with you and yet you still do not know me?' 'O you of little faith!' So often we glimpse this frustration, which is an inevitable part of love when it is not returned. The anger of God is real, *because God is love.*

It is when we see the pain we cause in God that we truly repent, not when we are terrified of being found out. And remember what the true meaning of repent is: *rethinking your life.*

The Word

When Jesus finally turned to the father he would probably have spoken very quietly, yet with authority, so that the miracle-mongering crowd would not hear. That is only a guess, but it makes sense of the story. 'Your son lives' is not a prediction, it is the *Word of Authority*, a statement of fact about something that has already happened. The Lord of Life had spoken.

Present or absent healing?

We note that in this case Jesus does not go with the father, even though he did go with Jairus (Ch. 10), and did begin to go to the centurion's house (Ch. 5). His physical presence was not needed for this boy and 'absent healing' was appropriate, whereas in Jairus' case his physical presence was needed.

And for us?

This story stresses a point we keep making, but it does so from another angle: we have to learn to respond to each sufferer in the way appropriate for that person.

Putting a name on the prayer list may be sufficient in one case but not in another. It may be essential to go to the house and lay hands on one person, but a waste of time for another for whom the prayer list would have been sufficient.

CONCLUSIONS

- It is important for us to know when personal contact is needed and when it is not.
- Healing involves real relationships, not artificial niceness. Where a healthy relationship involves anger, it has to be expressed.

A story

Finally a story which illustrates that in these areas time and space work rather differently. One Tuesday night at the Christian Fellowship of Healing in Edinburgh, we were clearing up to go home when somebody came with a letter that had slipped under the mat and had been missed. It was a fortnight old, and was from a lady who was very ill in hospital and who had been helped before.

In her letter she asked for our prayers, saying that she knew we would be remembering her at the 10 am service each morning and so she would 'tune in' each day at at that time. The poor soul must have been doing so for two weeks. So there and then we got down to pray for her, with our coats on!

A week or two later we got a letter from her saying that she had recovered, much to the surprise of the doctors, and that her recovery had begun dramatically one Tuesday evening.

She had shown her *faith* by tuning in at ten each morning, but what was needed to complete the circuit was 'two or three gathered together' to represent Jesus. That is what *in his Name* means. In this case, as in the story of the nobleman's son, *time* was relevant, *distance* was not.

17. THE VIOLENT LUNCH

Luke 14:1–23

And so it was that he went to 'eat bread' one Sabbath with one of the leading Pharisees, and they were watching him like hawks.

And look! There was a man with dropsy before him. Jesus responded by asking the legal experts and the Pharisees: 'Is it legal to heal on the Sabbath, or not?'

And they were silent.

He grabbed the man, healed him and released him.

And he said to them: 'If any of you should find that your son or your ox has fallen into a well on the Sabbath, won't you immediately pull it out on the Sabbath?'

And they were unable to reply.

Notes

Jesus' quotation from Deuteronomy has two close parallels:

1. In the story of the stonemason (Ch. 19)
2. In the story of the woman in the synagogue (Ch. 12)

The obvious conclusion is that, as Jesus went about the countryside, he followed this line of thinking in a number of situations. The Gospels give us three of them. Those of us who have preached and spoken in a number of places know the situation well: There are stories and phrases that crop up often when we are speaking. We know too that they never come out quite the same in each place.

Some of our more scholastic brethren who write commentaries but who have never done this, feel that they have to invent all sorts of theories about editors juggling manuscripts, etc. Surely we can take it that Jesus really did use this approach on several occasions.

Background

This story once again makes it quite clear that Jesus did not need to have an atmosphere of emotional suggestibility in which to work. He could work in the face of strong opposition. We thought about this when considering Jairus' daughter (Ch. 10). What did pose problems for him, however, was the complacent attitude which he had found in Nazareth (Ch. 6) – and perhaps finds in many churches today. God help us!

The patient

Dropsy is a form of heart failure in which the bodily fluids build up, draining down to the legs and bloating them. The fluid level continues to rise until it reaches the point where it is fatal to lie down. Effectively, to lie down is to drown.

The initiative

There is no clue as to why the man was there. Was he a trap as the stonemason in Chapter 19 would probably have been? Or just somebody so desperate that he was ready to gatecrash a dinner party? We do not know. Did he come for healing? All we know is that he stood there. There is no sign that he asked for healing, but it would seem that in this case the initiative was his.

How Jesus went about it

The Lord begins by challenging the elders. Then there is a surprising thing. It says that Jesus grabbed the man. It is the same violent word as was used in Mark 8:22–26 (Ch. 11). This was no gracious laying-on of hands! It was, once again, the act of an angry man. In this we see God's reaction to pride cloaked in religion. He who could be compassionate towards the crowd of 'sheep without a shepherd' takes a strong line with those who have turned religion into a power-base.

We are not told how Jesus healed the man.

Releasing

The next step is very interesting. It says that Jesus *released* him. It is much stronger than the 'let him go' which is what you will find in most translations. It is literally 'free-from'. It is the word used of Pilate *releasing* Barabbas, and in Luke 6:37: 'Forgive as you have been forgiven,' which is literally: 'Release as you have been released.'

Certainly the man needed to be released from the oppressive atmosphere of that lunch. Such healing needs time and peace to 'take', for his new life would still be fragile.

And for us?

However there is another level at which it was important that Jesus released him. Too many people in the healing ministry try to hold on to those who have been healed. In the Christian Fellowship of Healing on several occasions we have had to release people from some charismatic healing figure who had formed some sort of hold over them. It had become a form of bondage (see Ch. 12).

Of course some of the people who were healed by Jesus did later become followers – Bartimaeus and Mary of Magdala for instance – but most of those he healed were just released. Therefore, having healed people, we must be prepared to release them. There is a subtle but vital difference between loving aftercare on one hand and failing to release a person on the other. There is another subtle difference between the joy of seeing newborn people becoming part of the family and sharing in the work, and scalp-hunting to swell your numbers. *If there needs to be follow-up, it must be directed at helping the person to share in the ongoing life of the fellowship, not at a continuing relationship with the person(s) who ministered.*

The follow-up

Once the man is out of the way, Jesus returns to the attack. First of all he confronts them on their own ground, quoting Scripture: Deuteronomy 22:4, which states that if your neighbour's donkey or ox (or some say 'son') falls you have to help it up. Jesus adds 'if it falls into a well', putting it to them that surely even they would not condemn saving the donkey/son from drowning on the Sabbath.

What a wonderful comeback on them. Would they have left the poor man to drown in his own fluid?

Remember, too, what we have already noted: their rules forbidding healing on the Sabbath arose from their interpretation of what 'No work on the Sabbath' meant, and they did accept actual life-saving on the Sabbath. That is why they could not answer: they knew very well that there was nothing in the Bible which said, 'No healing on the Sabbath,' but they themselves had prohibited it. It was *their* authority which Jesus was challenging, and they were cornered.

Such enthusiasm to spell out in detail what the Commandment meant could spring from a real devotion to God and the Law, but underlying this there could be other motives which Jesus went on to lay bare. The Pharisees could only see zeal for the Law of God when they looked in their own hearts, while Jesus showed up the hidden pride.

For us too, no matter how much devotion and love for God and for people we began with, nasty, poisonous elements creep in when we are not looking. They need to be exposed.

Clerics of all descriptions make rules with the best of intentions, but then when somebody breaks the rules because the situation has changed, they see it as disobedience to God! That is painful for us, as it was for those Pharisees that day. Can we take it? Watch Jesus now at work laying bare their 'nasties'. (Follow the story in your own Bible.)

The sequel

Jesus began by laying bare the hidden pride even more clearly. He exposed their concern with precedence. 'Being given my place' is a sinful concern not unknown among eminent church leaders today.

He then followed it up with an attack on manipulative invitations. Hospitality is regarded as sacred in all religions, but to use it to curry favour or to further one's own selfish ambitions is to abuse it. Jesus could see the network of inter-manipulation going on under the surface, and challenged it.

Of course, to go to the other extreme and to refuse to welcome your own kith and kin is to go wrong on another count (Isaiah 58:7).

By now the atmosphere must have been such that a real storm was brewing. So we come to the oily guest who tried to pour some of his oil on the stormy waters.

Jesus often gave crushing replies to those who made vacuous pious comments. Remember the man who called him 'Good Master'? Jesus snapped back, 'Why call me good?' In other words, 'Don't use words like "good" unless you know what you are talking about.' Or the man who exclaimed, 'Blessed is the womb that bore you, the breasts that suckled you'? Jesus made short work of him: 'Blessed are those who hear what God says and do it.'

The parable of the invitations

Far from allowing that oil to calm things down, Jesus gave a parable that stirred things up even more.

To understand its explosive content you have to understand that in the days before diaries and calendars, the way you gave an invitation was first to tell intended guests that you were going to give a party, for instance, 'after the barley harvest'. They would then send messages back accepting the invitation. When the barley was eventually in, the message would go out: 'Come now.'

In Jesus' story the first invitation had been accepted, but the excuses began when the 'Come now' message went out.

The parable concludes with the teaching that God is desperate for people to come and share the heavenly Feast. This is still offensive to many religious people who harbour the belief that it is only people like themselves who will get in. To suggest that God is not fussy about who 'gets in to enjoy the party' is still bound to provoke a storm of protest in certain circles, as it must have done that day.

We often seem to be erecting fences around God's table rather than going out looking for folk willing to come in, even if they are disreputable!

In some cases we seem to be building the dogma up to more and more unbelievable heights to keep people out: 'You have *got* to believe this or else...'

In other cases we seem to be raising the moral standards so high that people give up trying. Sometimes it is even the way we dress, speak and conduct ourselves that raises the barriers. Heaven help the congregation that on the one hand seems to be offering healing, while on the other hand is subtly keeping people out.

These religious barriers are raised by the hidden pride and selfishness that Jesus attacked so ruthlessly. They are the sins of the religious – and if you are reading this, you probably come into that category.

While genuine love in the Name of Christ *will* have a higher level of goodness, it will be a goodness which is attractive to the lost, the poor, the failed, and those who feel that they are not good enough (Matthew 5:20).

CONCLUSIONS

- Two points are reinforced:
  1. Jesus did not depend on 'atmosphere'.
  2. Anger on behalf of others has a rightful place, in us as in God.
- Toothpaste smiles and oily words have no place in a healing ministry.
- Jesus faces us with the hidden motives beneath our religious exterior.
- Those who minister must be on guard against the temptation to hold on to patients.
- Beware religious pride which builds barriers to keep people out even as it laments that they will not come in, and condemns them for staying out.

18. TO THE DOGS

Mark 7:24–30 (Matthew 15:21–28)

He went away up to the coastal district opposite Tyre and, going into a house, he wanted nobody to know. And yet he could not be hidden, for straight away a woman came, having heard about him, for she had a daughter who had an unclean spirit.

Coming, she fell at his feet, she was a Greek, Syro-Phoenician by race, and asked him to throw the demon out of her daughter.

And he said to her: 'Allow the children first to be satisfied, for it isn't done to take the children's food and to feed it to the pet dogs.'

And she replied: 'Yes, sir, yet the dogs under the table eat the children's crumbs.'

And he said to her: 'For that saying: Go! The demon has gone out of your daughter.'

When she got home, she found her daughter flat out on her bed and the demon gone.

Notes

Matthew has that 'she came crying: "Have mercy, sir, Son of David, my daughter is badly demonised." But he never spoke a word. And his disciples came pleading with him to get rid of her "For she's crying out behind us." But he replied: "I was sent only to the lost sheep of the house of Israel." Then she came and fell down before him saying…'

Then Jesus' reply: ' "O woman! Great your faith! Let it be as you have wished." And her daughter was healed at that time'

Tyre was an ancient city built on an island off the coast of what we call Lebanon, near present-day Beirut, and it would seem that Jesus was on the mainland.

The description of the woman may be puzzling to the reader. The culture of educated people in that part of the world at that time was Greek. She would have dressed and spoken like a Greek, but would have been Phoenician by race, as we might say that a woman was Highland by race but English by culture.

There is a strange turn of phrase to describe how she found the girl when she got home. All English versions have that she was lying on her bed. Yet it is not the usual word for 'lying'. It suggests to me that she was flat out on her bed, maybe 'out for the count'. It is one of those slightly puzzling expressions which only the eyewitness could really understand, but there does not seem to be anything vital in it.

Dogs? The reference to dogs is unusual, but the Phoenicians were one of the first people in the western world to keep dogs as pets, rather than as hunters or scavengers. In St Mark's account the Greek word has a diminutive, and would perhaps be best translated 'doggies'. It is not the insulting word 'dog' as a Jew would use it. Jesus is using a homely illustration of the pet dog yapping for food, while the food is set on the table in front of the child.

Background

This story is one of the most disturbing and apparently most out of character incidents in the Gospels. It needs to be looked at very carefully.

The foreign country

This was foreign territory for a Jew, the great port of Tyre. It was the first of a series of journeys 'abroad'. From here, after this incident, Jesus crossed over to the country to the east of Galilee, to what we call the Golan Heights. Then he went northwards, towards Syria, and it was up in that foreign territory, at Caesarea Philippi, that Simon Peter made his great confession: 'You are the Christ.' It was from that point that Jesus turned to face Jerusalem and the cross. We see, then, that this was the first of a series of attempts to find peace, away from the crowds and from the demands for healing. He was obviously needing to be alone with his disciples to prepare for the great ordeal. He was doing so by going to foreign countries.

The patient

This Gentile woman must have heard about Jesus, but she could not bring her daughter as the father had brought his son (Ch. 15). In St Matthew's account she says that her daughter is 'badly demonised'.

The initiative

St Matthew's account makes it plain that Jesus took some time before responding to her. She had to keep on asking. The initiative is very definitely with her.

How Jesus went about it

She faced him with a very real temptation and it was obviously a genuine
struggle for him as the delay and the vehemence of his reaction show. It was
as if he were thinking aloud, trying to sort out conflicting demands. He knew
very well that he had only to do one miracle here and he would be caught up
in crowds of suffering people again, all hope of preparation gone.

We often forget that Jesus was really tempted to do the wrong thing.
Remember that at the Last Supper he commented to his friends: 'You are those
who have continued with me in my temptations.' How wrong we are if we
think that those three temptations in the wilderness, at the start of his ministry,
were also the last, and that he sailed calmly through the rest of his life on earth
without a struggle. This, then, was a real temptation, something like: 'Heal her
daughter, and that will open the gate to the Gentiles.' He had to struggle to
work out what the right thing would be.

At this point he could have been diverted into being a popular preacher
and healer on a world scale, and he could have avoided the cross. His surprising reaction shows how violent the temptation must have been. As with the
centurion, we note that there is no sign of Jesus having checked on the suppliant's religion. She was a person in need and that was enough for him. The
woman's reply delights him and he responds at once. He leaves the district
immediately, before a crowd could gather for healing.

And for us?

This story takes us on to further insights into deliverance. There are two points
to note:

1. This is the only case in which Jesus exorcises at a distance.
2. This is the only case in which Jesus exorcises silently.

As we have seen, the normal way in which Jesus delivered somebody was to
'throw out' the demon by a short, sharp command. Yet in this story there is no
sign of a 'throwing out', only the statement that the demon had gone. It would
seem, then, that in this case a silent command had been given.

We have found that this is indeed possible, especially where the person has become infected by a demon without an act of will.[5]

It is especially important to exorcise silently if the fear aroused by the whole business of exorcism would outweigh the good done by getting rid of the demon. Remember the example given at the end of the summary of the Exorcism section.

Therefore it seems that in this case 'deliverance at a distance' and 'deliverance by silent command' may have been possible because it was a child who was involved and she presumably was the victim rather than the agent.

There had been no involvement of her will. That may be why the ministry was very low-key. This leads to a possible general rule: *The deeper the involvement of the will, the stronger must be the act of deliverance.*

There are cases when the Word of Authority is best given silently, in order not to stir up fear. On the other hand, if the person has deliberately dabbled in the occult, or in the obscene, then there must be renunciation and repentance – in other words they have to get 'the whole works'.

CONCLUSIONS

- Jesus himself found some decisions hard to make. We must not be surprised if we too find ourselves facing difficult decisions.
- Eventually he responded to the woman's faith and need, giving this priority over the strategic need for a quiet retreat.
- Deliverance can be done silently and at a distance if the person has not been responsible for being infected.
- 'He was tempted in all things as we are' commented the writer of the Epistle to the Hebrews (4:15) and we raise a barrier between ourselves and Jesus if we minimise the struggle which he faced.

---

[5] Father Jim McManus in *Healing in the Spirit* (Darton Longman Todd, 1994) gives some interesting insights into such matters.

Summary OUT OF CHARACTER

No doubt this section will have upset some people, undermining the 'gentle Jesus meek and mild' picture they have built up since childhood. We have seen that he could be ruthless in some ways, that he could get angry, and that he was truly human, in that he needed to struggle to find the way forward.

On the other hand others will have found it helpful, for it shows a Jesus, and therefore a God, who deals with the real world. If we base our picture of God on the life of Jesus, then we lose that heavenly uncle who just wants the children to enjoy themselves and who, while meant to be almighty, does not interfere when the children torture, abuse and massacre each other. That sort of a god never did make sense of the real world.

The wrath of God

What we see in these stories fits rather the picture of God which we get, for instance, in the prophet Amos who blasts the rich for 'grinding the faces of the poor' (yes, that is Amos's phrase, not Karl Marx's), and who pours scorn on the worship, the twanging harps (guitars?), sacred songs and sacrifices, demanding that justice should flow down like waters and fair dealing in a mighty flood.

Isaiah too expresses God's anger at much of the religious business ('temple-tramping' he calls it scornfully) while the poor are exploited by the rich, and Ezekiel blasts the 'shepherds of Israel' (the leaders) because they have made themselves rich and fat at the expense of the poor (Ezekiel 34).

In Romans 1 St Paul lets fly, in the Name of God, at the corruption in the Roman Empire which was reaching new depths of depravity under Nero.

All that degrades, impoverishes, exploits and perverts people is evil and, being *love,* God is implacably opposed to it. Therefore those who identify with these things and wilfully indulge in greed, exploitation, prostitution and idolatry, will experience God's love as destructive and hostile: *wrath.*

As we saw at the beginning of this book (Matt 9:36, *The Call*) God in Jesus looks with compassion at the confused, misled, exploited masses, 'sheep without a shepherd', and gives us good news for them. But that is not always what comes across to the masses.

Healing anger

This applies further when we are dealing with individuals. Many emotionally disturbed people turn out to be those who have been frightened into 'being good' by the picture of an angry God and they need to be helped to understand God's wrath, *and be grateful for it*. They need to discover for themselves that God's wrath is always *on behalf of* the lost sheep, such as they are. Such people are rarely impressed by attempts to sentimentalise God. They need to discover, as we have seen in the stories in this section, that God's wrath is always *for us* and *against* all that tyrannises, exploits and frightens us. And especially against people who claim to be frightening us in the Name of God, as those Pharisees did in Jesus' day – and as some folk still do!

There are times when we too feel angry when confronted with human suffering. We feel, 'This should not be!' Then we understand why Jesus would have been angry when it was suggested, as we shall see in Chapter 20, that he might not *want* to heal the leper. Sharing in that holy anger helps empower us for the job to be done.

CONCLUSIONS

- The picture of God All-matey[6] lets us down in the real world.
- The picture of God the Bad-tempered leads to unhealthy, bad-tempered Christians.
- We need the anger of the 'God who is *with us*' – with us in a deeper sense than the usual picture of a shadowy presence beside us.
- We need to see where our anger brings us close to God.
- Our churches need more anger on behalf of the hungry, the homeless, the lost.
- Our healing and our churches' healing lie in that anger.

---

[6] I am not sure who coined this phrase. I heard it from George MacLeod.

Introducing TO ASK OR NOT TO ASK?

Any minister who is involved in the ministry of healing has a problem when visiting the sick: 'Do I broach the subject of "healing", or do I not?' On the one hand, I have heard some say: 'If a person does not have faith enough to *ask*, then he does not have faith enough to be healed.' But, on the other hand, how can people know that the Church has a ministry of healing if we do not tell them? Or again, some people are disappointed if we just sit and chat socially with them, while others, if we do offer to pray, react with: 'Oh my God, am I as ill as that?' The offer of prayer sounds like a death sentence to many folk. It is not easy to know what to do.

A personal experience may illustrate the problem. I took our Christian Fellowship of Healing Newsletter to the print shop to be printed, and found that the lady in charge could hardly get off her seat because of a sore back. She had never shown more than a passing interest in the material we brought in, yet something moved me: 'This is ridiculous! You can't print stuff about healing because of a sore back? We'll have to do something about this.' I went round the counter and laid hands on her back with a prayer something like this: 'Lord, this won't do. Please do something about her back.' And he did.

I had taken the initiative in Jesus' Name and it proved the right thing to have done. Yet I also remember only too many cases when I have tried something like this and nothing happened. Afterwards I heard that the unspoken reaction had been, 'I knew it wouldn't work,' 'I didn't like to say "no" but...' or some such negative attitude. I had done more harm than good. Those concerned were not ready for it, and I should have kept quiet. It shows a lack of sensitivity on my part, but it illustrates a minister's problem.

Therefore it is with some urgency that we are going to look at what Jesus did, and we shall take four instances. In two of them Jesus took the initiative and in two of them the sick person took the initiative. Of course we have already noted who took the initiative as we have been working through the cases so far. If you look back, you will see that each story has had something to say on this topic.

19. The Stonemason

Mark 3:1–6 (Matt: 12:9–14, Luke 6:6–11)

And he went to the synagogue once more, and there was a man with a withered hand.

And they watched him closely to see if he would heal him on the Sabbath.

And he said to the man: 'Stand up so that we can see you.'

And he said to them: 'Is it legal to do good on the Sabbath, or to do evil? To save life or to kill?'

But they were silent.

Looking round at them with anger and deep sorrow because they were so hard-hearted, he said to the man: 'Reach out your hand.'

He reached it out and his hand was made good.

Notes

An old version, not in any Bible, has the man say to Jesus: 'I was a stonemason, working for my living with my hands. I plead with you, Jesus, give me back my wholeness so that I do not have the humiliation of having to beg for my food.'

In Matthew it is the synagogue officials who put the question of legality to Jesus. He replies: 'If any of you has a sheep which has fallen into a pit on the Sabbath, will he not grab it and lift it out *on the Sabbath*? How much more valuable is a human life than a sheep's! So it is legal to do good on the Sabbath.'

In Luke it is Jesus who puts the question, and Luke mentions that it was his right hand which was withered. He phrases Jesus' quotation as 'a son or an ox has fallen into a well...' We discussed these variations when looking at the man with dropsy (Ch. 17).

Background

The situation in this story is quite different from that in any other, so we depart from our usual pattern by looking first at the man who was healed.

We note that unlike the boy who was let down through the roof, he was not brought by friends full of faith. It was the very reverse.

Nor is there any suggestion that he had come that day seeking healing.

Presumably, since Jesus was in the district, he could have asked for healing any time if he had wanted to.

Whose game?

It seems more likely, especially in the Matthew version, that he was placed there as a pawn in the murderous game being played out, and he must have known it. In this he was different from the woman in Chapter 12, for there was no suggestion that she had been 'planted'.

One might, of course, say that the poor man was now caught up as a pawn in Jesus' 'game', reduced to being a 'visual aid' to his sermon. That would be true, except that humanity is made in the image of God and we are only truly ourselves when we allow ourselves to be caught up in God's 'game', and 'God's game' is wholeness.

Murderous religion

When we looked at the story of the paralytic at the pool of Bethesda (Ch. 3) and at the man with dropsy (Ch. 17) we mentioned the evil that is evident when the 'religious' see suffering humanity as mere pawns in their religious game, and do not consider the suffering of the person. This story gives us an even more blatant form of it.

How Jesus went about it

Even faced with this, Jesus went ahead. He provocatively assumes the initiative and his healing reinforces his teaching. However, as we noted, in the non-biblical account the man seems more active than in the Gospel accounts.

Confrontation

So we come back to the story. The New English Bible has a wonderful way of putting Mark 3:5 '*Looking round at them with sorrow and anger at their obstinate stupidity, he said...*' What a picture! How often does he still look at us in the same way?

Anger

Once more we see Jesus acting in anger, and deliberately bringing out into the open the murderous religion of the officials by asking: 'Is it right to heal (the same word as 'save') life or to kill it?' (See Exodus 31:14 for the penalty for Sabbath-breaking.)

The healing

When it comes to the actual healing, Jesus does ask the man for a minimum of faith in that he commands him to stretch out his hand. However the man has been face to face with Jesus and presumably has heard at least some of the sermon which led up to the incident. It is probable that Jesus has awakened some faith in the man even if he had none when he came to the synagogue.

Jesus does not, however, lay hands on him. Once again he works by his Word of Authority alone.

And for us?

We come back once again to the contrast between Jesus' healing in the face of such opposition, and his not being able to heal much in Nazareth.

In our situation it is very often counterproductive to try to introduce 'healing' into the church situation, cancelling out any good one might do. By contrast 'things happen' in the most unlikely contexts. Yet again – the point cannot be over-emphasised – it depends on our sensitivity to what the Lord wants done in each particular situation.

A 'plant'?

I remember a man (I forget who) telling me that he had been conducting a series of meetings, including healing, in Northern Ireland. In one village hall he realised that the front row was made up of the local IRA come to break up this Proddie service. An old lady hobbled forward and was healed. She was the mother of a local IRA leader. There was no trouble in that meeting! But to begin with she was probably 'a plant'.

CONCLUSIONS

- The initiative was possibly with the men of ill-will.
- Jesus deliberately took over the initiative from them.
- The man was quite passive, but even if he had no faith in Jesus when he came in, he had been exposed to the Lord's words during the service.
- No touch was involved, but a small act of faith was called for.

---

20. The leper

Mark 1:40–45 (Matthew 8:1–4, Luke 5:12–16)

And a leper came right up to him, crying out and kneeling before him, saying: 'If you want, you can cleanse me.'

And, indignantly, Jesus reaches out his hand, grabs him and says: 'I do want. Be clean.'

And the leprosy left him at once and he was cleansed.

Snorting, he immediately threw him out, saying: 'See that you say nothing to anybody until you have shown yourself to the priest and made the offering laid down by Moses as evidence.'

Notes

Luke says that this took place in a city (walled town) which is surprising, because lepers were not allowed in towns. He also mentions that the man was 'full of leprosy'.

Indignantly In most versions of the Bible we read that Jesus responded 'with compassion', but in the NEB you will find that he responded 'indignantly'. One very old manuscript does give that term, although most others do not. The NEB folk, however, reasoned like this: You can imagine some scholar, copying out St Mark's Gospel, coming to this angry word and being puzzled. He would think, 'It must be "with compassion",' and duly put that down.

On the other hand if 'with compassion' had been the original, you cannot imagine anybody later changing it into 'indignantly'. So maybe 'indignation' is the original in Mark. I have therefore followed the NEB and, in the light of the rest of the story, I think it is right.

Got hold of him All the versions that I can find have 'touched him', but once again Mark uses the stronger word which can even mean 'embrace'. It is not *epithesis*. Again this fits with 'indignation'.

Snorted Every version I can find says that Jesus *commanded* the man to go, etc. Yet the Greek word here is not 'command', but 'snort ', the same word as is used in St Matthew 9:30 (Ch. 9) and in the story of Lazarus (Ch. 24). Again it fits with anger. Yet nobody dares translate it like that. Nevertheless it is there in Mark. (Luke has a word which means 'command', while Matthew just says that Jesus 'told him'.)

Threw him out   This too is what is there in St Mark, so what I have written above is what it actually says, Most translations, if not all, try to make the account more acceptable.

Until...   I have put it that the command was to say nothing *until* he had seen the priest. This is because in the old way of speaking this is what 'say nothing but go and show' meant. As we say 'There is nobody here but me,' i.e. 'apart from me', in the same way 'Say nothing but you see the priest' means 'Say nothing without having seen the priest.'

Background

This story contrasts in almost every way with the one about the stonemason. The setting is in the open air and there is no suggestion that the man had been hearing Jesus preaching.

The patient

In Leviticus 13 and 14 you will find the rules and regulations with regard to leprosy. The symptoms mentioned there make it clear that the word 'leprosy' at that time covered a number of skin diseases which today we would not call leprosy. It seems that 'leprosy' was considered a sign of God's special disfavour, so the leper had to be driven out lest God's anger spread to the community at large. A leper was 'untouchable'! Hence the leper's hesitant: 'If you want to.'

Priests

Priests lived scattered throughout Israel, working their own smallholdings until their turn came to serve at the Temple. In the meantime they were referred to in situations such as this. They had to know the symptoms of 'leprosy' among other things.

The leper's psalm

If you want to know what it felt like to be a leper, then read one of the most heart-rending passages in the Bible: Psalm 88, the leper's psalm. In it we are helped to feel their plight. What made the leper's situation even worse was that, in Jewish belief, after death there was only the prospect of 'sheol', where nobody would be able to worship God, and there was only darkness and mean-inglessness. So the psalm finishes in blank despair. The last word in the King James Version is 'darkness', and the NIV closes it with 'the darkness is my closest friend', i.e. 'when nobody can see the revolting mess that is me'. Nowhere is it plainer what a difference the Gospel made.

Inner conflict

This leper has two lines of thought in his mind. One is his desire to get better, and his confidence that Jesus can heal him, the other is the orthodox religious teaching, which makes him feel cursed by God.

The will of God

We come back to the question: Why might Jesus be angry? Surely it was at the very idea that it might be his will, or the Father's, that anybody should suffer this revolting disease. Jesus never questions the fact that he is doing God's will by healing. His healing might be limited by lack of faith, as at Nazareth, or by the shallowness of the disciples' prayer-life, as with the epileptic boy, but it is not limited by God's will.

If we change the wording from the archaic 'If it be thy will' to the modern 'If you want to', it is easier to see what that over-used phrase really means. Jesus was always clear that God wanted him to heal, but there are barriers on the human side. The only time Jesus used the phrase: 'If it be thy will' was with regard to his approaching death on the cross. He never used it with regard to illness. Our responsibility as disciples therefore, is to discern what God wants done in each case, and then to do it.

We are not to use 'If it be thy will' as a 'get-out' clause.

There is another point here. I have compared experience with others in this ministry, and we all have had experience of feeling angry at some disease – not at the person.

How Jesus went about it

Grabbing the man was an amazing thing to do – especially in the light of 'what the Bible says' about leprosy. It fits the word 'anger'. A man 'full of leprosy', as Dr Luke says, would smell awful, and to get hold of such a man would take a lot of the love of God!

It was not *epithesis* although I have heard sermons in which it was made out to be so. It seems more to have been sign language, saying: 'You are my brother. I am not driving you out.' Jesus then swept aside the religious teaching with an imperious *'I will.'* Then follows the Word of Authority. Then comes the snort!

The snort

We looked at the Greek word earlier (Ch. 9). That too fits with the word 'anger'. It may have been that the outpouring of life force to do this work was considerable, and made him snort, as we shall see again when we come to Lazarus.

Then it says that Jesus threw him out – another violent word. All translations I can find have that Jesus commanded him or some such. The Greek word for 'commanded' is nowhere to be seen. However, I understand it best in terms of what he might have said if he had been Scots. As the man began to get emotional Jesus would say, 'Aach! Away and see the priest!'

He had no time for sentimental bubbling. Just as he told Jairus' wife to go and get the girl something to eat (Ch. 10), so he brings this man down to earth with a bump, telling him to do the proper thing the Bible commands, and not to say anything until he has been properly certified as healed.

We note here that while Jesus had disregarded the Bible regulations with regard to this leper, here he enforces them. It was important for the man to get that certificate for only when he had it could he return to the life of his community. *Then* it would be right to tell people how he had been cleansed.

It is strange that Jesus seems to have taken a tough line with the man right through the story, and it ends on a tough note. There was to be no wallowing in emotion. He was to get the certificate. He was to get on with living.

So, in this, Jesus observed the Law in Leviticus, because it was for the man's good. As with the Sabbath, the Law was made for the good of humans (Mark 2:27). This matters more than the letter of the Law.

And for us?

It is a pity that more people who exercise a ministry of healing do not follow his example here. Only too often in so-called healing services people excitedly claim miracles long before the doctor (in our case) has certified that a healing has indeed taken place.

One particular international name in 'healing' has been shown up repeatedly as claiming miracles when none has happened. He has claims but not the evidence.

Our humanity and his

Jesus comes over in this story as intensely human, with strong emotions, so much so that translators have trouble putting it into English.

However, if we are to deal with the reality of suffering humanity, we need to know Jesus' true humanity, and so come to terms with our own humanity. You cannot heal from a pedestal.

Tom Smail was once speaking at a conference held by the Christian Fellowship of Healing in Edinburgh. He referred to the passage in which Jesus says: 'He who believes in me, out of his belly shall flow streams of living water.'

Tom commented that modern translations nearly all try to put it more politely: 'out of his heart', or 'out of his inner being'. He commented that this was a pity, because 'belly' is the best translation. Healing flows from the gut level, not from the head, or from the dog collar. Those who are afraid of real gut-level humanity cannot be healthy healers.

CONCLUSIONS

- It is the leper who takes the initiative, breaking the rules. His faith and his will-to-get-better are an essential part of the story.
- The fact that he still had a big question in his mind is brushed aside.
- Jesus deliberately breaks the biblical rules about contact with lepers, but observes the rule about the priests certifying that the man is cleansed.
- Touch was involved but not 'the laying-on of hands'.
- It was the 'Word of Authority' which healed, once again.
- The phrase 'if it be thy will' is confronted, making us rethink our conventional use of the phrase in healing prayer.
- If we are not in touch with our own real humanity, we are not in touch with that of Jesus either.

21. The ten lepers

Luke 17:11–19

And so it was that on his journey to Jerusalem he passed through Samaria and Galilee, and entering a certain village there met him ten lepers, who stood at a distance and cried out: 'Jesus, Sir, have mercy on us.'

And seeing them he said: 'Go! Show yourselves to the priests.'

So it was that as they did so, they were cleansed.

However one of them, seeing he was cured, returned with much 'glorifying God' and fell on his face at his feet, thanking him. And he was a Samaritan. Jesus replied: 'Weren't there ten cleansed? Was there none but this Gentile to give glory to God?'

And he said to him: 'Stand up! Away you go! It's your faith that has healed you.'

Notes

The lepers call Jesus by an unusual title, best translated as 'boss', literally 'over-stander'. I have avoided putting 'lord', because that suggests something more than is actually there.

If we look at Jesus' last words in the story, we see that he uses two different terms. He says that ten were *cleansed*, but this man was *healed*. The word here for 'healed' is, once again, the word for 'saved'.

The way the sentence runs in Greek, Jesus stresses that it is the man's faith that has healed him, once more giving the credit for the healing to the recipient.

Background

This group of ten men seems to have included a Samaritan, which is surprising in a way for, as St John says in his Gospel, 'Jews had no dealings with Samaritans'.

The Samaritans were descended from the people who were left in Palestine after most of the upper classes had been deported to Babylon. Other conquered nations had been brought into Palestine and had intermarried with those who remained. When the exiles returned seventy years later, they found this racially mixed group who still worshipped in the way that had been the style before the exiles left. There was bitter hostility between the two groups.

To this day a few Samaritans still remain who carry on the ways of worship that go back to a time before much of the 'Old Testament' was codified.

The patients

People in such dire straits as these lepers are drawn together in the fellowship of suffering, and understandably the old barriers had crumbled. A new, fitter person was valuable to help the weaker survive. The new person needed the comfort and help of the more experienced. In this way even those who had once been enemies could be drawn together. This group of ten, then, call out to Jesus as he is about to enter a village.

The initiative

The initiative here is with the group. It is they who call to him standing at a distance. Unlike the leper in Chapter 20 they observe the Law.

How Jesus went about it

There was no conversation or counselling at that distance. There was no touch or laying-on of hands, only the command.

There was a real test of faith in this. They had to make that step of faith to obey him. So it was that as this group made its way to where a priest lived, they were cleansed. We note the Lord's sorrow at the lack of response from the nine others.

This is the only example of healing a group, and at a distance.

And for us?

Giving thanks is an important part of healing. Compare it to taking in a rope at sea. Each time you take in a bit of slack, you make it fast round a cleat or bollard. If you do not, you are liable to lose what you have gained. So it is that thanksgiving 'makes fast' any blessing received.

CONCLUSIONS

- Jesus' work is silent. It is non-verbal, unexpressed by any action. He then sends the lepers away, exercising their faith.
- We note the importance of thanksgiving.

---

22. BLIND BARTIMAEUS

Mark 10:46–52 (Luke 18:35–43, Matt. 20:29–34)

And they come to Jericho, and as they were on their way out of Jericho, he, his disciples and a considerable crowd, there at the roadside was a blind beggar, Son of Timaeus (Bartimaeus).

And hearing that it was Jesus of Nazareth, he began to shout out saying: 'Son of David, have mercy on me!'

A lot of people tried to shut him up, but he shouted all the more: 'Son of David, have mercy on me!'

Jesus, coming to a standstill, said, 'Call him.'

So they called the blind man: 'Cheer up! Get up! He's calling you.'

So he threw aside his cloak, and leaping up came to Jesus.

Jesus, responding to him, said: 'What do you want me to do for you?'

So the blind man said: 'Rabboni, I want to see again.'

And Jesus said to him: 'Away you go! Your faith has healed you.'

Immediately he could see again, and followed Jesus on the way.

Notes

Matthew and Mark both have this incident as Jesus was leaving Jericho, but Luke has it as he drew near to Jericho.

Matthew has 'two blind men' and does not mention any name.

He calls Jesus by the title given to a rabbi, 'Rabboni', although Jesus was not one, as we have already noted.

Mark and Luke both quote Bartimaeus as wanting his sight restored. Matthew only has that they wanted to see.

Matthew says that Jesus touched their eyes, but not that he 'laid hands on their eyes'. In Mark and Luke no touch is involved.

Background

Jericho, the city with the longest history of any on this planet, was the stopping place before the long haul up to Jerusalem. The Lord is on his way up for the final confrontation.

We know from other contemporary accounts that there were many blind beggars in Palestine at that time. They would naturally throng the gate that led pilgrims to Jerusalem.

The patient

The fact that his name is given in Mark and Luke presumably indicates that Bartimaeus was known to the first readers, which is in accord with the phrase about 'following him in the way' that concludes the story. Before the term 'Christian' was coined, 'in the way' was the term used to mean one who followed Jesus.

The initiative

The point of this story is that Bartimaeus made sure that he was healed, risking his life and that of Jesus by saying something politically dangerous: 'Son of David'. It was a royal title, with messianic overtones. Jesus would lay claim to this title when he arrived in Jerusalem a few days later on what we call 'Palm Sunday'.

Here in Jericho, however, it could have started an uprising. Then, as now, it took little to start the stone-throwing.

It was crazy but it worked. Jesus had to stop lest a riot began. In this case the initiative was very definitely with Bartimaeus and his determination is the vital factor in his healing.

How Jesus went about it

Strangely, Jesus does not seem to have healed any but Bartimaeus, though there must have been many at the gate. Those who just ask for pity and charity may get some, but that is all they will get. This man, determined *to be healed,* is healed. This links in with what we saw in Chapter 3.

Mark says that he threw aside his beggar's cloak. Probably his stick and bowl would go for six too! 'I'll not need them any more.' It is not always easy to leave behind the things which have been your identity, even if they were unpleasant. Sometimes being healed involves a radical change in our lives – real repentance, rethinking.

According to Mark and Luke the healing was short and sharp. The Word of Authority: '*Go,*' then one word, *'See-again.'* No fuss, no sermonising, no prayer, no laying-on of hands. Then, once he sees, Jesus gives *him* the credit for his own healing, as in Chapters 4 and 21.

Note that Jesus did not take him aside, as he did with the blind man in Galilee (Ch. 11), and this 'work' is in strong contrast to the 'man born blind' (Ch. 2). Presumably this healing could be done publicly and with minimum words because of Bartimaeus's attitude.

And for us?

Yet again we notice the lack of religiosity, the direct, businesslike response from Jesus. Perhaps the Lord would work through us all the better if we were a bit less religious, a bit more direct. Yet there is the danger of generalising. Some preachers take Bartimaeus as the standard pattern, and suggest that if you don't feel like him, then you cannot be healed. As we have seen, that is not the case. Such assertions result in people going away feeling worse, not better.

Incidentally this is the last case of individual healing before the Passion.

CONCLUSIONS

- Bartimaeus's determination to be healed was a decisive factor.
- Jesus stressed this to him as he gave him the credit for the healing.

I remember one service in which I asked people to imagine what Bartimaeus would have experienced as he regained his sight: beginning to see light and shadow, the shadow taking shape. Colour comes and he's looking into the face of Jesus. All this led up to singing the chorus 'Turn your eyes upon Jesus, look full in His wonderful face'.

A young man who had been blinded in one eye in an assault found that his sight had come back in that eye.

Summary To ask or not to ask?

What are we to conclude from these four very different initial contacts between Jesus and the person to be healed?

- The stonemason was probably a mere pawn in the game of the 'religious' and therefore the initiative may have been evil.
- The leper broke the Bible rules in his determination to be healed, but with a real doubt as to whether it would be God's will.
- The ten lepers were insistent but respected the biblical injunctions.
- Bartimaeus's determination was an important factor in his case.

Reviewing *all* the cases we have studied so far, we note that in some cases Jesus takes the initiative (Chs. 2, 3, 12). In others the person seeking healing takes it (Chs. 4, 9) while in others the initiative is with a third party on behalf of the sick person (Chs. 1, 5, 7, 8, 10, 11,15, 16). Finally there are two cases where the initiative might have been with Jesus' enemies (Chs. 17, 19). Therefore there is no one rule about who takes the initiative.

The situation today

As stated several times before, the conclusion is that we just have to learn to be more sensitive to God and to the people who come our way. We must never make such rules and generalisations as those we referred to at the start of this section.

On the other hand, we have to face the fact that some people could have been healed if only we had had the courage to offer ministry. Sometimes to fail to take the initiative is shameful negligence. (God forgive us!)

It all comes back, once more, to what is called 'meekness' in the Beatitudes – being open to God's guiding as a good horse is responsive to the rider.

Conclusions

- Sometimes we do need to take the initiative.
- Sometimes it is right to take the initiative on behalf of another.
- Sometimes we have to wait for some sign of faith before acting.

Introducing RAISING THE DEAD

One of the surprising things about the Gospels is that there are only two exam-ples of the Lord's victory over death, apart from his own. Right at the begin-ning we looked at *The Call* and if you had read on in the Bible you would have seen that part of the marching orders for the Church was 'Raise the dead' (Matthew 10:8) as if it had been part and parcel of Jesus' mission. We shall come back to that passage later. Yet we only have these two stories of his rais-ing the dead. Of course some would add Jairus' daughter (Ch. 10), but I prefer to accept what the Lord said: 'She is not dead.' However, if they had gone ahead and buried her, she would soon have been dead, so it is an academic point. We look, then, at the two stories we are given.

It is puzzling, because Jesus must often have faced the situation of people dying. After all, the infant-mortality rate was high, and so was the rate of deaths in childbirth. The 'average life expectancy' was only about forty. So we are left wondering whether two stories out of 25 reflects the actual frequency or not. Raising the dead is so spectacular that one would expect all such instances to have been recorded.

Accepted beliefs

As a background, it is as well to remember that the Sadducees, priests, did not believe in an afterlife because it is not mentioned in the first five books of the Bible, which is all that they recognised as 'the Bible'. They maintained that when you were dead you were dead, living on in your children. The Pharisees believed in the eventual resurrection of the dead – 'at the last day' – but that meanwhile the dead went to Sheol, sometimes wrongly translated 'hell'. We thought about what that meant when we considered the leper (Ch. 20). They believed that the souls of the dead lingered around the scene of their earthly life for about three days.

Jesus shook the 'priestly' Sadducees by telling them that they were wrong (see Mark 12:26ff). On the other hand he seems to have used language and imagery which would have been familiar to the Pharisees. It seems that they had picked it up from the religion of Zarathustra, whence came the Magi to welcome the child Jesus. It certainly was not in the 'Bible' as they knew it (what we call the 'Old Testament').

The Old Testament had very little to say about the afterlife. Other religions, such as the Egyptian, might make much of it, but the Jewish prophets were notable for their concern for this life, for justice, and for right relationships right here in this world now.

It was in this respect that Christianity went beyond its Jewish roots, while remaining faithful to them. All of which makes it all the more surprising that we only have these two stories.

23. THE WIDOW OF NAIN'S SON

Luke 7:11–14

The next day he went to a city called Nain with his disciples and quite a crowd.
And as he drew near the city gates, there was, before him, a corpse being carried out, the only son of his mother, a widow.
Seeing her, the Lord had compassion on her and said to her: 'Don't cry!'
And coming up to the bier, he touched it, so that the bearers stopped.
And he said: 'Laddie! I'm telling you get up!'
And the 'dead man' sat up and began to speak.
And he gave him back to his mother.

Notes

The term 'city' only means a village surrounded by a wall, in contrast to an open village.

His words to the boy make two points clear:

1. He was a young man. I have put the Scots 'laddie' in, since there is not an English word to convey the meaning.
2. The speaker has authority. It is an emphatic 'I'.

Background

What a masterpiece of understatement this story is! Imagine what a modern newspaper reporter would have made of it. Or even how some of our modern 'healers' would have written up such a case.

All we have is a simple account of a chance meeting of two crowds at a village near Nazareth, providing us with yet another example of how simply Jesus worked.

The patient

We know nothing about the boy. However his mother was now in a precarious position in Jewish society with neither a husband nor a son. The wider family could just walk in and claim her house and property. No wonder the Bible continually stresses that kings and others must protect the widows.

The initiative

There is no sign of a cry for help; it was purely the compassion and sensitivity of Jesus which wrought this work.

How Jesus set about it

We find no magic gestures, no action such as Elisha's with the widow of Sarepta's son (which looks very like the 'kiss of life' to modern readers). He does not ask about her faith, or about the lad himself. All that Jesus does is to signal to the bearers to stop by taking hold of the bier. It is as if to say: 'Wait a moment!' Some preachers, however, construe it as indirect 'laying-on of hands', suggesting that the power flowed even through the bier to the young man. Personally I think Jesus was just saying 'stop'. Readers must decide for themselves.

Whatever one makes of that gesture, true to his 'man of few words' style, all that we can be sure of is that he told the young man to get up. His words are blunt, homely and to the point.

The Greek says that the boy began to speak – one can imagine him looking round bewildered and asking, 'What's going on?' It says that Jesus *gave* him to his mother. The words suggest a physical gesture, taking him down from the shoulder-high bier, and handing him over to his mother.

There is another interesting point about his touching the bier. As with the leper or the woman with the haemorrhage, Jesus became 'unclean' according to the Law, in this case because he had touched something in contact with a dead body. According to the Law he would require ritual purification before doing anything religious – such as raising the dead. Jesus must have been quite sure that the holy life of God flowing from him was enough to counteract the uncleanness. *And that was it!*

And for us?

When dealing with a case of death, we have to be very sure that the power, the anointing, has been given before we raise hopes. Compassion is not enough.

CONCLUSIONS

- Jesus took the initiative.
- There is no suggestion of 'faith' among the mourners.
- The element of touch is questionable.
- The Word of Authority is short, sharp and homely.

---

24. LAZARUS

John 11:1–46

After surviving an attempt to get rid of him, Jesus had withdrawn to a place in what we now call Jordan, and we take up the story from there.

A certain man was ailing, called Lazarus of Bethany, the home village of Martha and her sister Mary. (That was the Mary who anointed the Lord with ointment, and wiped his feet with her hair. It was her brother Lazarus who was ailing.)

So the sisters sent a message to him saying: 'Sir, your beloved friend is weakening.'

Hearing this Jesus said, 'This illness is not terminal; it is all for the Glory of God, so that the Son may be glorified through it.'

Now Jesus loved Martha, her sister and Lazarus. However, when he heard that Lazarus was weakening, he stayed where he was for two days.

Finally, he said to his disciples, 'Come on. Let's go to Judea again.'

The disciples protested: 'Rabbi, the Judeans were trying to stone you the other day – are you going back?'

Jesus replied: 'There are twelve hours of daylight, aren't there? If you walk in the daylight, and you have light, you will not stumble. You are going by the Light of the World. But if you walk in the night you will stumble, because you've no light.'

That is what he said. Then he said to them: 'Our friend Lazarus is asleep, but I am going to waken him.'

The disciples said: 'That's good. If he's sleeping he'll recover.'

Now Jesus had meant that Lazarus had died, but they thought he was refer- ring to restful sleep.

Then he said right out: 'Lazarus is dead. I'm glad for your sakes that I wasn't there. But let's go to him.'

Thomas (the twin) said to his fellow disciples: 'Let's go...and die with Him.'

Now Bethany is about two miles from Jerusalem and many Judeans had come out from the city to Martha and Mary to comfort them in the loss of their brother.

So when Martha heard that Jesus was on the way she met him, while Mary sat in the house.

Martha, then, said to Jesus: 'Sir, if you had been here, my brother would not have died. But I know now that whatever you ask of God, he will give it you.'

Jesus says to her: 'Your brother will rise again.'

Martha says to him: 'I know he will rise again...at the Last Day.'

Jesus says to her: 'I am the One who is Living Resurrection. The believer trusting in me, even if he dies, shall live, and all who are living and trusting in me shall certainly not die in the age.'

She says to him: 'Yes, Sir, I've always believed that you are the Christ, the Son of God coming into this world.'

So saying she went off to fetch her sister Mary, but secretly, saying: 'The Master is here and is calling for you.'

Having heard that, she rose hurriedly and came to him...he had not as yet entered the village, but was still in the place where Martha had met him.

However, the Judeans who were with her in the house comforting her, when they saw Mary get up in a hurry, followed her, saying: 'She's going to weep at the tomb.'

So Mary, when she reached Jesus, fell at his feet, saying: 'Sir, if you had been here, my brother would not have died.'

Jesus, therefore, seeing her weeping, and the crowd of weeping Judeans with her, snorted in the spirit (breath) and disturbed himself.

He said: 'Where have you put him?'

'Come and see, Sir,' they said.

Jesus wept.

But some said: 'Surely, if he could open the eyes of the blind, he could have prevented him from dying.'

So Jesus, snorting to himself again, came to the tomb, a cave. A stone was lying on it.

Jesus said: 'Lift the stone.'

Martha, the dead man's sister, said to him: 'Sir, by now he'll stink. It's the fourth day!'

Jesus said to her: 'Did I not tell you that if you trusted, you would see the glory of God?'

So they raised the stone.

And Jesus looked up and said: 'Father, I thank you for hearing me! Of course I know that you always hear me, but it's because of the crowd standing round that I said it, so that they may believe that you sent me.'

Having said that, with a loud voice he shouted: 'Lazarus, come on out.'

The dead man came out, wrapped head to toe in bandages, and a cloth over his face.

Jesus says to them: 'Unwrap him! Let him go!'

Many of the Judeans who had come with Mary, seeing what had been done, believed in him, but some went away and told the Pharisees what had been done.

Notes

People wonder why John, whom we regard as a Jew, refers to the people there as 'Jews'. 'Jew' literally means 'a person from Judea', the district around Jerusalem. However John, a Galileean, uses the word correctly, whereas we often use 'Jew' to describe a Hebrew, in the same way as some people use the word English to include Scots, Welsh and Irish.

We come across that word *snorted* again. It is interesting to see how again modern translations water it down.

Pneuma As mentioned when we spoke of deliverance, *pneuma* can mean 'breath', 'wind', 'spirit'. The Gospel puts these two words – *snort* and *pneuma* – together, setting a puzzle for translators. The other word, 'disturbed', a rather violent expression, is as in 'Let not your heart be troubled'. I have left the perplexing words as they stand, without trying to make a more readable sentence.

Background

Bethany is a village on the hill across the valley from Jerusalem. It is the bus terminus today, and when I was there the smell of diesel was awful.

To help in imagining the scene, it might be as well to describe the sort of cave-tombs which have been found from that era in Palestine. Any reasonably well-off family would have had its own cave-tomb ready. The soft limestone rock was carved out into two chambers. The outer one had a ledge, and on that ledge the latest occupant was placed, wrapped in linen bandages with fragrant spices placed in them. When another arrived, the previous body was removed to the inner chamber, and so on. There was something like a large millstone made to roll into place to seal the whole thing.

The patient

Jesus obviously had more contact with this family than we actually know about. For instance in Luke 10 there is the lovely Martha/Mary story. It clearly shows that he knew them well. This is the first mention of the brother, Lazarus.

Mary of Bethany is not to be confused with Mary of Magdala. This anointing is not the same as the one in Galilee by an unnamed woman 'who had been a sinner', and who also anointed Jesus' feet. 'She who had been a sinner' did it out of penitence and love. Mary of Bethany was quite different. She showed great intuitive insight, in that she *broke* the jar, part of the funeral rite, and *anointed* Jesus, part of the coronation rite. She seems to have been the only person who came near to understanding what was going on.

Jesus expressed appreciation of this. Hers is an act of recognition, leading to congratulation, whereas the Galilean anointing led to a declaration of forgiveness. Mary of Bethany's act is one of the few stories to be found in all four Gospels.

Thomas appears here for the first time. We know him as 'doubting Thomas', but here we see the man who is the realist. He knew what they were heading for if they went back to Judea, and yet he had the courage to be the one to say, 'Let's go.' The story in John 20:26ff which gives rise to his 'doubting' nickname shows that in fact he was the one who had the greatest grip on what was what. The others had drifted back to the Upper Room, 'but Thomas was not with them'. He saw the issue more clearly than the others. Eventually it was Thomas's 'My Lord and my God' which came to terms with who Jesus *is*.

Again we come up against the misunderstanding of 'faith'. Faith does not mean maintaining a cloud-cuckoo land over against reality. It means daring to come to grips with reality.

The initiative

Martha and Mary took the initiative by sending for Jesus when their brother became ill. They were obviously reproachful and disappointed in him. Why had he not come in time? However Jesus was waiting for his Father's initiative. We may compare his hesitation here with when the Syro-Phoenician woman asked him to heal her daughter, and when the two blind men followed him (Chs. 9 and 18).

How Jesus went about it

Verse 9 gives us Jesus' awareness that if he was doing *what* the Father wanted, at the *time* the Father indicated, he need have no fear. Nor need we, if we get our obedience and our timing right. If we do not, then admittedly we are vulnerable to the 'old enemy'.

Martha
Then Jesus has the conversation with Martha. It is fascinating to see Martha's faith rising and falling in a way that many of us know only too well. It is one thing to say, 'I believe,' when looking into the face of Jesus; it is another to say, 'I believe,' when face to face with a tombstone. It is one thing to sing hymns about trusting God on Sunday; it is another to sing them when faced with your redundancy notice.

Resurrection and life
'I AM.' When Jesus makes the great statement in verse 25, he uses *ego eimi* – *'I am the One who is'*. It is much stronger than just *I am*. It is the Greek for the Hebrew YHWH, the Holy Name of God which Jews were far too respectful to utter. It is hard for us to realise how awe-inspiring or how blasphemous (depending on your point of view) it must have been to hear a human being speak such words.

.
'I am the Living Resurrection'?
In Hebrew 'the good man' would be 'the man the good', so I take it that 'the Resurrection, the Life' means 'the Living Resurrection', that is to say: 'resurrection in the here and now'. The word 'and' would have crept in when turning it into Greek.

I have left the words 'in the age' as they stand in Greek, whereas most translations put them as 'never'…'never die'.

Later Jesus said that 'the life of the ages' (usually translated 'everlasting life' or 'eternal life') is to know the Father and Jesus Christ whom he has sent (John 17:3). Therefore the relationship with him is something which transcends death. Resurrection-life cannot be in the future when Jesus is in the present. This is utterly mind-boggling. No wonder that Martha fell back on more familiar terminology!

Martha in reply makes the crucial confession of faith: 'The Christ, Son of God.' Matthew ascribes this vital confession of faith to Simon Peter (Matt. 16:17). St John, however, ascribes it to a woman, Martha.

The meeting with Mary is quite different. Jesus does not try to use words for her. Hence, in this Gospel, we have:

- The great confession of faith – 'You are the Christ, the Son of God' – given by a woman: *Martha,*
- The anointing of the Christ (the Messiah) given by a woman: *Mary* and

- The first witness to the Resurrection being a woman: *Mary of Magdala.*

Was St John trying to say something ahead of his time?

Raising the dead

Now we come to a point which I know is controversial. I have had several experiences in my ministry that have made me look deeper into what the Gospel actually says about Jesus in this story. I have been forced to look past the translations and past the conventional interpretation. I believe that in moving towards the tomb, if not before, Jesus would know the build-up of the power of God within him. The power needed to do this *work* was enormous. Even *his* system groaned under it. His words were even shorter and sharper than usual.

This perhaps makes sense of those surprising words we looked at in the Notes above: 'He snorted in the *pneuma*' and 'he disturbed himself.' In fact the snort word is emphasised more strongly this time

William Temple in his *Readings in St John's Gospel*[6] writes: 'The passage represents the Lord passing through a time of most severe tension. The word *groaning* does not suggest grief, but intensity of feeling, with an inclination to indignation rather than to sorrow.'

I believe, however, that it was at this point that Jesus was literally struggling with death, snorting and breathing violently, with tears streaming down his face under the pressure.

Jesus wept

It is a pity to spoil a good sermon... I have preached on the text 'Jesus wept', and I have heard good sermons on the same text, stressing that we should not be ashamed of weeping at a funeral, for Jesus did. The point being made in the sermons was right enough, but I no longer think that this was what was happening at that point in the story, even though the bystanders thought it was.

I now believe that the snorting and tears were strain, not sadness. Such work is very costly. Raising the dead required such an effort that it could not be done often. The human frame could not take it. However, that is not the understanding which is generally accepted, although I was glad to find that William Temple shared my perception of the situation.

Finally, when the *power* had gone, he gave the order to remove the stone, and relaxed into that lovely childlike prayer, knowing that the job was done.

---

[6] Macmillan, 1949, p. 183.

Reactions
It is quite clear from various hints, scattered throughout this Gospel, that the writer had inside information and access to the High Priest's palace. That being so, he gives us the clue that it was this miracle which finally sealed Jesus' fate, from the earthly point of view.

The follow-up
We notice that here, as with the blind man who was sent to the Pool of Siloam (Ch. 2) and the paralytic (Ch. 3), St John shows us that Jesus had contact with the person later, unlike the other Gospels which seem to suggest that he just moved on. In this case it seems quite natural that they have a party to celebrate (John 12). Jesus was now ready to move on to confront death himself.

And for us?

I wonder! I remember once visiting a church and being told that two ministers I knew had tried to raise a dead person in it some weeks earlier. They had finished up thrown across the church in a state of shock. They had invoked a power too great for their systems. So back to the previous chapter. You would have to be very, very sure that you had 'the green light' before trying to raise a dead person.

Resuscitation and resurrection

Now let us compare carefully what happened to Lazarus that day with what happened to Jesus of Nazareth a week or so later.

- Lazarus had to have the grave-wrappings taken off. Jesus left them behind.
- Lazarus was there for all to see. Jesus was only seen by chosen witnesses.
- Lazarus continued with his day-to-day life. Jesus only appeared at times.
- Lazarus was back to normal. Jesus could move through space and time, materialising in Jerusalem, in Galilee, and then vanishing.

Quite clearly, utterly different processes were involved.

- Lazarus was *resuscitated*
- Jesus was *resurrected* – whatever that may mean. (See 1 Corinthians 15)

We know very little of what either process involves, apart from the fact that both involve conquering death

The greatest

The raising of Lazarus forms the high-water mark of all the healing works. If we come back to the four words which are used to describe the miracles, then it works out like this. *Erga* – it was the hardest *work* of all the miracles. *Dunamis* – it involved so much *power* that it taxed even Jesus' system to the uttermost. *Semeion* – it was the clearest sign as to who he was, is and shall be, and *Teras* – because of all of this, it was the greatest *wonder* of all.

It was in a different category from anything else. The Widow of Nain's son had only just died (bodies had to be buried within hours of death in those days). Jairus' daughter was on the verge, and several others were near death, but Lazarus had been dead four days (we would say three days). By their belief the soul was no longer around and had to be summoned from death, from Sheol, the dark, shadowy underworld in which the dead awaited the Day of Judgement. No human had the authority to do that. Furthermore, the body would have decomposed considerably, unless Jesus' prayer-work over those days had kept it from doing so.

CONCLUSIONS

- We note the Lord's sensitivity to the Father's timing, not moving out of mere human compassion.
- We get a glimpse of the costliness of such a work.
- Once again, the Word of Authority is the instrument which he uses.

Summary RAISING THE DEAD

We have now looked at the only two incidents in which it is claimed that Jesus raised the dead. They differ very widely.

In the first, the party of Jesus and his disciples meets the burial party, apparently by chance. In the second, it all seems to have been carefully worked out 'behind the scenes', and we watch the build-up to the great moment.

Jesus very definitely takes the initiative with the dead boy.

The sisters had sent for him to deal with Lazarus.

There was at least some degree of touch in that Jesus touched the bier on which the boy lay.

Lazarus responded to his command, with no touch at all.

The boy would only have been dead for an hour or so.

Lazarus's body would have been unpleasantly decomposed, as his sister commented.

The boy seems to have been a stranger to Jesus.

Lazarus knew Jesus well, and can be supposed to have had 'faith' before he died.

The boy was raised immediately, simply and without any sign of 'religious' activity.

Raising Lazarus seems to have been a complex and lengthy business.

Jesus and prayer

The raising of Lazarus is the only 'work' during the process of which we are told that Jesus prayed. It would seem from Mark 1:35 that usually he went away and prayed early in the morning. His contact with the Father re-established, his batteries charged, when he came across human need, the power was there already.

CONCLUSIONS

- Raising the dead may be right on occasions, but only rarely.
- It may prove a real strain on our mortal systems.
- There is no definite procedure or line of prayer to be followed.
- Yet again: we just have to wait upon God and learn to be sensitive to what is right in each case.

Introducing CROWD SCENES

Before we pass on to the final stages, we must consider the passages in which the Gospel writers tell us of Jesus dealing with crowds. So far we have looked at *individuals* whom Jesus met on his journey or who came to him for healing. Now we examine healings in the various 'crowd scenes'...

There seem to be random references to these scattered through the first part of each of the Synoptic Gospels and it is not possible to say dogmatically where each fits in with the other. Therefore, while I have put references to parallel passages I am aware that others might differ with regard to this.

We do not find any scenes of mass healing in St John's Gospel, although he does mention the crowds, especially when telling the story of the Feeding of the Five Thousand. Our examples, then, are limited to what we call 'the Synoptic Gospels': Matthew, Mark and Luke.

Coming back to the words for healing which we considered at the beginning of this book, we will note that in the crowd scenes it is the *therapy* word that is used in all but two cases. 'Jesus *treated* them' would be more accurate than '*healed* them'. It is in the *Gennesaret* story that Mark says, 'As many as touched the fringe of his cloak were *made whole*,' while Matthew goes even further and expresses it as *made thoroughly whole.* In the story we will be looking at under the heading 'At the Seaside', St Luke tells us that 'power went forth and *cured them*' (Luke 6:19).

25. CROWD SCENES

EVENING AT CAPERNAUM – Mark 1:32–34 (Matt. 8:16–17, Luke 4:40–41)

As evening came, at sunset, they brought to him all the sick and demonised.
   The whole population was gathered around the door, and he healed many who were ill in various ways, and cast out many demons, not allowing them to speak, because they knew him.

Notes

All three Gospels tell us that in the evening, after the demoniac had been healed in the synagogue (Ch. 14) and after the healing of Peter's mother-in-law (Ch. 7), a crowd gathered. They would have waited all day until the ram's horn in the synagogue had sounded 'Sunset', indicating that the Sabbath was over, for only then would they feel free to move around. Simon Peter's house was then mobbed, and Jesus dealt with this crowd.

   Mark says that Jesus healed *many*. Matthew says that he healed *all*. Luke says that 'he laid hands on every one and healed them'. However Matthew says that he cast out demons 'by his Word'…not by *epithesis*.

Jesus and prayer

St Mark follows this story by telling us that early the next day Jesus was up and away in a quiet place to pray (Mark 1:32-34. Matthew 8:16-17. Luke 4:40-41). This valuable insight accords with our conclusions in summarising 'Raising the Dead'.

MISSION GALILEE – Matt. 4:24 (Mark 1:39, Luke 4:44)

And his fame went throughout Syria. And they brought to him all the sick, people with various diseases and pains, and those who were demonised, and the moonstruck, and the paralytics and he treated them.

Notes

It seems that after these events on the Sabbath, Jesus had a mission around Galilee in which healing figured. Luke just says that he was preaching in the synagogues. Mark says: 'He was preaching and casting out demons...and they brought him all the sick, those afflicted with various diseases and pains, demoniacs, epileptics, and paralytics, and he healed them.'

Matthew's list is fuller and makes plain the wide scope of the troubles dealt with, including 'the moonstruck', or, to use the Latin-based word, 'the lunatics'. This is interesting in that it draws a distinction between the lunatics and the demonised.

AT THE SEASIDE – Mark 3:7–12 (Luke 6:17–19, Matthew 9:35 & 12:15–21)

Jesus and his disciples withdrew to the seaside and a great crowd from Galilee followed him...and from Judea, from Jerusalem, from Idumea, from Jordan, from the Tyre and Sidon region, a great crowd of those who had heard of the things he had done came to him.

And he had a word with his disciples to have a boat ready, because of the crowd, lest they should crush him, for he treated many...indeed they fell upon him in order to touch him, as many as had plagues. And the unclean spirits when they saw him fell down before him and cried out, 'You are the Son of God.'

After that first mission, it seems, Jesus withdrew to a quiet place in Galilee. This time the crowds came to him, rather than him going round the villages. They came from all over Palestine.

Mark tells us that it was after this that Jesus appointed the Twelve to cope with the pressure. The scene with which we began, in Matthew 9–10, fits in here. Matthew reduces it to few words, while Luke has much the same but adds the wonderful phrase: *for power went forth from him and healed them all.*

GENNESARET – Mark 6:53–56, Matthew 14:34–36

They began to bring the sick on pallets...and wherever he came, in villages, cities or country, they laid the sick in market places, and besought him that they might touch even the fringe of his garment. As many as touched it were healed.

Matthew has the same with less detail. Imagine the woman with the haemorrhage multiplied by a thousand. Since it says that 'as many as touched it were healed' we gather that there were some laid out who did not manage to touch, and so were not healed.

What is more, we wonder how very costly for Jesus it would have been if each time 'virtue went out of him' and he was aware of it, as he was with the woman (Ch. 4).

Naturally we ask ourselves: Did he not insist on facing each one, as he had done with that woman? Were there no blind folk who needed a shady spot in which to receive their sight? Were there no people who needed to be separated from their 'carers'? And how about those who needed forgiveness?

The costly care for each which has been so apparent in his works so far is hard to fit into the crowd setting, even if we are thinking of a session that lasted for days at a time.

Summary

Now let us put together the various points that we have made in the Notes, and try to compile a picture of what actually happened. It is possible that the result may not be like the picture we get in Sunday School or in films. For one thing the crowds in the Middle East are much more open and volatile than our religious gatherings.

Duration

Mark in his account of the feeding of the four thousand mentions that the crowds had been with them for three days. A 'crowd scene', then, might go on for days, with people sleeping in the open at night. We must not imagine that one of these sessions was over in an hour or two like a modern healing service. Healing and teaching would have been all part of the process, with give and take from people in the crowd. And we think that if a service goes on for an hour and a half it is rather too long!

Crowding This picture of the jostling crowd, and that of Jesus' need to use the high stern of a boat from which to speak stresses once again how different it all was from the picture presented by most modern healing services. For one thing, it is obvious that the healing was going on first, as they jostled him, and then he got into the boat to preach. We usually preach first.

What about the disciples?

As we try to visualise what actually went on, it is natural that we wonder what the disciples were doing in these settings. After all, Jesus had passed on his

Authority to them. Surely they were not just sunbathing!

Could it be that they were healing too and their healing activity was just included with his in the various accounts? We got a glimpse of this when we looked at the case of the boy at the foot of the mountain (Ch. 15).

In that case we know that the father had come for Jesus but had been dealt with by disciples, and it seemed reasonable to guess that on that occasion they had dealt successfully with others. Their very bewilderment at their failure with the boy suggests that they had succeeded elsewhere.

Therefore perhaps we should revise our picture of the crowd scenes even further. We can visualise the people being dealt with by the disciples in pairs, with Jesus moving from one pair to another, advising, correcting and completing the work where needed. He might have told a parable where relevant, and from time to time have proclaimed the Good News more formally.

This, surely, was his method of 'discipling' – training – them. Not by giving them lectures on theology and pastoral care, but by plunging them 'up to the neck' in crowds of suffering people.

Preaching and healing

We have mentioned several times that Jesus' healings were accompanied by proclaiming the good news that the Kingdom of God had come upon them. However, we remember that a number of the cases had *not* heard his Good News, for example because they were deaf. The good news may follow rather than precede, as it did on the occasion he requisitioned the boat as a pulpit.

Sermons

Of course, we should not imagine that when Jesus was preaching the gospel he gave a neat twenty-minute sermon. Matthew and Luke both give us specimens of his sermons, and they all begin with 'good news'. We call them 'Beatitudes' (Matt 5:1ff and Luke 6:20). They are variations on the same theme, but this seems to have been typical of the way he started.

People were used to this sort of beginning. After all the Book of Psalms opens with a 'Blessed...'. However, what people were accustomed to hearing was how blessed were those who strictly adhered to all the complicated rules and regulations of the Law and the Prophets, and did not deviate from its path by a single jot. Add to this a few curses on those who put a foot wrong and rabbinic sermons did not exactly sound like good news to ordinary folk. They would feel that according to the rabbi's reckoning they did not have much chance: 'Well, that's me out!' Jesus, on the other hand, begins with the blessedness of the spiritually bankrupt, the heartbroken and so on. They could all identify with those.

As suggested above, parables also featured. Perhaps it would be good to remember the point made earlier: 'He spoke to them through parables' (Mark 4:2). One can imagine Jesus telling a parable and then waiting for the response, questions and discussion, with perhaps one or two people being healed while that was going on. In fact Jesus' proclamation would probably have been far more participatory than what we are used to, so that preaching and healing could have been going on at the same time.

Jesus would have been closely involved with the crowd, physically and emotionally, not speaking from a remote pulpit and then descending to lay hands on anonymous people kneeling before him.

And so

Having tried to assemble the jigsaw from the many bits we find scattered throughout the Gospels, we find no single pattern emerging of which we can say: 'This is how it should be done.'

Preach and heal

We would want to say that any healing which the Church does in the Name of Jesus should be in the setting of the proclamation of Good News...and make sure that it is *good* news! However we must not assume that this justifies sermons as we have come to know them, with the congregation sitting silently for a long period. We have to remember, too, that people who are really suffering do not find it easy to sit through sermons.

However the one thing we have to do in our sermons is to point to Jesus. Point to him in such a way that love and trust are awoken in those who lack it. We have to be clear that people today know very little of him, and what fragments of the New Testament they have lying around in their memories may not be very attractive.

Where do we go from here?

We may wonder, pray and puzzle about these things, but the only danger is when people in the healing ministry build too much on single verses and on carefully selected phrases from the crowd scenes without facing the fact that there is a problem in doing this. The only advice I can offer is *not* to trust those who believe they know all the answers and have everything sewn up with proof texts.

We are left with a degree of mystery so that we have to begin afresh with each sufferer who comes to us, and in each parish situation in which we find ourselves. We have to depend on the guidance of the Holy Spirit to find the right way for each individual and for each local situation.

On the one hand we must say that there are no simplistic answers. But on the other we must say, equally firmly, that all answers must be simple, and that complicated answers are probably wrong, however clever they may be. The deeper we go into these things, the deeper the mystery. We accept that there are things we do not understand, and get on with living out what we do understand.

CONCLUSIONS

• You must draw your own this time!

JOHN THE BAPTISER'S QUESTION – Matt. 11:2–19 (Luke 7:18–35)

If we are left with a lot of questions, so was one of the great Bible characters.

The question came from Jesus' forerunner, who was also his cousin – John the Baptiser, imprisoned and later executed by the puppet king Herod – and we look at his question now, before we leave the crowd scenes.

It is important to face it, not because it tells us much about the actual treatment, but because it gives us a vital clue as to the light in which Jesus saw his healing work, and in which we should see ours.

Now John in prison had heard of the work of the Christ, and, sending through his disciples, asked: 'Are you the One who is to come or are we to await somebody else?'

Jesus answered them: 'Go and report to John the things that you hear and see: the blind see again, the lame walk, lepers are cleansed, the deaf hear, the dead are raised up, and the poor get good news.'

Notes

I have used the word 'Baptiser' instead of the more familiar 'Baptist' because I find that many people think that John was a Baptist as we today understand the word. Baptism had no official part in the religion of the Jews, but in this revival movement it came to symbolise making a clean start. The term comes from the Greek word for dipping cloth into dye.

John the Baptiser, said Jesus, was the greatest of all the prophets, (Matt.7:11) yet he was human and therefore puzzled. He brooded in his prison on Jesus' identity, and sent some of his followers to ask the vital question: 'Are you or are you not the Messiah (Christ)?' He was no longer sure, and was wondering whether he had been wrong in proclaiming that the long-awaited Messiah had arrived.

He had terrified people with his threats of what would happen when the Messiah came. Had he not said, 'The axe is laid to the root of the tree, the fire is burning,' as when a forest is cleared? Anybody who was not keeping exactly to the Law of Moses would be 'for the chop'. Sinners who had been expelled from the synagogue could expect the fire when the Christ came! Even being a king would not help. John certainly put the fear of God into everyone.

But where was the chopping? Where was the fire? This cousin of his, Jesus, seemed to have a reputation for being a 'friend of sinners' when he should be destroying them.

What was worse, John heard that Jesus seemed to take the Law of Moses lightly, and was even accused of being a Sabbath-breaker. And as for the sick, had they not 'done something to deserve it'? How come, then, that Jesus spent so much time healing the sick instead of lecturing them?

The fact is that John had got his prophecy partly right, but he was still a child of his own culture and understood his message accordingly. This is a warning to us: If even the greatest of the prophets could not get his prophecy a hundred per cent right, we have to be careful about accepting a hundred per cent of what any modern prophet says. Consider also how much trouble has come about because people have uncritically accepted that the Old Testament prophecies are a hundred per cent right for all time.

Jesus hears the question and carries on quietly with what he is doing. For a time he goes on healing many and delivering those who need it. Then he turns to John's two messengers and gives them the message to take back to the Baptiser.

Of course, that did not answer the question the way John wanted. John on that occasion, like many today, had to 'rethink' what was meant by the word Messiah (Christ). However Herod was soon to put an end to John the Baptiser's questions. He had John executed, and then no doubt the great prophet would 'know as he was known'.

The sign of the Kingdom

How did Jesus see his healing work, then? He clearly saw the *work* of healing as the *sign* that the Kingdom of God was present in their midst. However, he was unlike previous 'Christs': military conquest did not come into it. The new order, the new age, had arrived.

The turning point

After these various missions we find Jesus concentrating on the Twelve. He was no longer going around his own country preaching and healing. Rather he sought privacy by going into the neighbouring lands, as we noted when we looked at the Syro-Phoenician woman's daughter (Ch. 18). There are fewer crowd scenes as the story moves on.

At last, up in foreign territory, on the slopes of Caesarea Philippi, he confronts the Twelve with the question: 'Who do you say I am?' Peter gives the answer: 'You are the Christ, the Son of the Living God.' After that Jesus faces Jerusalem, and the cross.

St Mark gives us an awe-inspiring picture of Jesus striding on ahead, with the disciples trailing behind, afraid, awestruck. It seems they were quite out of their depth. He no longer teaches and chats as they walk (Matthew 10:32). We are told of no more crowd scenes such as the above until the final one at which we look in the next section.

Introducing
WORKING THROUGH THE DISCIPLES

One of the main themes of this book has been that Jesus healed in his capacity as the 'Son of Man', or, as we might say today, 'the representative of true humanity'. It is therefore important that we explore further how, almost from the beginning, he was concerned to involve the disciples in the work he was doing. This takes us back to where we started.

In the story 'Why couldn't we?' (Ch. 15) we noted that people were dealt with by disciples, with Jesus taking over when they failed. In the summary of our study of 'crowd scenes' we asked what the disciples were doing. Now we turn to see how he sent them out without his being there to help and advise them...or to sort things out when they failed, as they had done with the lad at the mountain foot.

It is not easy to work out from the Gospels exactly how often Jesus sent his disciples out on mission, and scholars vary in their opinions on this matter. However, that does not prevent us from looking at three passages about mission, and learning what we can from them. We can leave the experts to argue about the rest!

26. OUR GOD IS A GOD WHO TAKES RISKS

THE FIRST MISSION – Matthew 10:5

We looked at 'the Call' of the first Twelve right at the beginning, but now we look at their mission. Following on from the names of the Twelve, we read:

These Twelve Jesus sent out, ordering them as follows:
> *'Don't go into Gentile country, nor into any Samaritan places.*
> *'But go rather for the lost sheep of the House of Israel.*
> *'As you go, preach saying: "The Kingdom of Heaven has come near."*
> *'Heal the sick. Cleanse the lepers. Raise the dead. Throw out demons. Freely you have received, freely give.*
> *'Don't carry gold, silver or brass coins in your bags. Never bother about a rucksack, spare shirts, tunics or sandals. "A workman deserves his food"...'*

Notes

These are instructions for a lightning tour of the local villages. There was no call even for weekend luggage!

The temptation to spread the net too widely was well known to Jesus, as we have seen (Ch. 18).

Authority

When we were looking at *The Call* we noted that Jesus gave them *authority* (not 'power') to heal the sick, cast out demons. This is an important point, as we have seen in studying his works. It was by his Word of Authority that Jesus healed, although sometimes he used other means.

It was his Authority he passed on. We usually think that the disciples received some kind of electromagnetic power in their hands which had a healing effect. Such 'power' is known apart from Christianity altogether, as we have noted several times. That was not what they were given. As the Lord's main method of healing was by the Word of Authority, so their words spoken as his representatives (in his Name) would carry his Authority.

Now, there are people who receive gifts of healing which are more physical and psychic, but Christian healing is primarily by that Word which was to be preached and applied to the individual in the power of the Holy Spirit, whether by the laying-on of hands or not.

Some of us do *not* have a particular gift for healing by the laying-on of hands, but it is a great mistake for those who find no such gift in their hands to think that therefore 'the ministry of healing' is not for them.

The true healing ministry for Christians is in giving expression to the Word, both in word and in action in the Name of Jesus. It depends for its effectiveness on the depth of unity between the 'two or three gathered to represent him' (Matt 18:20), and on how deeply they are tuned in to God's purposes.

So it was that these 'learners' were sent out in pairs *with authority.*

Surprising?

Yet how surprising that is. Reading further on in the Gospels it is plain that they still had many wrong ideas about Jesus, and about the Kingdom of God. That is what surprises us. Yet he sends them out with his Authority.

What they *did* have was a deep loyalty to Jesus, and it was on this basis that he sent them out. Today most ministers would want to check that their members had their theology right before entrusting them with such authority. Jesus, however, knew that we learn our theology and we learn how to pray out there in the field, facing impossible odds.

If we think that we should make sure that we all have correct theology, have read all the appropriate books about healing, and have attended umpteen courses on the subject, then we will never start.

The starting point is real devotion to Jesus. The rest we learn when we are ready, guided by the Spirit.

It is this personal devotion that is lacking in so many churches.

Good news

This brings us back to something that has been underlying all we have said. The job the first trainees were given was to tell the world about *a fact*, not to spread a theory. They were to point to *a person,* not to propound a proposition. They were not sent out to preach nice sermons, giving good advice on how to stay respectable. They were to proclaim that the Kingdom of God had arrived and that people could enter it *now.* The healing was testimony to that fact, and it would happen wherever people allowed themselves to be ruled by God.

PREACHING AND ANOINTING – Mark 6:ff

Here we have much the same story, but there is a difference in that it adds *that they went and preached that people should rethink, casting out many demons and anointing many sick people with oil, healing them.*

Notes

This is interesting in that there is no mention of Jesus using oil, and it is the only mention of the disciples anointing. Of course anointing was quite a normal medicinal practice, often using sweet-smelling oil, a sort of aroma-therapy. We mentioned anointing as something soothing, pleasing, when we spoke of *kyrie eleison* in Chapter 9.

In the parable of the Good Samaritan Jesus said that he poured oil and wine into the wounds of the wounded man, and in the 23rd Psalm we have refer-ence to being anointed with oil as a soothing, healing act. Anointing for heal-ing does not appear again until we read about it in James 5, which we shall consider later.

There is a nice touch at the end of Mark's version of the story: Jesus invites them to come to a quiet place and rest for a bit.

Keeping our noses to the grindstone is very inadvisable. Overwork is not a Christian grace. Unfortunately it is common.

THE SEVENTY-TWO – Luke 10:1–20

After this the Lord appointed seventy-two as well, and sent them two-by-two before him into each village and city to prepare the way for him.

Notes

Following the above, there is a long passage in which Jesus gives them their orders, much as in the previous account.

This time seventy (Or was it seventy-two? The versions vary.) are sent out. Much of what Luke records is strangely similar to the orders for the earlier mission. We note again that they go two by two. This seems to have been the normal pattern.

The important thing here is what happens when they report back, thrilled that even the demons were subject to them when they used his Name. We looked at this in the summary of the section on Exorcism.

Power!

However it is worth having a second look at this. The thrill of *power* is always a problem. The teenager on a motor bike is bad enough, but the higher up the scale one goes, the more power corrupts. Therefore we are not to be too excited by the fact that a demon or two has been chucked out, and a disease or two healed. What is important is to realise that we are becoming truly the children of God. It is the new relationship with God which matters.

Power must always be subject to *love*

There have been tragic examples in the healing ministry among people who have been carried away by finding that they had a ministry of healing or of deliverance, but have forgotten that this is secondary, and not what they should have been getting excited about.

And for us? Our God is a God who takes risks

God entrusts his work to ordinary people and sends us out when by human standards it would seem foolish.

In our churches we very often try to act sensibly, so we never get anywhere.

Any teacher will tell you that a class will learn little if they do not have expression-work, but in our churches we tend to wait until we are sure that people have the right qualifications of faith and behaviour before we trust them and give them 'expression work', i.e. mission.

It is only as you hit the snags that you really appreciate teaching about how to tackle them. This applies in every sphere of life including the spiritual.

The heart of it

What we really need is devotion to Jesus. Then, even if the theology and much else leave a lot to be desired, the Lord will work through us. He gave thanks that it was through 'spiritual babes' that wonders had been worked, while the clever clerics and the qualified Pharisees guddled around in their intellectual mazes.

For ministers

Sometimes we ministers in our sermons are so concerned to make sure that people have correct theology and morality, that we lose the quality of person-to-person devotion between the worshipper and the Lord.

Imagine what would happen if we had weekly lectures on marriage but never fell in love. Or imagine what would *not* happen!

CONCLUSIONS

- GO AHEAD!
- Pair off
- Get out of the church rut to contact the 'sheep without a shepherd'.
- Preach good news
- Heal the sick
- Cast out demons

  The LOT!

Introducing THE FINAL STRUGGLE

So far the healing works have been grouped by subject matter, with no regard to where they came chronologically.

Our last three healing works take us close to the heart of God as we follow on from the Lazarus story, through Palm Sunday and out beyond Easter.

We could fill libraries of books writing about the Passion. For the purpose of this book we focus on the healing aspects of the story.

27. In the Temple

Matthew 21:12–16, Luke 19:45–6, Mark 11:15–19 (see also John 2:13–17)

And Jesus entered the Temple, and threw out those selling and buying in the Temple, and upset the tables of the money-changers, and overturned the seats of those selling doves, and he said to them: 'It is written: "My House shall be a House of Prayer" but you are making it a den of robbers.'

And the blind and the lame came to him in the Temple, and he healed them.

And when the chief priests and clerics saw what wonderful things he did, and the children shouting out in the Temple: 'Hosanna to the Son of David,' they were furious, saying: 'Don't you hear what they are saying?'

And Jesus replied: 'Have you never read, "Out of the mouth of children and babies Thou hast produced praise?"'

And he left them and went out of the city.

Notes

The Temple was not like a church. The outer courtyard was rather like the biggest school playground you can imagine, an open, paved area. Within it was a series of courtyards. *Anybody* could come into that first yard. Then there was a barrier beyond which only *Jews* could go. Then an area into which only Jewish *men* could go, then one for *priests* only, and so on until the most holy place of all, a high building into which only the *high priest* could go, and that once a year.

The market was in the outer court, in the open air.

Hosanna The children were singing excerpts from the Temple liturgy. The word comes from Psalm 118:25. It was originally a cry to 'save us', but as the Church forgot Hebrew, it came to be thought of as praise, as in some of our hymns.

Jesus is being sarcastic when he asks the priests if they have ever read Psalm 8. They all knew it by heart and had sung it thousands of times.

Background

It is important to see this final time of healing in its setting. It might be advisable to read the whole passage in your own Bible. A key verse is: *'in Christ God was reconciling the world to himself'* (2 Cor. 5:19). Through this we get a glimpse of what the place of worship is meant to express: God's longing to be known and loved by humankind, who belong to but have fallen away from God (see Jeremiah 31:33–4).

The conflict

The conflict between human sinfulness and God's goodness had to be brought to a head if there was to be peace between God and ourselves. It is not always right to 'pour oil on troubled waters'. Subtle evil has to be brought to the surface and faced.

To do this, Jesus had to confront the religious and political rulers head on. We saw as we read Chapter 15 that he had a real temptation to avoid this and just become another travelling healer. The raising of Lazarus, the triumphal entry of Palm Sunday and this final episode in the Temple meant that there was no way that the clash could be avoided. He had laid claim to the ultimate Authority, and the religious and political rulers could not allow it to pass unchallenged. They had to challenge his Authority and either anoint him as the Christ or crucify him as a blasphemer and a threat to peace.

It becomes even clearer when you remember that, still today, in the east, when a new ruler is appointed, he is expected to take some action which will symbolise his policy. A number of people who had claimed to be the Messiah had started off by attacking Roman soldiers. Therefore, when Jesus had received and accepted a royal welcome on what we call Palm Sunday, people would have been waiting to see what symbolic action he would take. His driving out the market and bringing in the beggars for healing was his carefully worked out symbolic action. The fact that he did *not* attack the Romans had profound political implications for the people of those days. Not to align yourself with the nationalists in such situations is to invite their accusation that you have betrayed your people…and then…

The market

Of course, the Temple market had begun as a help to worshippers. When the first regulations about sacrifice were laid down, every family had sheep, so that lambs for sacrifice were provided by one's own flock. However, by the time Jesus came, most Jews were city dwellers, and had to buy whatever animals were needed. We know from historical records that people came from every corner of the Roman Empire to the Temple, and could not possibly have brought their own lambs or doves with them. All this meant that the provision of sacrificial animals was an essential service.

Money-changers

One complication was that Roman coins had on them a 'graven image' of the Caesar, who claimed to be a god. It was against the Ten Commandments to bring such coins into the temple to buy your lamb – hence the need for the money-changers who could provide coins with no offensive image. Again, by their way of thinking, this was an essential service.

Such is human nature that these essential services to enable people to worship God had become a racket. People referred to it as 'Caiaphas's market', and the high-priestly family was making a fortune out of it. When you remember that historians have estimated that about a million people converged on Jerusalem to sacrifice at the Temple each Passover, you can imagine the amount of money involved.

There was another aspect of that great outer courtyard of the Temple. There were colonnades round the outside, in the shade of which the great rabbis of Israel sat and taught. Not only ethnic Jews but people of many nations came to hear what they said. Jesus himself as a boy stayed behind to avail himself of this opportunity, 'both hearing them and questioning them' (Luke 2:46).

This courtyard was a step towards fulfilling that vision of Isaiah's (Isaiah 2) to which we have referred several times: a world in which swords would be beaten into ploughshares and spears into pruning hooks because people of all nations would come up to Jerusalem to learn how God wanted them to live – in peace.

The tragedy of human history is that what is best and what is worst are often found very close together. And here in the Temple courtyard we see it: On one hand, the wonderful vision of a temple to focus the concept of world peace under the rule of God (the Kingdom of God), and on the other, the tawdry exploitation of religion for the sake of money and power.

John Richards (Renewal Servicing) comments that the Devil's main tactic is not so much to tempt us to do wicked things, but to take what is good and to distort it. We see that exemplified in the Temple.

It is this distortion that Jesus faced and brought to a head. Behind his response to human suffering he faced the fundamental twist in humanity – call it 'original sin' if you wish – the human ability to get *anything* wrong.

How Jesus set about it

Jesus did two things:

1. He cleared out the clutter of money-making stalls.
2. He brought in those who were usually kept outside begging.

This was no sudden, impulsive outburst, but a carefully planned operation to make it clear what his mission was about. It was when the Temple had been cleansed that the work of healing began. As the sufferers poured into the outer court of the Temple, it was, perhaps for the first and only time, being used as God wanted it to be used.

Once again Jesus was affirming that healing and worship are linked. He had previously made this point in local synagogues, but now he does so in the Temple itself. It cannot be stressed too emphatically *that those whom the priests kept* outside, *in order to safeguard the decency and order of the Temple worship, Jesus now brings* inside *to receive healing.*

And how about us?

How many people are kept outside our churches to safeguard the dignity of our worship? As it was only in the cleansed Temple that healing took place, perhaps in our churches too we need a cleansing. It is too glib to think that this only applies to the tatty bookstall at the back of the church, which probably loses money. Look at some examples of how we go wrong today:

CHURCH HEALTH WARNINGS

- Having received over the years newsletters, etc., from many 'healing centres', I have seen how often the early issues are about healing, but after a year or two they move slowly round to being full of appeals and advertisements for their wares – all of them, of course, 'aids to devotion'. Of course! Yet subtly the emphasis has changed.
- At a more personal level, most ministers begin with a real sense of vocation, yet how easily it slips into being 'my profession'.
- At ordinary congregational level, we begin by 'serving a church', but gradually it becomes 'my church'. Most people who serve the Lord in churches or in healing movements begin with a real sense of privilege at being allowed to serve him, but over the years strong personalities build up little empires and react forcefully if somebody else comes along who seems to threaten them.

- At the individual level, somebody finds that he or she has a real gift of the Spirit, say for healing, and in no time that person wants the whole life of the congregation or movement to revolve around their gift. It has become *their* 'thing'.
- Our churches should indeed be places where people can find healing, and places where people can give expression to their gifts.
- However that does not mean that we create 'healing' centres which pander to people who want 'healers' to provide easy cures so that they can get on with their selfish lives.
- Nor does it mean that the church should provide a stage on which people can show off and have ego-trips.
- There can be no true healing unless people see that the way humanity is living is contrary to the love of God, and that it is a struggle to the death between the way *we* want to live and the way God wants us to live (i.e. God's will).

Perhaps we too need a cleansing by God's creative anger. (Read St Mark 12:1ff in the light of this.)

The children

One other detail in this story may be relevant. It seems that children were dancing round as Jesus healed, singing bits of the Psalms and items of worship which they had heard (Matt. 21:15–16). It is strange, in the Middle East, how children appear from nowhere, and how quickly they pick up what is going on, mimicking it. In the case of our armies, it does not require great imagination to realise what they mimic. However, in this case they were coming out with the priests' solemn incantations. The priests were shocked and asked Jesus to check the urchins. He refused.

Once more we see highlighted something which is typical of clerics down the ages: They are shocked at the wrong things, they denounce the wrong things, and they react violently to the wrong things. In this case, they had not been shocked and moved to do something about the suffering of the beggars on their doorsteps, but they were shocked at the songs of the children, and moved to take action against Jesus.

What shocks us Christians? What do our churches denounce? What leads us to take action?

This is the last public healing session in the Gospel story. It is perhaps the one which is most clearly a *sign*...a sign we all need to read for ourselves and for our churches.

CONCLUSIONS

- Our churches exist in order to proclaim to suffering humanity that *God rules*.
- But we proclaim a God who rules in love and not through fear.
- A God who comes to us from among the poor and the outcast.
- A God who would heal the sick, but through human brains and hands.
- A God who turns human values upside-down,
- A God who challenges us, but who lets us crucify him.
- A God who will not give up, but who rises above death and destruction.
- We have to be careful to check all aspects of our church life for distortion, no matter how well-intentioned they were to begin with.

God save us from the distorter, and cleanse our churches. Then perhaps we can see healing happening in them.

28. MALCHUS' EAR

Luke 22:40–54 (John 18:1–11, Mark 14:32–50, Matthew 26:36–56)

The scene is the Garden of Gethsemane, after Jesus and his disciples had shared 'the Last Supper'.

While he was speaking, a crowd came up to them, heading for Jesus, including Judas Iscariot, one of the Twelve, who came forward to kiss him.

Jesus said to him: 'Judas, do you pass on the Son of Man with a kiss?'

Then some of those around him asked: 'Lord, shall we strike out with the sword?'

And one of them struck the high priest's servant, cutting off his ear.

Jesus said, 'Just let me do this...'

Getting hold of his ear, he cured him.

Notes

Judas Iscariot

In *The Stature of Waiting*[7] the English theologian Vanstone makes the interesting point that nowhere in the Greek is the ugly, judgemental word 'betray' used with regard to Judas, although it appears in most English translations. In all four Gospels the word used is *to pass on*, as when Paul writes about Communion: 'I *pass on* to you that which I had passed on to me' (1 Cor. 11:23). I have used that word in the above rather than 'betray'. People who are puzzled by Judas Iscariot would do well to read Vanstone.

The word for 'kiss' refers to a friendly greeting, not an erotic one. That involves a different word. In many countries it is still normal practice to greet somebody with a cheek-to-cheek touch.

Malchus

He was 'the high priest's servant' – possibly a sort of security man. St John gives us the name Malchus, probably because he had become a well-known figure in the Church.

Strangely, the first three Gospels all mention this incident, giving no names. Only Luke tells us that Jesus cured him. The word here is 'cured', not 'made

---

[7] Darton Longman Todd, 1982

whole'. Only John tells us the names of those concerned, Peter and Malchus.

Background

This is the final healing miracle, and once again we have to see it in its setting in order to appreciate it. It takes place in one of the gardens which wealthy people in Jerusalem kept outside the city, so that they could get away from the heat and the smell. John tells us that Jesus often met with his disciples there (18:2), so some wealthy supporter must have given him the key.

We usually assume that Judas would have led the squad to the house in which the Last Supper had taken place, and, finding that the party had left, would have guessed that Jesus would be in the garden.

In fact you can still see the steps, dating from that era, from the old city down into the Kedron Valley beside the church built on the site of Caiaphas's palace. Jesus must have gone down them that night.

Peter

Knowing that it was Simon Peter who bravely lashed out gives us a very interesting insight into his character, for a few hours later he was to deny his Lord three times. This is true to life, for many a man who showed great courage in battle has yet lacked the courage to stand out against the possible mockery of his fellow-officers on a moral issue in the mess later.

Jesus himself

The full dimensions of 'Jesus' agony in the garden' are beyond the scope of this book. It is as well, however, to look briefly at the Agony, for too often people think of 'healing' as something beautiful and romantic.

In reality, as we grow in sensitivity to the Light, we also grow in sensitivity to the Darkness. It begins to appal us as we realise the awfulness of what we are doing to the earth, to each other, and to God. This is 'the suffering of Christ'. St Paul sums it up by saying: 'I want to *know* Christ, the power of his resurrection and the fellowship of his sufferings, becoming like him' (Philippians 3:10). If we are to heal 'like him', we must enter into both the resurrection and into the sufferings, his pain over the sin of the world.

As we think of the power involved in this healing miracle, we must also remember his awareness, as set out in Matt. 26:53, that he could have applied for 'twelve legions of angels' (the Roman garrison was six legions) to help him escape, but he did not. This shows that he was still struggling with temptation.

The initiative

In this final miracle, there is no doubt as to the initiative. There is no reason to suggest that Malchus had 'faith' – in fact there is a hostile atmosphere. Nor is there any hint that Jesus asked Malchus to repent.

How Jesus set about it

The Greek word for 'touch' here is once again the strong one. It implies that Jesus really got hold of the ear. It was not just a light touch. We do not know the extent to which the ear was cut off. If it had been cut right off, it would probably have been lost in the darkness. It is more likely that it was still partly attached. Head wounds are very messy, and always appear a lot worse than they really are.

The last miracle, then, embodies Jesus' teaching: 'Love your enemies, do good to those who hate you.' This is an important *sign* for those with eyes to see.

This is the only healing work that deals with something which we would call 'surgical' rather than 'medical'.

CONCLUSIONS

- The initiative is entirely with the Lord.
- There is no sign of faith in Malchus or in the others around, in fact the reverse.
- This is the supreme example of Jesus refusing to use his power *over* people, but using it *for* somebody, regardless of merit.

A final thought

Do you wish to be saved? The Master will only say to you: 'Take the cup of Salvation and call upon the Name of the Lord.' Do you wish to be mightily used of the Lord in the office of raising the sick from their beds and giving life to those who are dead in sin? You will hear Him asking the searching question 'Can you drink of the cup that I drank of and be baptised with the baptism which I was baptised with?'

(A.J. Gordon, *The Ministry of Healing*) [8]

---

[8] New York, Fleming H. Revell Co., 1882

29. SIMON PETER'S HEALING

John 21:17

Notes

In all previous cases we started straight in with the Bible account. In this case we start with a note. Some explanation is necessary before reading the passage.

A very deep bond is forged between men who in war-time have been 'in action' together, depending on each other in life and in death. Something similar is found among fishermen and miners. One finds it among the women too in such communities, where births and deaths are community affairs. The Old Testament calls it *chesed* (often translated 'mercy' as in Psalm 23 – 'goodness and *chesed* shall follow me' – although 'mercy' means something different from what we today mean by the word).

The New Testament calls it *agape* (rhymes with *canopy*). It is not the same as 'liking somebody', which depends on having common interests, on temperaments which go well together, and is expressed by the Greek *phileia*. Nor is it the same as sexual attraction, which is taken care of by another word, *eros*. We get tied in knots because in English we use *love* for all three of these words.

Those of us who have experienced this *chesed/agape* know that it is the most valuable thing in life. In fact St John says that *God is chesed/agape/love* (1 John 4:7), and to know this love is to know God.

In the story that follows, I have followed the NEB footnote in translating *agape* as 'love' and *phileia* as 'being a friend'.

After breakfast, Jesus said to Simon Peter: 'Simon son of Jonas, do you love me more than these?'

He answered: 'Yes, Lord, you know I'm your friend.'

He said to him: 'Feed my lambs.'

Then a second time he asked him: 'Simon son of Jonas, do you love me?'

He said to him: 'Yes, Lord, you know that I am your friend.'

He said to him: 'Feed my sheep.'

Then a third time he said to him: 'Simon son of Jonas, are you my friend?'

And Peter was upset because Jesus had questioned his love a third time.

And he said: 'Lord, you know everything. You know I'm your friend.' And he said to him: 'Pasture my flock.'

Background

It is about three weeks after the resurrection. Peter, with some of the others, has gone back to the fishing. They had to live. But also, having failed so miserably as disciples, it was perhaps good to get back to something they knew that they *could* do well!

Or could they? Not a ****** thing all night! The sense of failure must have been complete: 'I can't even fish now.' Then a fire glimmers on the shore...the smell of cooking wafts across the water. A familiar voice calls out, 'Caught anything, lads?'

Then there was the big catch, breakfast, much needed, and finally the Lord turns to Peter, and that is where we take up the story.

The patient

Simon son of Jonas, nicknamed Peter (the Rock), who feels very un-rocklike, having denied the Lord three times, and having failed at his job.

The initiative

The Lord does not wait for Peter to grovel, but takes the initiative to restore him.

How Jesus set about it

Getting breakfast ready on that rock beside the lake was the first step, coming to them as a servant, not as a glory-figure. How typical of Jesus to do such a menial task for men who, having been working the night shift, were cold and hungry.

The inner healing only began after he had re-established his friendship for them in this practical way.

The conversation

Having looked at the introduction to the story, perhaps you have been spared the embarrassment that most people feel when 'Do you love me?' is read. The story makes a lot more sense once the different senses of the word 'love' are sorted out. We know that the Lord had already appeared to Peter (Luke 24:34), so he would have known that he was forgiven for denying Jesus three times. Something deeper yet was needed to heal that memory, so...

Once more it is dawn and a fire is burning, just as at the denial. Once more three questions are asked. First of all Peter has to undo the boast he had made at the Last Supper: 'Even if *all these* deny you, I would not.' Now he is asked: 'Do you still claim to love me more than *these*?' Jesus uses the *agape* word.[9]

Peter does not dare to use it of himself; he claims only friendship. Then he has to be stripped down even further, until in the third question Jesus uses the friendship word, questioning even that. Peter now makes no claims at all, casting himself entirely on the Lord's understanding. But notice that as Peter appears to go *down* the staircase of self-confidence, the Lord leads him *up* the staircase of responsibility: from the child's job of tending the lambs, up to the man's job of feeding the sheep in the field, and finally up to the skilled task of taking the flock out on to the hill-pastures with all the dangers there.

Reinstatement

Here was a healing which had to be done in front of the others, for the three-fold denial had been public. This memory could not have been healed privately when the Lord met Peter that first Easter day. Peter had to be given back his job as leader in full view of the others. Yet it was only given when he had lost his self-confidence, and could never trust himself again. Instead he had learned to trust the Lord completely, even with his weaknesses. Only then was he ready for spiritual authority and power.

And for us?

This is the only instance in the Gospels of what we today call *inner healing*, an important aspect of the healing ministry.

When we have had a traumatic experience which has really shown up our weakness, we may try to forget it – but that is useless. We may try to compensate for it, and are then caught up in a process of continual tension, always trying to live it down. The best way is to open it to God in Christ, and face it with him.

For instance, I remember a man who came with a physical complaint which would not clear up under medical treatment. After a few questions we found it went back to an incident in the war. He never told me exactly what it was. However we called on the Presence of Jesus, and as we did so the patient 'saw'

---

[9] If you look it up in your own Bible you will find that some versions interpret 'these' as referring to the fishing tackle, and insert words accordingly. It seems obvious to me that the reference is to Peter's previous boast. 'These' are the other disciples. However, the reader can decide, for it can be taken either way.

the cross over the incident, with the peace of Christ pouring down to Germans and to British. A few months later, visiting a church, I found him in the choir: 'I'm fine now,' he said.

Of course in psychotherapy something similar is attempted, but it involves making the person relive the incident, experiencing all the horror of it, and then helping him or her to come to terms with it by sharing it with the therapist. *When we focus on Jesus, the emphasis is on* his *love and peace, and it is this which is the healing element.*

Those who have experienced both the Lord's 'healing of memories' and the psychotherapeutic method speak of how more gentle and beautiful is the former, even though we find it hard to do this healing of memories with, for instance, the person to whom the Name of Jesus means little. That may be either because they are like his neighbours in Nazareth (Ch. 6) or because they have had unfortunate experiences of Christians. They have been 'inoculated' against reality. Non-Christians are sometimes easier to treat because they are more open. After all, the secret of the 'healing of memories' is the Presence of Christ, and no technique or ritual can ensure this. Open, loving hearts who depend entirely on him will truly know when he comes with his peace. *Until that presence is real to both the ministrant and the patient, any delving into the past can be dangerous for both.*

Notice that the healing process itself only begins after Jesus has re-established his earthly friendship with the disciples. For us it is usually wise to avoid the clinical setting such as counsellors use. Such a setting, with its objective relationship, is right in some circumstances, but 'loving one another as he loved us' is the starting point for inner healing. Perhaps not fish and bread, or even chips!…but making the person a cup of tea may be the first step.

The conditions for power

The final point to note is that the Holy Spirit was poured out at Pentecost, not on people who had proved themselves good, loyal, faithful people, but on those who had faced their weakness in the light of the cross, and who knew that they could do nothing on their own. Their leader was the one who had learned this lesson most painfully.

In the same way, if we are following Jesus, his power will come to work through us, but not as a reward for being good Christians. It is not a case of 'Are we good enough?' *Our spiritual growth comes through a process of stripping* down *our self-confidence, and stepping* up *our confidence in him.* People who try to short-cut by resorting to learning psychological techniques or by dabbling in the psychic are on dangerous ground.

CONCLUSIONS

- The focus of such healing is Jesus, not the incident.
- Jesus is Lord of past, present and future. All time is *present* when we are with him, and all can be healed.
- We cannot alter the past, but Jesus can alter the effect it has on us.

The big question

When all is said and done, there is only one question that is important for any human being – God's question to each of us: *'Do you love me?'* The first Commandment, the number one priority, is: *Thou shalt love the Lord thy God with all thy heart and soul and mind and strength.* Get that right and all else follows. Get that wrong and nothing will work out right. Because most of us do not get this right, we get into an increasing hell of a mess (I use that word advisedly).

The basic healing (salvation) is when a puny human being actually begins to love God. If God is like Jesus, despised, rejected, battered and bruised, yet still coming back to us saying 'Peace!' then perhaps we can begin to love him.

This story of Peter facing the big question is really the only one that could come at the end of the four Gospels, although its writer could never have foreseen that, for people did not think in terms of books, only of scrolls – a separate scroll for each Gospel – and these would have come in no fixed order. Yet in the mystery of the Holy Spirit this story concludes the Gospels in the form we know – God in Jesus asking humanity in Peter, 'Do you love me?'

We stumble, as Peter did, hardly daring to use the word *love*, but we fling ourselves on the mercy of God as Peter did: 'You know everything. You know that I, sort of…well, I…you know'. Then he knows that it was worth the whole bloody business. (I use that word advisedly again. Just remember how bloody it was.) He has saved us, healed us, by winning our love at last. If through our healing ministry we have led people to respond with love to Jesus' love, then we have succeeded, even if we have not healed people physically. If we have just removed symptoms, we have failed.

SECTION TWO

Healing works in Acts

TO BE CONTINUED...

As we have seen, Jesus meant his healing work to be continued. We now turn to the Book of Acts, written by Luke, whom St Paul calls 'the beloved doctor'. It is really a 'volume two' of his Gospel. In this second volume he tells of the first thirty years or so of the Church's life, and healing plays an important part in that story.

In the writings of the 'fathers', the great theologians of the next few centuries, it is plain that they, too, took healing for granted. Around 490, St Serf, who lived in the area in which I now write, had a reputation for healing, and so in the next generation did St Columba of Iona. Bede writing in Northumbria in 731 records that St Cuthbert, who came from near what we now know as Edinburgh, performed many healings, and he seemed to take it for granted that healing and exorcism were part of the life of the Church. It is clear that healing was not confined to biblical times.

It would seem that the power to heal was lost as bishops (a word that comes from the Greek word for a foreman, *epi-skopos* = over-see-er) began to have political power, to live in palaces and to be 'lord bishops' with secular power. There was a big difference between the 'overseer' of a little group of persecuted Christians in a town, and what came to be thought of as the bishop of that town.

Today, however, as the Church loses political power, her leaders/overseers have to be men/women of God or nothing, and so spiritual power is being given back.

Back to the Bible

However, before the story of healing could be continued, two important things had to happen:

THE ASCENSION (Luke 24:50–51, Acts 1:9–10, Ephesians 4:9–10)

It is not easy to work out from these very brief accounts what actually happened, however glibly Sunday School pictures may show it. If you have ever had a 'spiritual experience', even a small one, you will know that it is just impossible to find words to describe it. Therefore it is no wonder that *Matthew* does not try to describe the Ascension, although he implies it, *Luke* in the last words of his Gospel boils it down to one mystifying sentence, and

John does not tell the story at all. There are a number of endings for *Mark,* one or two of which refer to it briefly. *Luke* in the opening of Acts tries to tell the story more completely, but even here he cannot explain it in such a way as to make sense. For instance, he tells us that the apostles saw Jesus 'going away' and yet were full of joy!

Whatever 'the Ascension' was, however, it had clear effects:

1. It left the apostles clear in their minds that Jesus would no longer be physically in their midst.
2. He would no longer materialise and dematerialise as he had been doing for some weeks.
3. They would find him 'filling all things' (Ephesians 4:10), which is to say that in everything that happened they would be dealing with *him.*
4. The mission was in their hands now.

In one way it was as if the driving instructor had got out of the car and said, 'You drive now, in the way that I have shown you.' Yet that is not a completely valid illustration.

PENTECOST (Acts 2)

On the fiftieth day after the Sabbath of Passover, the Jews still observe another 'festival', called Pentecost (meaning 'the fiftieth'), celebrating the giving of the Ten Commandments on Sinai. Those Jews who had become Jesus-followers would naturally head for Jerusalem, and be drawn to the apostles once there. Again it is hard to work out what exactly happened. Words are strained to their limit to describe that spiritual experience. It was '*like* wind, *like* fire'. Such words fail to describe what they actually experienced. Attempts to paint pictures of it just confuse us.

Whatever it was that they experienced, they knew that the *life* which they had seen in Jesus now switched to being *in them.* From that point on, and until today, God is to be experienced as the inner power of love, working through us to reproduce the Jesus-life in whatever situation we find ourselves. This is where our driving instructor picture falls down: in one sense 'we are on our own now', but in another sense he is even more 'with us' than he was with the first Twelve.

The new Church

As the result of all this we read in Acts 2:42–47 the description of the sort of life which the Holy Spirit produced in the believers. Let us now look at the two vital elements: *togetherness* was the keynote for, after all, Jesus had said that love for one another was to be the hallmark of his followers. The Greek word that describes this is *koinonia*, translated as *fellowship, communion, sharing, partnership.*

This *koinonia* becomes one of the keynotes of Christianity, for being Christian, like football, is something people do *together*. There may be individually good folk, just as there are people who are good with a football on their own, but until people get together with others in some sort of team, they do not really know what either Christianity or football is all about.

There is no such thing, then, as an individual Christian, for the Christian is called to a truly corporate experience. There are good, kind individuals, and there are very religious people, yet they need to be part of a team before they know what the 'game' is about. That is why the word *koinonia* refers to the central act of Christian worship; 'communion' (with-one-ness) is the translation we usually use.

The new Church members were receiving *'the apostles' teaching'*, were taking part in house-to-house meetings with the *'breaking of bread'* and sharing in *'the prayers'*. The word *the* seems to suggest something definite rather than just 'prayer'. What is more, their sharing was in *'all things'*. It was a shared life, not just a Sunday get-together.

These verses give us a picture of the Church which would scare off most church folk today! They would be terrified of being asked to share at such a level. That, perhaps, is why so few healings take place today in churches.

Power to heal and to communicate with God and with other people (tongues) flows from this *koinonia*. The authority to heal, for instance, depends on the strength and depth of the sharing (*koinonia*) among the followers of Jesus. It was not a case of the apostles 'being healers' but rather that the love-power generated in the *koinonia* found expression through them in healing. We shall be looking at this in more detail as we go on.

REINTRODUCING SIMON PETER

It is comforting to know that God does not require us to be perfect before working through us. This comes out clearly as we follow Simon Peter into action. Once more Peter takes the lead, now that the trauma of his denial has been dealt with. Of course, Peter was still the fallible person he had always been, and we shall see this in the way in which he seems to have failed to pick up the international implication of the Gospel.

He received a number of pointers to the fact that their mission was to break out of the closed circle of Jewishness.

1. The 'marching orders' given at the Ascension mentioned 'all nations'.
2. Pentecost gave a further sign of international outreach, with its 'tongues'.
3. In Acts 10, quite a few years later, Peter got yet another jog to point him to breaking out of the Jewish rut.

Yet Paul tells us in Galatians 2:11 that he had had to withstand Peter to his face for being inconsistent, being fussy about kosher food while he was with Jewish Christians, but eating freely when he was with others. In spite of all he had experienced, he could not break out of his Jewishness, and it fell to Paul to take up the mission to the wider world.

For Simon Peter, as for us, the twin processes of growing spiritually and of learning go on throughout our lives. Those of us who have known some of the great Christians personally know that they too had their faults, just as we do. Yet God works through us. It is this awareness which enables us to take up the challenge of God's work.

No matter how committed we are, there are still points at which we need to learn and grow. No matter how much we may respect a person as a Christian, there will still be points at which we are painfully aware of the need for his or her growth.

What's his name?
He started off in life known as *Simon* (it should rhyme with *alone*) son of Jonas. Jesus gave him the nickname *Kephas* (rock). When he went into Latin speaking areas that became *Petrus* (rock), which was anglicised into Peter, and if he had come up to Scotland he would have been Craig!

30. THE CRIPPLE AT THE GATE OF THE TEMPLE

Acts 3:1–4:21

Peter and John were going up to the Temple for the three o'clock prayer time.

A certain man, lame from birth, was being carried to his place at the 'Beautiful Gate', where they used to put him each day so that he could beg.

Seeing Peter and John he asked them for alms.

Peter looked right at him, and so did John. Then he said: 'Look at us!'

He looked up expectantly.

Peter said, 'I've no silver or gold, but what I do have I'll give you! In the Name of Jesus Christ of Nazareth WALK!'

And gripping him by the right hand he lifted him up.

Immediately his feet and ankle bones were strengthened, and leaping up to his feet he went with them into the Temple, walking and leaping and praising God.

Notes

The Greek seems to suggest that the beggar's family or friends were in the act of placing him back in his usual 'pitch', presumably after the 'siesta'.

The three o'clock prayer time was part of the daily ritual of the Temple. Only the really devout went to it.

The disciples

We note that Simon Peter and John are together. We note too that they still behave like good Jews, going to the Temple, unaware as yet that the death of Christ has made the Temple with its sacrifices redundant.

We note their togetherness. Remember that in Mark 6:7 we read that Jesus sent them out two by two, and that the lists of the Twelve always give the names in pairs. Usually Simon and John are paired with their respective brothers, Andrew and James (Jacob), but here the pairing is different. We cannot stress too often that 'two together in the Name of Jesus' is the basic tool of Christian work, and we have to be very careful of anybody who works solo.

But notice further that St Luke places this story directly after the description of the *koinonia* of the first church (Acts 2:42–47). As we noted, healing flows from the *koinonia* and the principle remains clear. *The effectiveness of the church in healing, as in all else, depends on the depth and strength of its* koinonia. *The deeper the* koinonia, *the more effectively it will be able to heal in the Name of Jesus.*

Or, to put it another way, the more the pattern of the life of a congregation or fellowship approximates to the description in Acts 2:42–47, the more they will be able to produce the effects which that *koinonia* produced by the power of the Holy Spirit when they set forth in pairs to do the Lord's work.

The beggar

We wonder where he was when Jesus was healing the beggars in the Temple (Ch. 26). Was he too crippled to get in? Apart from that, if his place was at the gate of the Temple, then Jesus must have passed him many times, so why had Jesus not healed him?

We noticed in Chapter 22 that there must have been other beggars asking for alms apart from Bartimaeus, but only Bartimaeus was healed, and that was because he had pushed himself forward. Yet this man, it seems, had *only* asked for alms.

The right time

Perhaps he had never been ready before, in the same way as we often find people whom we know could be healed, but they continue to be ill. They are not ready for healing. We waste our time and resources trying to help those who are not ready. Mere compassion, good intentions and 'correct' theories about healing on the part of those ministering are not enough. The Spirit who searches the hearts of both the sick and 'the healer' knows the right time. This is where we need the gifts of discernment and knowledge.

We do not know if he had heard Jesus preach or not, although surely he must have heard about the execution of Jesus. On the other hand, it would not seem that he recognised the two main disciples. We would gather, then, that there was little faith of any sort to begin with. He was certainly not 'looking with faith' to these two strange men from the start.

The initiative

The initiative in this case is entirely with the apostles, or rather the initiative is entirely the work of the Spirit in them. They do not pick the man out on any human grounds. It is just that they had an inner knowing that this specific healing was being given.

In the summary of the section on the Laying-on of Hands we referred to a good example of this, in 1 Corinthians 12:28, where the term is *gifts of cures*, suggesting that each healing is a gift in itself.

We should not take such an initiative, then, unless we are clear that we have a gift for this particular person, or, as some people put it, that we have an anointing for them. We thought about this in Chapter 10.

And how do we know that? It is not easy to describe, but there is on occasion a deep knowledge, sometimes accompanied by a physical sensation, and different people have different ways of knowing. Each person must work it out for themselves. If, facing a sufferer, we have no such anointing, we have to behave in a compassionate way, doing what we can at the physical level.

The healing

There is no laying-on of hands in this incident, nor is there any word of preparation, only the command, 'Look at us.' That would have been a surprise, for people usually look away from beggars, even if they do toss a coin or two to them. The insistence on eye-contact could be an important point. However, note what Simon Peter does here: he first utters the Word of Authority, then he grips the man by the hand to lift him up. Once again we note that this is not the laying-on of hands, and once again we see that touch comes in *after* the Word. That in itself was an act of faith and love on the part of Simon Peter.

As the story unfolds we see clearly the characteristics which indicate that it is in fact the continuation of the work that Jesus began. In what he says to the amazed crowd, Simon Peter specifically denies that he is a healer or is saintly ('no power or godliness of our own' in the language of the KJV – Acts 3:12). He had healed the man, not because he had 'achieved his highers' in things psychic or spiritual, but because he had given expression to the Jesus-life present in the *koinonia* in the Upper Room.

Faith healing or divine healing?

This comes perilously close to 'faith healing', with the 'look at us' verging on hypnotism. If they had not been sure that the power had been 'switched on' for this man, it would have been dangerous for him.

As an example of this danger, I remember one Evangelist-healer who came to do a service in Stirling. He got a woman out of her wheelchair by sheer force of suggestion; he was shouting, 'Look at me!' and was gripping her hand, doing the Simon Peter 'thing'.

She walked back to her seat, and he claimed a miracle on a par with the one we are considering. However, when she went back to the Infirmary the specialist said that she had done irreparable damage to her hips. A lot can be achieved through the use of suggestion and hypnotic techniques, i.e. faith healing, but that is not the same as Divine Healing. We have to be very careful to differentiate. That 'healer' had slipped down on to 'faith healing'.

The trial

The rest of the story is well worth reading for yourself. It is vivid and has the marks of a genuine memory. For one thing, as we read it we find unusual terms referring to Jesus. There seem to have been ways of speaking about Jesus which dropped out as their thinking developed. For instance, Peter refers to Jesus as God's *pais*, which means 'boy', although most versions translate it as 'servant'. We only find this in Peter's early sermons, because later the term 'Son of God' took over.

Peter also refers to Jesus as the *Archegon of Life*, and *archegon* means *one who goes before*, the pioneer and leader. This is another way of speaking about Jesus which dropped out later. We only meet it again in Hebrews, notably in 12:2.

These two hints point us to the fact that the great doctrines of the faith had not yet been worked out, and that the terminology of the apostles was still fluid.

We note too that in Acts 4:13 it says that the priests were impressed that these men who spoke so fluently and courageously were unschooled, having no proper theological education. They were ordinary working men. Like Jesus, they did not speak out of books and with theories, but with blunt reality. This reminds us that the true work of the Holy Spirit is to make us *earthy*, as Jesus was, and as his apostles were. Highfalutin religiosity is *not* a sign of the Holy Spirit!

CONCLUSIONS

- The Holy Spirit continues to work through the body of believers as It did through the body of Jesus.
- Our ability to heal as Jesus healed does not depend on gaining more psychic knowledge, theological training or psychological techniques, but on deepening our fellowship within the Church along the lines of Acts 2:42–7
- The basic instrument of Christian healing is 'two together in the Name of Jesus', not a 'healer'.
- We must be careful to move into this sort of initiative only if we are sure that we have 'an anointing' to do it.

31. SIMON PETER AND THE PARALYTIC

Acts 9:32–35

And so it was that Peter went round the whole area, and came down to God's people in Lydda.

And he found a certain man who had been bed-ridden for eight years, paralysed.

And Peter said to him: 'Aeneas, Jesus Christ cures you. Up you get and pull yourself together.'

And he rose up at once.

Notes

Lydda is where the airport is today, between Jerusalem and Tel Aviv.

God's people: literally 'the holy ones', usually translated 'saints'. It is difficult to know how to express it. The word 'saint' has taken on a special meaning for us. The word 'Christian' had not come into currency by then, but even that has many meanings, depending on who uses it.

Pull yourself together This is a puzzling word. Some translate it 'make your bed'…presumably meaning to pick it up ready to take it away. Yet the word for 'bed' does not come into it. The same word is used about people casting their garments in front of Jesus on Palm Sunday. It is also the word that Jesus used when he sent the two disciples to prepare the room for the Last Supper…there it seems to mean 'furnished'. It may mean to 'gird yourself', i.e. get properly dressed. Perhaps I am wrong in translating it the way I have, but it seems as good a guess as any.

Background

This incident took place during the lull after the first wave of persecution, which seems to have ended after Saul of Tarsus (whom we know as Paul) had been converted. So we are probably about five years on from Pentecost.

Note that it says that Peter 'came down to God's people in Lydda and found Aeneas'. This seems to imply that Peter came to Lydda as part of a pastoral visit to the church there, and that Aeneas was part of the *koinonia*. It is possible that Aeneas was lying in the street begging, but on the whole one would tend to understand that Peter, finding him as part of the fellowship, took the initiative. However, one cannot be dogmatic about it.

The fact that Peter calls him by name is unusual, and would seem to indicate that he knew the man personally. So we assume:

1. that the setting is in the gathering of the *koinonia* at Lydda,
2. that Peter takes the initiative,
3. that this paralysed man had been part of the fellowship, and yet was unhealed.

Faith

If the faith had already been there in Aeneas and in the fellowship, he would have been healed long before this. Presumably 'the saints' at Lydda had already prayed for him, but their *koinonia* had not been deep enough. We are back to thinking in terms of the boy whom the disciples could not heal (Ch. 15). It must have been the preaching of the Word in this case that sparked off the deeper faith which in turn made the healing possible.

While Peter is not noted in this account as having been paired off, as he had been in the previous work, here he is acting as part of a *koinonia*, not solo.

Similarity with 'The paralytic boy' (Ch. 1)

It is, however, interesting to compare this story with the story of the lad let down through the roof in Mark 2:1 and Luke 5:18. Modern scholars often suggest that St Luke has deliberately made this and the next healing resemble the Lord's healings in order to make a point. Yet if one had been with Jesus while he was healing, as Peter had been, and if, like Peter, and like many of us, you had spent years meditating on these works, is it any wonder that there are similarities? Of course Peter's reaction to sufferers would echo his Lord's, and one hopes that our reactions today echo them too.

There are times when 'scholars' are too clever. It is not necessary to suggest undue 'editing' on the part of Luke. We note a further point: that St Luke uses the slang word for bed in verse 33, just as St Mark uses it in Mark 2:11. Yet when Luke tells the story of Jesus healing the boy, he puts a more polite word in our Lord's mouth, as if he did not like the idea of the Lord using slang. However he seems to have no qualms about putting slang in Peter's mouth!

Furthermore, in the Greek, Peter's words are quite different from those of Jesus in Mark 2 and Luke 5. There is also a different word for *rise,* a different word for *heal* and then that puzzling word mentioned above which means: 'pull yourself together'/'make your bed'. This, then, is no editorial concoction. It is a story that stands up in its own right. The healing of Aeneas is the work of the One Spirit. It therefore bears a resemblance to the accounts of Jesus' works – and that is as it should be – but it is not a carbon copy.

CONCLUSIONS

- Aeneas's case required 'a higher voltage' of power than the local church could offer.
- The preaching of the Word created the conditions in which the healing could take place
- We have to accept the limitations of our local churches, and realise our urgent need to grow in the Spirit.

32. SIMON PETER AND DORCAS

Acts 9:36–43

Now in Joppa there was a disciple called Tabitha (in Greek: Dorcas), who was always doing good, concerned for the poor.

And so it was at that time that she began to ail and eventually she died.

They duly washed her and laid her out in an upstairs room.

Since Joppa was not far from Lydda, and they had heard that Peter was there, they sent two men for him, urging him to come without delay.

Peter got up and went with them. On his arrival they took him upstairs to the room, where the widow-women were all weeping as they showed him all the shirts and cloaks which Dorcas had made while she was still with them.

But Peter threw them all out, knelt down and prayed. Then turning to the body he said: 'Tabitha, get up.'

And she opened her eyes and, seeing Peter, sat up.

And he gave her his hand, helping her up.

He called the people of God and the widows, and presented her alive to them.

Notes

Joppa, or Jaffa, is now part of the city of Tel Aviv, but in those days it was a port on its own, ten miles from Lydda. It would have taken those men about three hours to go uphill to Lydda, but perhaps less for them to walk downhill along with Simon Peter. Therefore it would appear that Dorcas had been dead for about six hours by the time Peter got to her.

Background

It would appear that Peter's work in Lydda was cut short by the arrival of the messengers with this urgent request.

The healer?

It is surely natural to think that when Dorcas was ailing, the first reaction of the local church would have been to pray for her, even to lay hands on her. Yet she had died. Whatever their line of thinking, they felt that Simon Peter should be sent for. They knew that they were at the end of their spiritual resources, and needed somebody whose knowledge of the Lord was deeper than theirs.

Dorcas

One interesting point is that Dorcas is mentioned as 'a disciple' in her own right. That in itself was unusual. Women were usually mentioned as appendages to men. Yet here already we see a woman regarded as a fully fledged disciple. The clothes she made, presumably for the poor, showed that she was working out her discipleship in a traditionally womanlike way, but it was *her* way.

Special gift?

The idea that some are more effective in healing than others is very offensive to some people. I remember one minister, whom I greatly respect, objecting: 'I don't believe in a God who has favourites, a God who answers one man's prayer for healing more than another's.' This good man was missing the point: healing is, as we have seen, *work* which God intends us to do. It is not a matter of wheedling favours.

Of course, we sometimes have to ask other people for help. We may be too emotionally involved to be able to pray effectively, and need the prayer of somebody else who is more removed from the situation. We may realise that somebody's trouble is beyond our power to deal with, and see the need to call in those with greater faith and experience of Jesus. We may also see that God expects us to call on those to whom healing gifts have been given.

Faith and initiative

The usual questions about faith and initiative are difficult to work out. The message from Jaffa, as we have it, did not specify the raising up of Dorcas, but of course we only have a shortened account. We do not know, therefore, whether 'the saints' were asking for her to be raised or not. Obviously they were people of faith and so must Dorcas have been. We have to leave these questions aside in this case.

The raising

When it comes to considering the method used, we find a very interesting point. First of all, as Jesus did with Jairus' daughter, Peter puts out the mourners – and the word once more is a violent one, as if they did not go willingly.

Was it that he blindly followed Jesus' example, or did he realise that these over-emotional women would do more harm than good by their reaction as

Dorcas opened her eyes?

The next point is also very thought-provoking: this is the only case we have come across so far in which prayer was offered on the spot, apart from the raising of Lazarus, also an instance of facing death. It seems natural for us to pray before tackling the actual healing. Yet this is not what we find in the New Testament. In all other cases the prayer, the communion with God, had been established already, so that all that was needed was the Word. Yet here it is specifically reported that Peter went down on his knees and prayed. There is only one further example of this, as we shall see when we come to look at Paul. Perhaps after that hurried walk he needed peace and quiet for a bit before taking action. Whatever the reason, he utters the Word, and then, when Dorcas has already sat up, he reaches out to help her to her feet. There is no laying-on of hands or other action. We leave her reunited with the *koinonia*.

Finally we note (v. 43) that he stayed there in Joppa for some time, lodging in the house of Simon the tanner by the sea. This is very interesting: Tanners were 'ceremonially unclean' because they handled dead animals. An orthodox Jew would not have stayed with a tanner. Also in those days the seaside was the place where the poor lived, and where smelly work like tanning was done. The rich lived up on the hill where there was a cool breeze. So we see Peter lodging with one who was in both senses 'on the fringes of society'. This is a true Jesus-like touch. – unlike some prominent Christian 'healers' and 'evangelists' today who, when they come to a town, stay in a luxury hotel, not in a council estate.

Prayer

This brings us to another important lesson about prayer: Prayer does not mean sending messages up into space hoping that God will hear and have a change of mind with regard to the sick person. We do not need to persuade God to act like Jesus. That is how God wants to act – it is *God's will*, to use the phrase we have come to misuse (see notes on Ch. 20).

What is necessary is that we have to understand *how* God has chosen to work, and then work in cooperation. Since, as we have seen, it is God's will that in this age divine healing should operate through the *koinonia* of the disciples of Jesus by the power of the Holy Spirit in us, there will be times when the result of prayer is that we are directed to seek healing through some chosen human channel.

God means us to be interdependent, for that is what loving one another means. We are meant to value each other's gifts, and to bring out the best in each other. We are much mistaken if we think that Peter or anybody else, including ourselves, can 'go it alone'.

Of course there are dangers, as we have noted several times. The person into whose hands the Lord has entrusted some healing gift may use it to boost his/her own ego. Yet that person will depend on others in some other way. A healthy *koinonia* will counteract the temptation to play at 'being a healer'.

St Paul summed all this up in the chapter we have referred to several times, 1 Cor. 12, likening us to one single body in which we all have different parts to play. We are not all preachers, and we are not all healers. We need each other to be complete. We need that 'togetherness' if the work of Christ is to be done, for we are, as Paul says, *The body of Christ, and each of us is a member of that body.*

To come back to our story, the 'saints' at Joppa were right, then, to send for Peter, and if they had not done so Dorcas would have stayed dead. Good would have come out of that situation too if it had occurred, providing that they had surrendered it into God's hands. In this case, however, God's will was to raise her up through Simon Peter. Because they did the right thing, God's will was done. Again we must avoid the temptation to idealise Peter. Peter knew his weakness better than any, as we have seen. He can have suffered from no delusions of sanctity, and that is the secret of spiritual power. Only those who have faced their sinfulness and weakness, and have accepted it in the mercy of God, can be trusted with the power of the Holy Spirit.

CONCLUSIONS

* There are times when it is right to accept our spiritual limitations and ask for help from those who know the Lord better.
* It is not always right to accept death as 'the will of God'.

33. THE OTHER SIMON

Acts 8:5–25

Then Philip went down to the city of Samaria and preached to them about the Christ.

And the crowds listened attentively to what Philip was saying, united as they saw and heard the signs he was doing.

For many who had unclean spirits were crying out loudly as the spirits came out, and many who were lame or paralysed were healed, and there was great joy in that city.

Now there was a certain man in that city called Simon, who had been practising sorcery, astonishing the Samaritans. He was claiming to be somebody great. Great and small hung on his words, saying: 'This man is the "Power of God".'

For a long time they had paid attention to him because he had astonished them by his magic.

However, when they believed what Philip was saying about the Kingdom of God, and about Jesus Christ, they were baptised, both men and women.

Simon believed too, and fastened on to Philip, amazed to witness the signs and 'powers' being done.

Now, when the apostles in Jerusalem heard how the Samaritans had responded to the Word, they sent them Peter and John.

On arriving, they prayed that they might receive the Holy Spirit, for as yet It had not come on any of them, but having been baptised they were nominally in the Name of the Lord Jesus.

Then they laid their hands on them, and they received the Holy Spirit.

And when Simon saw that through the laying-on of hands the Holy Spirit was given, he offered money saying: 'Give me this power too, so that when I lay on hands people may receive the Holy Spirit.'

But Peter said: 'To hell with you and your money! Do you think you can buy the Gift of God? You're nothing to do with us in this matter! Your heart is not right before God. Rethink this whole thing, and face your wickedness. Ask God and perhaps he will forgive you for the thoughts of your heart. For I can see you steeped in bitter gall, in bondage to wrong.'

Then Simon answered: 'Pray to the Lord for me, that none of the things you have said may happen to me.'

Notes

There is an old text which goes on to say that Simon 'wept much and clung on to Peter and John'. In the next century another Simon from Samaria appeared and caused much trouble. The two are often confused.

This is an extraordinary story, and even though it is not one of the healing miracles, it must be looked at closely. To do so, we must consider the whole setting. This brings us back to one of the first snags which the Church hit – a very common problem...

The row

In Jerusalem there were the 'locals' and, as in any capital city, a lot of in-comers. These latter, although they were Jews, were often Greek-speaking, dressed in the fashions of the Empire, and had Greek names. It seems that there was tension within the *koinonia* because the incomers thought that the local widows were getting priority treatment over the Greek-speaking widows. (Ministers who have had to supervise giving out the harvest thanksgiving gifts will appreciate the problem!)

Wisely the Church set up a committee including Greek-speaking Jews such as Philip (a Greek name). They were to take over serving meals for widows and orphans, removing the burden of this chore from the apostles, who would then be free to get on with the main work: preaching the Gospel.

Philip the server

As so often happens, things did not work out like that, for this Philip who had been appointed to organise meals for widows then went on to conduct an amazing preaching/healing ministry. The Holy Spirit 'blows where it wills', as Jesus said, and our neat organisations are often left in tatters. This need for flexibility comes up again later in the story in the accounts of people 'receiving the Holy Spirit' after the apostles had laid hands on them. They had been baptised into Jesus Christ under Philip's ministry, but the Holy Spirit was only given after the apostles laid hands on them. However, this is not the consistent pattern, for in other cases people are baptised *because* they manifest the sign of having received the Holy Spirit (Acts 10:44). There is no one set procedure in Acts, much as our ecclesiastical lawyers would wish that there were. It would be convenient if one could say: 'Do A, then B, then C and you will receive the Holy Spirit.' However it does not work that way.

The Holy Spirit and organisation

There is a painful lesson here for those who like to see the Church's ministry neatly and properly organised. The Church needs structures, organisational and intellectual. *Yet once we think that we have the Holy Spirit neatly in the structure,* we find that God has other ideas. The True Vine needs a trellis on which to grow, but it is always putting out shoots where we have not planned.

Back to the story

When word reached Jerusalem that Philip was having a phenomenal success in Samaria, the Jerusalem church sent the two apostles to check that all was in order. (Note that the church sent them – Peter was not the boss in the usual sense.) This shows us that the early Church did have supervision and order of some sort, even though there was flexibility. And so Simon Peter met the other Simon, as we read in the above passage. It is interesting that this other Simon could see that the power of the Holy Spirit was superior to his, and that he duly became a member of the *koinonia* by baptism.

A thought

How often do those who work with psychic gifts recognise a Higher Power operating in our church?

The trouble began when Simon the magician saw that in laying hands on people, the apostles received the gift of the Holy Spirit, and he wanted the *power* to do that too. It would seem that the apostles, quite rightly, were hesitant, for he went on to offer them money for it.

Simon Peter just about exploded! He did not mince his words. The man was interested in *power*, not in the grace of God. The *desire for power* and fascination with *the supernatural* are two of the most dangerous things in spiritual life. No wonder Peter dealt very firmly with him.

Psychic and spiritual power

Agnes Sanford, one of the great teachers in the Christian healing movement, said that the power of the Holy Spirit and psychic power are like AC and DC currents in electricity. If you try to mix them you get an explosion. That was just what was in danger of happening here. Simon the magician might have started using his psychic gifts in the church, and in no time there would have been terrible trouble.

Gifted people

The same thing happens whenever a gifted person comes into the Church: the gifted musician, organiser, flower-arranger...anything. However it is especially so with psychic gifts. It is, of course, right that the Church should encourage people to use their gifts to the glory of God. It is right that people should feel that they are valued in the Church. Yet beware the subtle twist and distortion which results in people using the Church as a theatre in which to show off – especially if this involves healing.

A guideline

How can we deal with people such as Simon who come to the Church claiming psychic gifts, such as 'healing'? In the Christian Fellowship of Healing we worked out an approach which seemed effective. When such people came saying, 'I'm a healer, can you use me?' our reaction was to invite them to become part of the Fellowship as it studied the Bible, prayed and befriended people. We would tell them that later, once they had truly become part of the Fellowship, we *might* find it was right to use them.

On most occasions such people went away, often with a sneer. One or two stayed and found that the Bible study was what they had really been looking for. Eventually any psychic gift that had been part of their basic nature was caught up into the higher work of the Holy Spirit. Once things are in the right order, there is no clash. Here we have a very important basic rule, which Simon Peter had obviously learned the hard way. It forms our conclusion.

CONCLUSIONS

- All natural gifts, including psychic gifts, can be used rightly or wrongly.
- All these gifts come into their fullness when they are used to the glory of God, not to the glory of the individual.
- Any natural gift, especially psychic ones, must be renounced, offered up to God, and only used under the direction of the fellowship.
- When a person comes into the church only interested in 'doing his/her thing', that person will cause trouble.
- Those with gifts for organisation, committee-work and order have their places too, but they must not be allowed to dominate either.

I deal with these issues more fully in my book *Across the Spectrum*.

34. Shadow and Take-away Healing

There is one reference to Peter's healing ministry, in Acts 5:15, which seems to be the exception to the rule that his work reflected his Lord's. It tells of how people used to lay their sick in the street, hoping that Simon Peter's shadow would fall on them and heal them. This is unlike anything said of Jesus. It seems to have happened in Jerusalem at one particular time. It is not referred to again, and does not seem to have been the general rule. A similar thing is reported of Paul and his friends in Acts 19:12, except that in their case the people carried away napkins and handkerchiefs which the Apostles had handled. Although these two incidents do not occur at the same time, we shall deal with them together.

A good thing?

On occasion I have heard sermons in which such healings were held up as 'a good thing' – yet were they? As we have seen, Jesus did nothing of the sort. Remember the occasion on which the woman tried to sneak a healing from Jesus without his knowing (Ch. 4). Jesus would not have it. She had to face him. Healing, for Jesus, was part of a personal relationship, and we have studied a number of incidents which show how often he took trouble with individuals.

The impersonality of 'shadow healing' and 'take-away healing', without any real person-to-person contact, puts them in a different category altogether from the rest of the healing in the New Testament. Could there have been a touch of mass hysteria and a cult of personality? This raises a lot of questions. I do not pretend to know the answers.

Proxy healing

There is another way in which people seek healing for others without the personal confrontation: *proxy healing.* In this a person does not just ask us to pray for somebody, but offers to receive ministry on behalf of the sufferer.

This involves something much deeper than asking for prayer. It is not the same as getting into an apostle's shadow or asking for a handkerchief from him either. So we have to say that there is no example of proxy healing in the Bible. It seems to have come in through the Anglican Church early in this century and many have been blessed through it.

There are one or two guidelines:

- Sufferer and proxy must be in communion with each other and with the Lord.
- It should, if possible, be agreed between sufferer and proxy beforehand.
- We must never try to bring spiritual power to bear on somebody who does not want it, or who is not ready for it.
- Any such ministry should end with inviting the proxy to release the problem into the hands of God. Over-identification is dangerous.
- Beware religious busybodies who revel in coming as proxies, whether they have been asked to or not, and who are kidding themselves that they are exercising a healing ministry. They take up valuable time and space, and bring the ministry into disrepute.

Summary SIMON PETER

We have now looked at each of the individual cases in which Simon Peter is recorded as having exercised a healing ministry, and at the rather strange 'shadow healing'. It is quite clear that he continued the emphasis that we saw in Jesus:

- The Word of Authority is the main instrument of healing.
- Peter is recorded as laying-on hands to pass on the gift of the Holy Spirit, but not in healing. He does however reach out to help people to their feet once they are healed.
- Each healing was directly linked in some way with the preaching of the Gospel.
- While there are strong similarities to our Lord's work, Peter's ministry was no carbon copy.
- We have also seen that while he had a special place in 'the Body of Christ', he never acted as an isolated individual when exercising a healing gift.

Introducing ST PAUL

We come now to St Paul, one of the towering figures of the Bible. We meet him first as Saul of Tarsus, although when he 'went international' he took to using his Latin name – Paulus, Paul (= little man). There is an ancient description of him: short, bow-legged, eyebrows which met in the middle, rather ugly, but his face could light up like an angel's.

It seems that he did not meet Jesus in the flesh, which is strange, for he tells us that he had been a student of Gamaliel, a rabbi who was contemporary with Jesus, and who is still today much respected for his liberal teachings. Perhaps Saul came up to Jerusalem to study from his home in Tarsus (in Turkey today) after Jesus had completed his mission. However, by the time Stephen, the first Christian martyr, was stoned, Saul seems to have been taking a leading part in the persecution of Christians.

It was while he was involved in this that he was converted by a vision of Jesus, and immediately set out on a flurry of activity on behalf of the very people he had been persecuting. In Galatians 2 he tells how he then spent fourteen years back in Tarsus, mellowing a bit perhaps, until Barnabas remembered him and fetched him. It was then that his famous journeyings began, at first as Barnabas's assistant. His letters were written in the course of these journeys and imprisonments.

Paul's main activity, then, took place between about 50 and 68 AD when he was martyred, which means that his letters are the earliest documents in the New Testament. The Gospels, beginning with St Mark's, came into being after Peter and Paul had been executed. By that time there were fewer eyewitnesses left, hence the need for written accounts of the teaching of Jesus.

People who speak of 'the simple Jesus of the Gospels', and accuse Paul of having made it complicated, have the cart before the horse. Mark and Luke both worked with Paul, and Paul was dead before they wrote their accounts of Jesus.

His letters

Strangely, there are very few references to healing in Paul's letters. He refers briefly to having wrought 'signs and wonders' in Romans 15:19, and in 2 Cor. 12:12. He refers to the Galatians performing miracles (Gal. 3:5). Only in 1 Corinthians 12 does he refer to healing as a part of the normal Christian life, and that was because things were going badly wrong at this level. However his faithful companion, Dr Luke, recorded some of his 'works' and we turn to these now, beginning with a healing in which Saul is at the receiving end.

35. SAUL AND ANANIAS

Acts 9:10–19

*At Damascus there was a disciple called Ananias, and the Lord spoke to him
in a vision saying: 'Ananias!'*

'Here I am, Lord,' he said.

*And the Lord said to him: 'Get up and go to Straight Street. Ask for Saul
of Tarsus in Judas' house, for he is praying, and he has 'seen' somebody called
Ananias coming in and laying his hands on him to get his sight back.'*

*Then Ananias answered: 'Lord, I have heard a lot about this man, and the
harm he has done your people in Jerusalem…and how he has come here with
authority from the high priests to arrest all who call on your Name.'*

*But the Lord said: 'On you go. He is my chosen vessel to carry my Name
to Gentiles and kings, and to the children of Israel. I will show him how much
he must suffer for my Name's sake.'*

So Ananias duly went, entered the house, laid hands on him and said:

*'Brother Saul, the Lord has sent me…Jesus, that is…the one who appeared
to you on your way here…so that you might get your sight back and be filled
with the Holy Spirit.'*

*And immediately scabs fell from his eyes, and he got his sight back. Up he
got and was baptised.*

Notes

I have tried to capture the jerky feeling of Ananias's greeting to Saul. Somehow his nervousness comes across in the Greek! I have translated what fell
from Saul's eyes as 'scabs' whereas it is usually translated 'scales', as in the
scales of a snake.

Saul and Ananias

The first thing that strikes us about this story is the 'double vision' – one to
Saul and the other to Ananias. Now, direct guidance of this kind does
occasionally happen, but it is not the normal thing. There is another example
in the next chapter of Acts, when Simon Peter is guided to visit a Roman
sergeant-major.

Guidance

Such direct guidance happens only when God requires us to do something which even the most sanctified common sense could not lead us to do. It is quite plain when we read Acts and St Paul's letters that the early Church did its decision-making through prayer and discussion. That was the normal way. After all, we are here to grow up into mature children of God, and how would children mature properly if at every turn their parents were giving them the right answers to everything? Over-protective parents are a menace. So we have to learn to make decisions the hard way. There is sometimes a danger in charismatic circles that we depend too much on guidance. The very nature of direct guidance is such that it usually comes when we have not asked for it, as in this case.

Under protest

Vision or no vision, Ananias knows the Lord well enough to be able to protest: 'This is ridiculous!' Just in case he had not noticed it, Ananias reminds him of the persecution. Some people might see this as a sign of a lack of faith, whereas in fact it shows that his relationship with the Lord was real.

Blindness

Now we look at Saul's blindness. One does not need to be a psychiatrist to recognise that there was an element of shock here. Not shellshock, but something very similar. About twenty years later Paul, as he was by then, wrote to the Galatians mentioning that they had been very helpful and kind to him when he had been in a bad way, so much so that they would 'even have plucked out their eyes to give him' (Galatians 4:15). Obviously he had been having trouble with his eyes again. Some suggest that this is a clue to his 'thorn in the flesh'. (We shall consider this later.)

Shock?

A lot is written about Saul's experience on the Damascus road, and it could fill the rest of this book. Let us only point out that when the risen Christ asks, *'Why are you persecuting me?'* the Greek word is *hunting me*. Like many persecutors, Saul had become fascinated by the very object of his 'hunting'. The inner tension would build up, and when he finally found himself 'one of them', it would be a shock to his whole system. It is usual for shock to affect the weakest part of one's body, and in Saul's case it seems to have been his eyes.

A brother's welcome

Whatever hesitation Ananias had felt at first, once confronted with the reality of this blinded, distraught traveller, he moved into action. The power of the Spirit welled up within him, and he knew what to do. That is so often the way when we are confronted with a big challenge. We lay our hesitation and bewilderment honestly before God, as very frail human beings, but once we move into action the Spirit is there and we know it.

The healing

In this case Ananias lays hands on Saul before saying anything. There seems to have been no build up at all. This is one of the rare occasions on which the laying-on of hands is mentioned and it was not just for healing but also 'so that he might receive the Holy Spirit'.

To be addressed as 'brother' by one of the people he had come to arrest must have been a healing experience in itself. Ananias's acceptance would be an important step in this process.

The physical healing was immediate, and so also was the infilling of the Holy Spirit.

Answer to prayer

Ananias's greeting to Saul is all the more impressive when you realise how the Christians in Damascus must have prayed to be spared this man's attention. When he arrived in the city, it must have seemed that their prayers had not been answered. Of course, God had indeed answered their prayers, but not as they had expected. That is usually God's way.

Baptism

Then Ananias moved straight on to baptism. Most churches today would be shocked at such precipitate action by a layman.

The house must have been a considerable one, since Saul and all his party were staying there. Such houses were usually built round a courtyard with a pump or well. This would probably be where Ananias baptised Saul, using the water that was also drunk by the horses and camels – something that many people today would find surprising.

Baptism is primarily the sign of becoming part of the Christian family, a disciple, and in those days people expected to 'receive the Holy Spirit' after baptism in a way that was clearly evident. By this sensitive but authoritative action, Saul's inner tension which had caused the shock is dealt with firmly.

A new man in Christ

So it was that Saul found himself part of the Christian community which he had come to wipe out. (Strangely, he did indeed 'find himself'!) There was nothing for it – Saul had become 'one of them', and he was on the way to becoming 'St Paul'. To put it another way, using the picture he himself used in Romans 6: *Saul the Pharisee was buried in the waters of baptism. Paul, the Man in Christ, was raised up.*

CONCLUSIONS

- In the first three of the four cases of blindness at which we have looked (chs. 2, 9, 11, 22), touch in some form played a large part.
- In this story, as in the others, the laying-on of hands is only part of a much wider process.
- It is also plain that in this case the laying-on of hands for healing merges with the laying-on of hands for the receiving of the gift of the Holy Spirit.

36. PAUL AND THE CRIPPLE AT LYSTRA

Acts 14:6–20

There was a man at Lystra, sitting with no strength in his feet. He had been like that from birth, never having walked.

This man listened to the preaching of Paul, who seeing that he had the faith to be healed, said in a loud voice: 'Get up, on your feet, stand!'

And he leaped up and walked.

Notes

Lystra was a city in Galatia, up in the hills between Turkey and Syria. The people of this area were Celts, speaking a language like that spoken in Gaul, ancestor of modern Welsh.

The rest of the story, after the healing, is quite fascinating. To understand it one has to know why the Lystrans take Barnabas to be Jupiter in disguise and Paul to be his messenger Hermes. Obviously Barnabas was the more impressive of the two.

It went back to a local story that once the two gods Jupiter and Hermes had visited Lystra in disguise, and had been treated inhospitably, except by an old couple. The result for Lystra had not been pleasant, and the Lystrans were afraid of making the same mistake again! Hence the excitement and the preparation to make sacrifices.

Background

It is in his letter to these Galatians (4:13–14) that Paul refers to the fact that he had originally come up into their mountain area because of physical weakness. Perhaps he had had malaria down on the coastal plain. He mentions that he was in such a condition that they might have despised him and, as we mentioned earlier, it appears to have been eye trouble. It seems that there had been no miraculous healing for Paul. It is interesting that Luke does not mention the health factor as the reason for coming to Galatia.

The disciples

Barnabas and Paul, then, arrive in Lystra. In most Mediterranean towns then, as now, there would have been a plaza, or whatever the locals call it, where farmers would sell their wares, friends gather for a drink, beggars sit hopefully, and where visiting speakers would naturally open up to whoever was there. It would appear that this healing occurred in such a public place, rather than in the *koinonia*, as had happened with Aeneas (Ch. 31). Apparently Barnabas presided, as an older man, and Paul preached. The healing is straightforward. As usual, there are the two disciples together: 'two together in Jesus' Name' – the condition for spiritual power.

The initiative

Paul takes the initiative. There is no sign of the man asking for healing.

The healing

There is no laying-on of hands, only the Word of Authority, but in this case Paul does not even use a phrase such as 'in the Name of Jesus'. Since he had been preaching in Jesus' Name, perhaps it was obvious in whose Name he acted, without specifically using the phrase.

Faith

One interesting aspect of this story is that Paul sees the man's faith as a prerequisite for healing, but this was never written of Jesus, although we do find him looking at the faith in those bringing *others* for healing (Ch. 1). He never demanded faith from a patient *before* healing, apart from the occasion with two blind men (Ch. 9). On the other hand, Jesus did sometimes refer to it *afterwards.*

The sequel

At the end of this passage from Acts, the crowd tries to stone Paul. It is only too true that emotional crowds can switch moods easily. However, Lystra was a Roman colony run directly by Romans, and would have been well organised. A proper stoning would only have been permitted after a trial, and there is no word of this. Hence it looks as if it was just a spontaneous outburst of stone-throwing.

Raised from the dead?

One can hear sermons and read books which assert that Paul was raised from the dead after this stoning. However, Luke is usually precise in what he says, so let us look at the Greek, word by word, even if it does make clumsy English: '...*stoning Paul, dragged him outside the city, assuming him to have died, but, the disciples surrounding him, rising up he came into the city.*' It does not say that they prayed over him, although surely they must have done so! It does not say that he was dead, but that they *thought* he was dead. To read into it that they raised him from the dead makes a good story, but it does not necessarily reflect the reality.

Trainees

One interesting sidelight is that the Greek speaks of '*trainees*' surrounding Paul. The Greek word *mathetes* means people who are undergoing training. It does not say 'the saints', or any such word. Therefore it would seem probable that Paul had had time to begin to train people there, and this healing was not something that happened as soon as he got there.

This whole story is bristling with things to think about! Instead of conclusions we leave this incident with five such points to ponder:

1. Paul's ill-health.
2. The fact that he picked on this man because he *saw* that he had faith to be healed.
3. His simple healing of the lame man by the Word of Authority alone.
4. The fact there were trainees.
5. The mystery of what actually happened after the stoning.

37. PAUL AND PYTHON

Acts 16:16–19

And so it was that as we went to the prayer-place we were met by a girl who had a spirit of Python, and who made a lot of money for her masters by fortune-telling. She followed Paul and us yelling out: 'These men are slaves of the Most High God, and they are telling you the way of salvation.' She did this on a number of days, but Paul was upset and turning to the spirit said: 'I command you in the Name of Jesus Christ to come out of her.' And it came out at once.

Notes

The story goes on to tell how the slave-masters tried to prosecute Paul for interfering with their trade. Paul and Silas were flogged and put in prison, but that is another story.

Us Another thing to notice about this story is that Luke uses 'us' instead of 'them'. In other words he is saying quietly that he was there. At the beginning of his Gospel and Acts he assures the reader that he has, as we would say, researched his sources thoroughly, but here he is speaking from first-hand experience.

Python The Greek words describing the spirit in the girl mean literally 'the spirit of Python'. A python is a big brown snake, of course, but also Python was the snake supposed to live in the depths of the Delphic Oracle to which many people went for guidance. In fact I know some who have gone there in our own day.

Paul and Python

This seems to be a straightforward story of exorcism, continuing the pattern set by Jesus. We note that as with the man in the synagogue and the man at Gadara, the spirit confesses Jesus, when from the demonic point of view it would have been better keeping quiet! It seems once more that the person concerned was in sufficient control to ask for help even while the demon was protesting, and we might say that the initiative was with the patient.

Python

Perhaps the best comment, however, is a story. A lady – we will call her Jean – asked us for help. She was a very committed Christian, but felt that there was something not right, since her family had been involved in spiritualism. Several of us met for prayer before her appointment, and two of us had the strong feeling that it was 'the spirit of divination'.

She duly came, and we commanded it to come out. We then went on to have Communion together. After that was over she said: 'It was strange, when I took the cup, I felt as if a great big brown snake was coming up and out of me.'

On the way home I was thinking about it, and wondering about the phrase 'spirit of divination'. It struck me that it came from the story of Paul and the slave girl. Then my hair just about stood on end, for I remembered having read not long before that the Greek was 'the spirit of Python', the Oracle at Delphi. In other words what 'Jean' and the slave girl were suffering from was an offshoot of the Python of Delphi. I checked later and confirmed that Jean and the others who had been present were quite unaware of the connection between divination and Python.

These stories are a reminder that an ability to foresee the future is not necessarily 'of God', and that there is something potent and dangerous in many of the old religious beliefs. Perhaps consulting the Oracle at Delphi was the best available to people of that time but, once the Christ had come, the second best became the enemy of the best.

Query

Luke tells us that the girl had been following them for 'many days'. We wonder why Paul did not act straight away, but delayed as he did. Was he perhaps unsure, seeing that the girl was proclaiming the truth? Perhaps Paul, Silas and Luke needed time to talk and pray about it before they were sure that it was unhealthy.

The exorcism

This exorcism, as noted above, was in the Jesus-pattern, and now we look at it in more detail. There are 'two together in the Name of Jesus', Paul and Silas as well as Luke. There is no ritual, none of the complications which exorcists of the time used. Paul issues a short, sharp command in the Name of Jesus, and that is it.

The phrase 'that same hour' is a bit of a puzzle: I have translated it as 'at once' but it might imply that it took some time, inside an hour.

The sons of Sceva

One further point before we leave this subject: In Acts 19:13ff we read that there were some Jewish exorcists who noticed how effective the Name of Jesus was in exorcism, so they tried to use it too, commanding the demon out 'in the Name of Jesus whom Paul preaches'. The result was disastrous. It answered: 'Jesus I know, Paul I understand, but you...who are you?' The patient then attacked them violently, and they fled naked and battered.

That is the deep meaning of the command not to take the Lord's Name in vain: we should not use it when we have no right to do so.

CONCLUSIONS

- Authority over the demonic continued into the life of the Church.
- We should not accept what appears to be support from psychic sources.

38. EUTYCHUS

Acts 20:9–12

And on the first day of the Sabbaths, as we were assembled to break bread, Paul was lecturing them in view of the fact that we were due to leave the next day. He went on until midnight.

Now there were a lot of lamps in that upper room, where we were gathered, and a certain young man called Eutychus, sitting in a window-seat, was overcome by a deep sleep, for Paul had been lecturing on for a long time. Thus overcome by sleep he fell from the third floor, and was taken dead.

However Paul, going down to him, fell on him, embracing him saying: 'Don't panic. There's life in him.'

Then going upstairs again, breaking bread and partaking, he went on in conversation until daybreak. Then he left. And they led the lad away, living, and they were considerably comforted.

Notes

'Sabbaths' – a strange phrase. Most English Bibles have 'on the Sabbath'. It means the first day after the Sabbath, i.e. what we call Sunday.

We notice once again that Dr Luke was present, telling this story as an eyewitness. It takes place in the town of Troas (Troy) on the coast of what we call Turkey.

Third floor For British readers this means the 'ground floor plus three' – 18 ft. For others this means the 'ground floor plus two' – 12 ft, most houses being lower than ours today.

'Was taken dead' Now that is a strange phrase. This Greek word for 'take' in other places always has the sense of 'taking something or somebody *from* somebody', or 'lifting something *out* of…'. What can it mean here? Some suggest that they picked him up dead. However the story indicates that Paul went down to where he had fallen.

Background

Christian worship

Here Dr Luke gives us one of the few glimpses we get of how Christians worshipped in the first century, and in the light of this we can make sense of a number of things that Paul says in his letters.

The Sabbath

First of all, note that already the Christians had departed from keeping the Sabbath, which, for Jews, lasted from sunset Friday until sunset Saturday. Already Christians were gathering on what we would call Sunday evening, after they had finished work. They called it 'the first day of the week' or 'the Lord's day'.

In fact we find in Colossians 2:16 that scorn is poured on those who still keep Jewish customs such as the Sabbath. We gather from other sources that the first part of the meeting consisted of expounding the Scriptures, and singing psalms and hymns.

The worship

Then, as we see in this account, they went on to the breaking of bread and, of course, the sharing of the cup of wine. This was done as a real meal, so much so that Paul had to rebuke the Corinthian church for the fact that some had too much to drink and over-ate while others went hungry (1 Cor. 11:20–22).

The scene

Now we come back to the story itself. The upstairs room was probably the dining room of a wealthy person's house, a rectangle with an apse, a semi-circular recess for the family, at one end. Many old churches are of this shape. It was an upper room, and – however you reckon it – it was a nasty fall indeed. The reference to the fact that there were a lot of lamps is a nice eyewitness touch. All those oil lamps burning would have made a stuffy atmosphere, and one can understand a young lad being drowsy after a day's work.

Injury or death?

Either way, it is the only example of an injury being healed, apart from Malchus' ear. When I set out to write about Eutychus, I thought I was going to be discussing Paul raising somebody from the dead. However I was surprised at what I found when I looked more closely, and now I am not sure. Let us, then, consider the story in detail.

Dead?

Strangely Dr Luke does not follow his usual careful practice of giving us a diagnosis, as he does in the next story. Surely the lad must have had some injury, unless something broke his fall. The congregation rush down, pick him up and 'he was taken dead' (see Notes). It also says that Paul 'fell on him', suggesting that he was on the ground. But even these points are not definite. It is difficult to form a mental picture of what happened. We come back to those two words, 'taken dead'. They certainly thought he was dead, and Paul's opening words suggest that they were making a great fuss.

The treatment

Now we have to note very carefully what Luke says: 'Going down Paul fell on him, embracing him.' This is rather like what Elisha did to the lad with sunstroke in 2 Kings 4:18ff. The word used means to wrap yourself round. It is far more like an attempt to establish whether or not there was life, checking heartbeat and breath. There is no suggestion that Paul prayed, no sign of a 'word of authority' such as, 'Rise up!' All we are told is that Paul said: 'Do not panic,' and declared, 'There is life in him.' He does not say: 'The Lord has healed him,' or any such thing. In fact it seems that Eutychus did not walk back into the house upright on his own, as he would have done if he had been healed. Rather it says that they led him – we assume back into the house.

The response

The story does not say that they gave thanks for his healing, or that they glorified God that he had been brought to life, only that they were relieved that he was alive. Now, one can present this as a story of raising from the dead – but is it?

I am not sure what conclusion to draw. I do, however, know the danger of ardent Christians reading miracles into situations which do not warrant it. It is an 'occupational disease' in 'healing' circles!

CONCLUSION

- I repeat, I am not sure whether this was a raising from the dead.

39. PAUL IN MALTA

Acts 28:1–10

Our final story about Paul takes us to Malta. He arrived there as the result of a storm and shipwreck, and it is worth reading the story of that disaster, because once more it is a 'we' account of the event. The New English Bible version is superb, apparently done by a sailor who knew ships. However we take up the story at the point at which Paul, Luke and other prisoners, with their guards and the ship's crew, land on Malta, cold, hungry and shocked. Once more we stick to Luke's own story.

The barbarous people there were very kind to us, kindling a fire, and welcoming us into shelter because the rainstorm was obviously coming on, and it was cold. When Paul had gathered a bundle of sticks and was laying them on the fire, the heat brought out a viper which fastened on to his hand.

When the local people saw this poisonous snake gripping him they said among themselves: 'He must be a murderer. He escaped drowning but vengeance has caught up with him all the same.'

But Paul just shook the viper off into the fire and carried on as if nothing had happened. When the locals saw that he did not swell up or die, they changed their minds and decided that he must be a god.

Now the official who ruled the islands, a man called Publius, had an estate nearby. He welcomed us and put us up for three days, very courteously. It so happened that his father was prostrate with a high fever and dysentery. Paul went in, prayed, laid hands on him, and cured him.

After that anybody on the island who was ill came for therapy.

Notes

Soundings A naval officer stationed in Malta took soundings in the bay where St Paul was said to have landed, and found that the Bible account was accurate.

Therapy I have kept the Greek word here. It is unusual.

And so Paul and Luke go on their way to Rome, laden with gifts and provisions.

The snake

The story of the snake is fascinating, especially since once again it is an eyewitness account by somebody who has proved to be a careful observer. It is not, then, a legend which grew up later. Yet it leaves us with questions as we remember a group of extremist 'Christians' in the USA who deliberately subjected themselves to snakebites in faith that they would come to no harm. They died. They were depending on one of the several possible endings to St Mark's Gospel, in which immunity to snakebites is promised. However nobody can be really sure as to how that Gospel ends, and therefore as to what was really promised. Incidentally, note that Paul was gathering sticks, for as a prisoner he would have to do the donkey-work.

The healing of Publius's father is of real interest. We note that Dr Luke is careful to give a proper diagnosis in terms of the medicine of his day. It might appear that here Paul breaks the rules we have been working out as we have followed through the work of Jesus and the apostles, for he appears to be acting as an individual healer. Yet, remember that this is a *'we'* passage, and therefore Dr Luke himself was present and would have played a greater part in it all than he himself acknowledges.

Again it is strange that no preaching is mentioned. Perhaps his approach was different because previously he had been dealing with city folk who had been in contact with Greek culture and Jewish religion, whereas these were people referred to by Luke as 'barbarians', with whom one had to start from scratch. However one point stands out for us: *The account of the healing of Publius's father is the only time when we come across the mention of both prayer and the laying-on of hands for healing.*

We have noted that in the cases of Lazarus and Dorcas there was prayer first, but no laying-on of hands. All the other cases of healing are notable for the way in which Jesus and his apostles moved straight in, for the prayer-power had already been gathered in the *koinonia* of the Upper Room or wherever it was that they gathered. All that was needed therefore was to give expression to that prayer-power.

Yet here we find a procedure familiar to us: 'prayer and the laying-on of hands'. The actual words of the prayer are not given us in this case. The sentence finishes with 'cured him'.

The outcome, for a change, is a happy one. So often Jesus told those healed, 'Say nothing,' yet they blabbed and caused trouble, or conversely in Nazareth (Ch. 6) and in Chapters 12 and 19 the reaction was hostility.

CONCLUSION

- We have found an example of 'prayer and the laying-on of hands' at last!

And that is the last healing work in the New Testament.

GENERAL REFERENCES TO HEALING IN ACTS

There are, of course, a number of references to healing in Acts and each one tells us something.

The koinonia (Acts 2:43 and 4:32–5) We have referred to these passages a number of times, for they stress the close connection between the *koinonia* of the Upper Room and the work of healing.

An example of prayer (Acts 4:30) This is part of a prayer and it shows us the place which healing had in the mind of the early Church.

The Temple (Acts 5:15ff) Here we have the interesting information that it was actually in the Temple that the apostles worked at first. The story goes on to describe the 'shadow healing' to which we have already referred in Chapter 32.

The other Simon (Acts 8:6–7) This is part of the story of Philip referred to in Chapter 33. The healing is very definitely linked with the proclaiming of the Gospel. Note the reference to the demons coming out with shrieks, as in Mark 1:21–28 (Ch. 13).

Peter's sermon (Acts 10:38) Here, in Peter's sermon, we have one of the few recorded references to Jesus' healing work by the apostles. You will observe that Peter assumes that Cornelius knows about what Jesus did, and does not need to spell it out.

Signs and wonders (Acts 19:11–12) We looked at this when we considered 'take-away healing' (Ch. 32), so that all we note here is the strong connection between the lectures, the arguments, the preaching of the Gospel and the healing. Paul's priority is trying to convince them who Jesus is, with the signs and wonders backing up what he said.

We have already come across most of these passages, but it is interesting to look at them together, in order to get the overall impression. Nothing emerges that we have not already said, but a number of points are reinforced.

40. THE THORN IN THE FLESH

(2 Cor. 12:7–9)

We cannot leave St. Paul, the 'wounded healer', without looking at the mystery of the 'thorn in the flesh'. He tells us that three times he prayed to be rid of it, but that the answer was: 'My grace is sufficient for you.' He accepted this affliction to counteract his pride, of which he was very conscious, and to which he alludes constantly in his letters. (It is very hard to avoid pride when you are sure of some truth. We slip so easily into an arrogant 'I'm right. You're wrong.' We may not notice the pride in ourselves, but others do.)

What was this trouble? In Scots we have a word *stab* meaning a bit of sharp wood – a fence-post for instance. It also means something painful, as in English. That word gets the meaning of the Greek word perfectly: a stab in the flesh. Nobody tackles this better than Dr John Wilkinson in *Health and Healing*, but all we are concerned with is that St Paul did not find a miraculous cure for his condition; he had to learn from it.

In fact, he finds positive meaning in his weakness, for he says (2 Cor. 12:9), 'I will boast of my weakness for then the power of Christ will pitch his tent over me.' I cannot find a translation which has that tent image, but it is there in the Greek. And remember that Paul was tentmaker to trade. Remember too what we noted when we looked at his visit to Lystra (Ch. 34). It might have been his thorn in the flesh which made it essential that he go up to the cooler air, or it might have been something else. Whatever it was, the answer was not 'prayer' but a change of climate.

He was not the only one not to be healed. In his letters he mentions that his fellow-worker Epaphroditus (Philippians 2:25–30) had been so ill that he nearly died, and that Trophimus (2 Timothy 4:20) had been too unwell to travel with St Paul. Furthermore it seems that his young friend Timothy (2 Timothy 5:23) was having stomach troubles, and St Paul does not suggest the laying-on of hands for him, but that he take a little wine with his water – a very sensible bit of advice!

So it seems that even in those early days when there were many wonderful healings, some ordinary Christians were ill and had to get better by normal means, although no doubt helped by prayer. This is still our experience today, and many, if not all, of those involved with the ministry of healing have had to go to the doctor like anybody else. Indeed it is not surprising, for if becoming a Christian were a guarantee of good health, people would become Christian for the wrong reason. God seeks to win our love through the Gospel, not as an indulgent parent who hands out goodies on request to people who toe the line.

CONCLUSION

- Beware of people who preach inspiring sermons suggesting that, if we only believed all the right things, we would be perfectly healthy.

Summary ST PAUL'S MINISTRY

What, then, do we learn from St Paul about the Church's Ministry of Healing? We cannot deduce much from his letters, for they were written to deal with specific problems which had arisen in specific churches and therefore they do not give a balanced view of what he taught, especially to those new to the message of Jesus..

Acts has given us more clues, but we note that there is only the vaguest mention of healing in the summaries of Paul's sermons. On the other hand, it is made clear that healing is done as a by-product of the preaching. Of course, St Paul must have included stories of Jesus' healing work when he was developing the life of the new Christian communities; and remember that two of the Gospel writers, Mark and Luke, were both Paul's 'trainees' at one time or another, who would have reflected their teacher's line to some extent when they wrote their Gospels. However, we must confine ourselves to what is actually said, and not guess too much about what is not.

CONCLUSIONS

- Paul's main, passionate concern was with the new relationship with God made possible through Christ, and the new relationship between people resulting from that.
- This is a balance that we too must keep, never letting 'healing' creep into the top place.
- We must therefore be very careful and prayerful before we organise 'healing services' or 'healing centres'. *The Gospel must be the focal point in everything.*

41. THE REST OF THE NEW TESTAMENT

We are still left with quite a lot of the New Testament that does not derive from Paul. Since the earliest centuries scholars have debated which letters were actually St Paul's and which were not. The discussion continues. We, however, are not concerned with who wrote what, but with what the letters say about healing, whoever wrote them.

As already referred to, there is a passing mention of healing in Galatians 3:5 and in 1 Corinthians 12. Also, as we have noted already, we find references to Trophimus and Epaphroditus as being very ill, and Timothy being advised to take a little wine with his water, all of which suggest that Christians had illnesses like everybody else. Then, of course, there is Paul's thorn in the flesh.

However, the fact is that the letters and Revelation say very little, with one surprising exception.

St James

The tradition is that the Epistle of St James was written by 'James, the Lord's brother'. It is a very practical book. It is all about conduct, and there is little of the theology which we find in all the other epistles. How surprising then that it is the one to bring in healing. James gives instruction to church members that if they are ill, they should send for the elders of the church, who should pray over the patient, and anoint with oil for healing.

Anointing with oil

Anointing with oil is mentioned in Mark 6:13 (Ch. 26) as being what the disciples did when Jesus sent them on a mission. However, as previously pointed out, there is no mention of Jesus anointing with oil, although he did anoint with spit (Ch. 11). Remember what we said about it there.

Notes on anointing
The initiative should come from the patient, or from those concerned. The agents of healing are those who are leading members of the *koinonia*, not necessarily 'healers'. As in other spheres of healing, some people seem to have a special aptitude for anointing, while others do not. We know that in the early Church people used to take home oil from the lamps in the place of worship,

in order to anoint members of their families when they were ill. There was no sign of the use of this oil being a function of priests or suchlike. It was only later that it became specialised as a safeguard against misuse.

Another vital point is that what is commended is prayer *over* the patient, not *for* the patient – literally 'the prayer of the faith'. That is to say, it is a confident invocation of the power of the Lord, not a pathetic plea to the Lord for help. Confession is mentioned but the connection is not clear. Some would say that there is a direct connection between the verses on healing and the command to confess.

If there is, we note that this instruction is concerned with what to do if members of the *koinonia* fall ill; it is not instruction in healing in evangelism, which is the setting of most New Testament healings. We have already seen that Jesus and his disciples were notable because they did not take the moralistic line.

Perhaps those who are Christian are required to look at the possibility that the cause of their illness lies in themselves, in a way that the 'lost sheep' are not. More is asked of the children of the house than of visitors!

CONCLUSION

- Anointing is a sacrament of healing, not the 'last rites'.

  (Note that in the Roman Catholic Church anointing has been reinstated as a sacrament of healing, and is no longer the 'last rites'.)

SECTION THREE

Looking back on it all

IN CONCLUSION

At this point the reader might well expect a summary of summaries, a conclusion of conclusions. However I am tempted to leave several blank pages for the reader to 'DIY'. After all, it is your conclusion which matters, and that may be different from mine!

There is, however, one impression I would share. Having gone over these works in detail, I am impressed by the variety of our Lord's response to those who needed healing. I do not think that any of the Gospel writers could have made up such stories, and therefore a greater Mind than the storytellers' lies behind it all. I am sure that if they had been making it up, there would have been far more emphasis on the laying-on of hands, since, as we have noted, this was the expected thing.

At the human level, I do not think that the Gospel-writers understood a lot of what they reported. They were guided to pass on what they had received and that was all that was asked of them. Comparing the different versions of any one story, you realise that both, or all three, point to something far beyond themselves.

In the light of this, I am convinced that the healing miracles really did happen, and were not made up for propaganda purposes. As I mentioned in the Introduction, I began by accepting the moral teaching of Jesus, but relegating the miracles to the realm of fairy story. Study and experience have changed my mind. I believe that Jesus did heal, and that he meant us to heal too.

So much for my impression. How about yours? You may have enjoyed reading this book, and have agreed with some parts and disagreed with others. But would it not be a good idea to sit down and work out what it really means for you?

And talking of your reactions...

We have become used to the 'TV mentality'. One programme follows another without any time for reflection. Nothing really sinks in to the extent that it makes a difference. That tends to affect everything. Having read something, or having heard a sermon, we just move on to the next thing without really absorbing the message. Therefore a time of reflection is needed:

- when you can clarify your own picture of Jesus,
- when you review your understanding of the Gospel,
- when you can think about your attitude to the suffering in the world,
- when you can be open to what God is saying deep down within you,
- and when you can face what it might all mean for you in action as an individual, as a member of your church.

Inevitably I will have some things wrong, and you will perhaps be able to learn from my mistakes. Very often, in fact, it is what we disagree with that makes us think and grow, whereas what we agree with slips past us and is lost.

However...

The first people to read the manuscript of this book made comments which led me to feel that I needed to emphasise one or two of the conclusions I had come to in the course of writing. A section dealing with these follows.

42. TECHNIQUES

One surprising thing about the New Testament is that in spite of there being so many stories of healing, there is no teaching about it. The laying-on of hands is mentioned, but there is no instruction on how to do it. Does one lay hands on the head or on the afflicted part? Does one leave them on for some time, or is it just a touch? Apart from the incidents mentioned in the two stories we studied (Chs. 11 and 12) there is not a word to help us. It is the same with anointing. Does one pour sweet-smelling oil liberally over the sufferer in Middle-Eastern fashion or just smear olive oil on the forehead? We are not given any instruction on these matters.

Another strange thing is that there is no example of Jesus dealing with somebody with depression, or with ordinary mental illness, even though in our day these are the most common problems with which we are faced. There is no practical guide as to how to deal with such people. In these and in so many ways the New Testament leaves us groping.

We are promised that the Holy Spirit will lead us into all truth, and we just have to get on with it. Faith always launches us out into the deep, and it is a lack of faith if we want to be experts in some technique before we feel ready to launch out.

Signs and wonders confirming the Word

The fact is that New Testament healing is the work of the Holy Spirit, and is a sign to reinforce the preaching of the Word. It is as we are open to the Spirit that healing flows. It is not necessary to have techniques of healing if one is being guided by the Spirit. Of course, the original disciples spent time with Jesus watching how he did it. They saw how he laid on hands and watched him dealing with people. To some extent they did learn by observation and by taking part in his work. And that goes for us too. We remain disciples – 'trainees' – and we will always have spiritual L-plates as well as crosses hanging round our necks.

Other levels

Of course if people work at the medical, psychological or psychic levels they have a responsibility to develop the most effective techniques. In New Testament healing, however, there is only openness to the Spirit. As we thus develop, becoming more sensitive to the Spirit's guidance, we shall be guided on each occasion as to what to do. The point is made by Martin Israel with his dual background as priest and doctor. He tells that when he sits with a patient as a medical man, his mind is going over how he treated people with these symptoms before, what he has read about them and so on. However, when he sits down with somebody as a priest, his mind must be quite clear, with complete openness to God and to the patient.

The tool-rack

However, the Holy Spirit is not an excuse for laziness. There *is* a learning process, too, for us. We are expected to get to know our Bibles so that we can refer easily to passages which would be relevant. We must meditate on the stories of Jesus, as we have done in this book, so that they become part of us. We may indeed learn from those who are more experienced in the ministry, but it is as we become simpler, more loving and more sensitive that we can expect an increase in signs to accompany the preaching of the Word.

Yet all this is secondary. Compare it with a tool-rack. I must ensure that the rack of my mind is stocked with 'tools' which the Spirit can lift off to use in any particular case. Yet the initiative is always with the Spirit, and it is God who heals, not us.

Therefore it is the Holy Spirit who will guide us as to where to lay hands and how long to keep them on. The moment we think we have the know-how, we fall back to the level of psychic or psychological healing.

Fashions

There are many books that try to make good the Bible's 'omission'. They attempt to describe the techniques. Often they do contain valuable insights, but they cannot show us how to continue the work which Jesus began. We find people with a special slant, for instance 'giving thanks in everything', 'healing the family tree', 'inner healing', 'Christian listening'. They write books giving examples of how this technique has healed so many.

Well-meaning people then read these books and try out the techniques on everybody who comes along, often with disastrous results. It becomes a sort of spiritual fashion until the next trend surfaces. We may well learn something from each of these methods, but if we stick to the basic New Testament emphasis, we shall not be led astray by the fashions which come our way.

Healing is by the Name of Jesus – his Authority, in the power of the Spirit. We respect those who are called to heal at the other levels, such as doctors and nurses, and at times we shall find ourselves looking to them for help. If we are called by God to serve at one of these levels, then we must do so with all our hearts and minds and strength. Yet, as I have stressed repeatedly throughout this book, if we are to preach the Gospel with 'signs and wonders', it is not a matter of techniques, but of love for God and for each other.

43. The Word of Authority

While looking at the story of the nobleman's son (Ch. 16) we tried to define 'the Word of Authority', but many people still find this puzzling, and understandably so, for little is said about it in sermons or in books on healing. Therefore, before closing the book, perhaps we should sum up what we have seen.

Remember some of the Words: 'Your sins are forgiven.' 'Pick up your kip and away home with you!' *'Talitha cumi.'* 'Your son lives.' 'You have been released from your weakness.' 'Stretch out your hand.' 'Lazarus, come on out.' 'He rebuked the fever.' 'Be muzzled (Shut up!).' These are either commands, or statements of fact as to what has already been done at the spiritual level. They are not spoken with impressive 'biblical' language, in fact the very reverse. Sometimes, but not always, when spoken by an apostle or disciple, they are preceded by 'In the Name of Jesus'.

While there are many examples of the Word being spoken to the suffering, there are no examples of Jesus or the early Christians *asking* God to heal somebody. Where prayer is involved it is an opening of oneself to be used by God in the work of healing. This is then followed by giving expression to what has been received from God.

True authority

We cannot stress too often that there is nothing authoritarian about the Word of Authority. No amount of posturing or posing, dressing up or dramatic gestures can give us authority to speak in Jesus' Name. No church can ensure that whenever we speak, we say the words that he would speak. There is no magic formula, no mystification, and no question of 'getting the right words'. Remember, once again, that the only two examples we have in Jesus' own language are both very earthy and commonplace. There is no equivalent to 'a spell' in which it is important to get the words right, and which can be passed on to initiates.

Above all there is no authority *over* the sufferer, only *for* him/her. Beware of those who use imposing rituals or who work up emotions by hypnotic music and overpowering preaching. Always suspect any 'healer' or preacher who requires a lot of noise! It is a way of saying, 'I have power over you, and I will manipulate your emotions.' (cf. Isaiah 42)

How do we learn to speak the Word of Authority?

The Beatitudes point the way (Matthew 5:1ff). First we must face our own spiritual weakness, our inability to help people ('poor in spirit'). Having done so, it is tempting to fall back on gaining more head-knowledge about healing, but this is not the way, even if a certain amount is needed. The main area of growth is in growing simpler.

That brings us to the next stage: being broken down by compassion for the suffering ('they that grieve'). Going through these two stages, we find that a lot of our little private agendas dissolve and we become more sensitive to what God wants ('the meek'). Lesser ambitions and fears are swallowed up in a great passion for *rightness*, true health, in oneself and in the world ('hunger and thirst for rightness').Then we no longer play games such as 'being a healer' or 'being a successful minister'; rather we see people with a deep understanding ('merciful'). It is this single-mindedness ('pure in heart') which enables us to see God and hear God without 'interference' from our hidden agendas. We then become the ones who bring *shalom* – that great Hebrew word which means total well-being – into the lives of those around us ('peacemakers').

The ministry of healing for ministers

It is important to realise this primacy of the Word, for the over-emphasis on the laying-on of hands has led many ministers and priests into disappointment. This is in fact what causes many to give up the whole idea. Finding that they have no particular gift in their hands, and that nothing much happens when they lay hands on people, they assume that this ministry is not for them. Yet there remains the Ministry of the Word, applying it to the specific situation of the sufferer, and this is more fundamental than the laying-on of hands. Without it the laying-on of hands should not take place.

Those of us who are ministers have had much training in how to apply the Word to a congregation in preaching and through the sacraments, but little in how to apply it to the individual in a person-to-person setting. Yet the 'Ministry of Healing' is only a matter of applying to an individual what has been given to the congregation as a whole. It is the lack of this personal application which is the weakness of most congregations. People come into a church and go out again without any in-depth *personal* application of the Word to their inner lives. They are expected to apply what has been said to themselves, but very few actually do so. *In fact you will probably only see what the Word really means for you by sharing it in the* koinonia, *even if that consists of no more than one other person who really understands the Gospel and you.*

Therefore, those who are not aware of a gift in their hands should concentrate on applying the Word to individuals, and see where it leads them. They may well find that on occasion, in the right setting, the laying-on of hands 'works' even for them. They may also find that their ministry is as partner to somebody who does have that gift in their hands.

If a person's concern is sincere, and if they have a real love for the Lord and true compassion for the suffering, then a ministry will emerge for them around the Word. It will be a distinctive ministry.

The gift

If you *do* find that you have the gift of healing in your hands, then beware of using it when it is not subject to the Word, in the *koinonia* of God's people. Again the warning: *Beware of doing a solo act!*

The steps in ministry

As a rough guide (knowing that the Spirit never obeys the rules we make!) one can observe three steps in the Church's ministry. A spiritually sensitive person can cover them all in seconds; others may take hours or days.

Step 1. Sit beside It is right that we should be like those in Mark 2 (Ch. 1) who brought their paralysed friend to Jesus. We too 'bring' our friends and families to him in prayer. We begin by establishing a real understanding between the sufferer and ourselves. To put it as a picture: we sit *beside* the sufferer in order to listen.

Step 2. Kneel beside We express his/her cry to the Lord. Our words may be short and sharp, but they must do two things. They must express the deep feelings of the sufferer. They must convey a real loving faith in God. The tone of voice and the body language are more important than the actual words. It does not matter if your prayer has bad grammar, or if you hesitate or stumble, so long as love for the person and love for God come through the words. That is not something which you can force. Either it is there or it is not there. What matters is that we speak to God in the name of the sufferer, perhaps saying things which he or she could not say.

Step 3. Stand in the Name of Jesus We wait beside the person until a Bible verse or picture comes to our minds. Then we *stand up* and speak to the sufferer in the Name of Jesus in terms of the Word which has come to us, expressing the Word with whatever may seem the right actions. We must be very careful not to begin to speak in Jesus' Name if we do not in fact have the inward assurance that what we say is from him – that is to say we must not take the Lord's Name in vain.

We must only speak in this way if we are very sure that this is what God is saying, not what our theory of healing says. We may perhaps only have authority to speak words of reassurance and love, in which case we must not go beyond that.

The live line

All this assumes that the line between God and us is *live*, and one hopes there is no need to stress again that this depends on the depth of the *koinonia* of which we are a part. Of course, each of us as an individual must have the live line, but all the promises of answered prayer are addressed to *you* in the plural: 'Whatever *you* ask in my Name', etc. It is not the numbers that count, it is the quality of the *koinonia*. (John 15:16–17)

Nobody is infallible

Of course, we all get it wrong sometimes. I can think of a number of cases in which I moved in too fast, on the basis on *my* faith, and realised later that I should have built up the person's faith in Jesus a lot more before moving on to step two. Remember how Jesus took people aside, building up the relationship with them (Chs. 8 and 11). I think of other cases in which I allowed myself to be pressurised into laying on hands when I should have done something else. This happens only too easily if one takes part in a 'healing service'.

Getting it wrong

I was impressed that John Wimber, the very high-pressure American evangelist/healer, stressed that of course we all make mistakes and get things wrong in the healing ministry, and 'if you are afraid to make mistakes, don't start!'

The learning process

We all do have to learn painfully and carefully to move beyond the asking stage to giving expression to the Word. The degree to which we can effectively do so depends on our being 'in tune' with God's purposes as revealed in Jesus. Unfortunately most of us have so many little 'hidden agendas', selfish pre-occupations and buried resentments that our authority to speak in Jesus' Name leaks away.

Once more: no matter how long we have been in this ministry, we are always disciples. We always have our spiritual L-plates on; we are never completely Christ-like.

SUMMARY

- The Christian ministry of healing happens when we bring the creative, healing love of God to bear on a person, as Jesus' representative (in his Name), speaking the Word of Authority.
- Praying *for* people is the background for the healing ministry, and on occasion is all that is needed, but usually it is only the first step.
- The Word of Authority we speak must be simple, short, loving and not necessarily 'religious' or impressive.
- We may use many actions, applying our hands, anointing with oil, etc., but only when in and through these actions we are expressing the Word of God.
- Although the true Authority flows from the *koinonia*, it is usually expressed by 'two or three in his Name'. One of these is often an ordained minister.
- Ideally our prayer-life as a *koinonia* of the Holy Spirit should be such that long prayers are not needed when we are with the patient. A great show of religion, religiousness and religiosity is a sign of weakness, not of strength.
- Any technique or form of worship which seeks to establish power *over* people has no authority from God. It is 'taking God's Name in vain'. Any miracles resulting from such 'services' are likely to do more harm than good in the long run.
- We grow in the ability to heal in Jesus' Name not by boosting our self-confidence (disguised as faith) nor by learning more techniques, but by learning to be more utterly dependent on God and by strengthening the *koinonia*.

44. HOW DO YOU UNDERSTAND PRAYER?

All New Testament prayer begins with some variation of 'Abba', 'Father'. It never begins 'Almighty God'. We never have to attract Abba's attention, he is trying to attract ours. We do not need to persuade God to be interested and concerned in the person and situation we are praying about. It is we who need to be sensitive to what God wants done in the situation, and to channel God's power and love into it.

Realising all that, we have to work out a better concept of prayer.

The triangle of prayer

How then does it work out in practice? The usual idea of prayer is that it is like a triangle: I look up to God asking for help for X. I hope God will look down on X and heal him. That picture of prayer makes *me* the initiator, trying to persuade God to do the right thing, but that is all. *It is pretty insulting to God!*

If, however, Jesus is God's own self-portrait, God's ikon (Coloss. 1:15), then that is not the right picture of prayer. Let us change it a bit. I look up to and open myself to God on behalf of X. The Holy Spirit flows into me to heal X. I pass it on to X by word and action.

Of course, in both cases there is another side to the triangle: the link between X and God. That is not my business. When we look at it this way we see that what is in question is not God's willingness to act today as he did through Jesus, but rather how open we are to the Holy Spirit in order to be able to speak and act with God's Authority.

45. BIBLICAL MEDITATION

Another question I have been asked is: 'How do you get all that out of these stories, most of which we have heard dozens of times before?'

Let us have a look at how to go about it, realising that in the long run it is something personal between the Lord and you, and no system can *make* it happen.

In this form of meditation there are three main steps: *intellect, imagination, stillness.* It is perhaps easiest to think in terms of television: How would you go about preparing a scene in a play showing Jesus performing a healing work?

Intellect

You first gather all the information you can about the incident. For instance: What is the scenery? What is the background of the characters taking part? What is known about the disease being healed? Having some idea of the scenery is important. For example, take the first healing at which we looked in this book, the boy let down through the roof. We commented at the time on how important it is to get the picture of the house right.

At this stage one may consult commentaries such as William Barclay's notes, or even my own book *Growing Knowing Jesus*.[10] However one has to remember that while scholars who write commentaries often know a lot about scholarly things, they very often have very little experience of actual healing 'in the field'.

It may also help us to imagine the incident accurately if we have some idea as to the medical background of the case. John Wilkinson's book *Health and Healing* is invaluable here.

We may well look at different translations of the New Testament, noting the differences, and seeing which one gives the most vivid picture.

Then, of course, we search our own experience for similar examples, or note examples we have come across while reading or while listening to people who do have experience.

In this way we assemble the scenery and characters, getting ready to produce the 'play'.

---

[10] Published by St Andrew Press, now out of print.

Imagination

Now 'the play begins' as we start to imagine the scene, looking at it perhaps from the point of view of one of Jesus' followers, or perhaps even from the point of view of the person who was healed. Remember the story at the end of Chapter 22.

Stillness

As the 'picture' fades, for instance as you 'see' the sufferer going on his way rejoicing, you are left in the presence of Jesus, perhaps sitting quietly at his feet, waiting to see if he has anything to say to you.

When the stillness is over, you should have a little more love for God in Christ, a little more understanding of yourself, a little more light to give the world. So sing a hymn of thanksgiving.

The use of imagination

Our ability to imagine things is one of our greatest gifts. It can either help us to come to grips with reality, or, getting it wrong, provide us with an escape from reality. In this form of meditation our concern has been to use imagination to explore reality in order that we may better serve our Lord, and be of more use to suffering humanity.

The more deeply we are committed to following him, the more likely it is that we will have experiences which help us to 'see' what actually happened.

Earth and aerial

To put it another way: each of us needs both an aerial and an earth. If I have developed a terrific aerial soaring up to heaven but am not deeply earthed in the realities of human life, then I become a dreamer – a spiritual crank, even mentally ill.

If I am deeply immersed in human suffering and misery, but have no aerial reaching up to tune in to the Word of God, I will have nothing much to give. In fact, I may find that the world gets me down rather than that I lift it up!

Biblical meditation as outlined above requires, then, both earth and aerial. We must be earthed in the sufferings of humanity in the Name of Jesus, and we must have our aerial linking us with heaven as part of a praying, learning, serving fellowship, tuning in to God. Without such an aerial we can get bogged down by the human situation. Without real earthiness our religion is a sham.

Of course, life is seldom as neat and tidy as the schemes we make, and this is very much the case here. Moreover, while the *intellect-imagination-stillness* scheme is basically sound, in practice it may not happen in this order. However, in a healthy spiritual life all these elements should have a place, even if sometimes the order varies.

We are to love God with our *minds*, and there is no excuse for intellectual laziness. We have to love God with all our *hearts*, for intellectualism is fatal. Beyond intellectual arguments and warm emotions we must love God in our *spirits*, which involves taking the Jesus Way, often at great cost.

Who is right? Who is wrong?

It may well be that, if you meditate on one of the works in this book, you will come up with a different picture from mine – in which case thank God.

In the spiritual life, while there are some things which are definitely *wrong*, there is no one right answer for everybody at all times. For instance, I see quite different things in the Gospels now from what I saw forty years ago, and you may see aspects which I do not. Later on you may see the Gospels differently again. There is no one right answer which will get you a gold star!

That is why we must be careful to avoid getting into religious arguments in which we take the line: 'I am right and you are wrong.' The old enemy loves to get Christians at each other's throats like that. If I see one truth, and you see a different one, we should both explore the possibilities in the other's point of view, look for where the lines converge, and then leave the other to sort out their own truth.

CONCLUSION

All this boils down to the fact that you, good reader, if you have not done so already, have an exciting discovery to make:

- these stories of Jesus' healings are for real,
- Jesus is for real,
- so is the suffering of humanity around you,
- and you have to *do* something about it.

What your life is about, from now on, is your response to Jesus and to the world around you. But in the meantime, spoil yourself! Treat yourself to the luxury of a quiet hour or so a week when you can settle down and do some biblical meditation, and see where it leads you.

EPILOGUE

Let us end with a biblical meditation on the Last Supper. It was probably in a domed room, with a round or U-shaped central table. Around the table would be divans, and each man would lie, leaning on the table with his left elbow, feeding from the central dish with his right hand. We gather that John was lying in front of Jesus, and Peter was in front of him. Their feet would be over the edge of the divans, so that it would be quite easy for Jesus to go round washing them. Judas Iscariot was lying behind Jesus, close enough for Jesus to speak to him without the others hearing.

This, of course, is not the conventional picture of the Last Supper, but it is the way in which the Jews dined, and it makes sense of a lot of details in the story which are puzzling if you think that they were all sitting on chairs at a western-type table. I offer here a free rendering of the story, and the reader would do well to look up St John's Gospel, chapters 13 and 14, to see the original.

The Last Supper

They had been reduced to a shattered silence as Jesus put on his robe again, and lay down again in his place at the table. For him to wash their feet…! It was unthinkable. Even a Jewish slave would not be asked to do such a dirty, humiliating job as that.

'You call me LORD…and quite rightly, for that is what I am. But if I, your LORD, do the menial job of washing your filthy feet, then you must do likewise. There is to be no master-servant relationship among you.'

No wonder they looked uneasy. Not long before, the brothers John and James had tried to book their places as Prime Minister and Chancellor of the Exchequer when Jesus became king – the places on a king's right and left hand. There had been a flaming row about orders of precedence, and it is obvious that the twelve still thought fondly about how they were going to be top-dog at last when Jesus came into his own. They had wondered at the time what Jesus had meant when he said grimly that the places on his right and left were already reserved. They were soon to find out.

They looked even more bewildered when Jesus went on: 'One last thing I ask of you all: Love one another. The hallmark of my disciples is love for one another. That is how people will know that you are my disciples, that you have this special love for one another. You are to love each other as I have loved you.'

'Are you going somewhere?' asked Simon Peter. There was no immediate reply. 'Where are you going? Can I not come with you?'

'Where I am going you cannot come – not yet. But you will...later.'

There was a hint of grim humour in his tone, and it brought Simon Peter scrambling to his feet: 'Why can I not come now? I'd die for you.'

Jesus' next words came out jerkily, as from somebody under great pressure. 'You'd die for me, would you? I tell you this. Tonight, before dawn-cock-crow, you will have denied me. Three times.

'Do not let that worry you, just trust God and me!

'There is room for all in my Father's house. I would have told you if there had not been.

'On the journey home, I am going ahead to get everything ready for you all, so that you can travel on with a quiet mind. At each stage of the journey, once I have the next stopping place ready, I will come back and lead you on to where I have been.

'Now, you do know where I am going and you do know the way.'

This was too much for Thomas the realist: 'Lord, this is beyond me. We do not know where you are going and so we cannot know the way there.'

'You know me, Thomas. I am the Way...the true and living Way. I'm the only way to the Father. In fact, if you know me, then you know the Father already. You have seen what the Father is like.'

There was a puzzled silence until young Philip had a bright idea: 'Just show us the Father – a real vision – that's all we want.'

'Oh Philip, have I been with you all this time and you still do not know me? When I washed your feet a few minutes ago, what do you think I was doing? I was showing you the Father. When I took you to eat and drink with people no decent folk would have anything to do with, what do you think I was doing? I was showing you the Father. When I healed the sick and cast out demons, what do you think I was doing? I was showing you the Father. In a few hours' time when you see me lifted up, I shall still be showing you the Father. See me...see the Father. How can you ask to be shown the Father after all that?'

By now they did not know where to look or what to say.

'Can't you see the Father when you look at me? Can you not see the family likeness? Are you still stuck with the old pictures of God? Has it not dawned on you that I speak with the Authority of the Father, that I am not just voicing human opinions?

'It is vital that you believe me, so that his work in the world may go on.

For the sake of that great work, will you get it into your heads that the Father and I are ONE. The Son is the very image of the Father and does the Father's work, and this work that I have been doing, you are to go on doing, and you are to do greater work than I ever did.'

Poor Philip wilted and the rest just gaped.

Perhaps one day the truth will actually dawn – on Philip, on Peter, on Thomas…on you, on me.

Then

> The love of God will at last pour through our broken hearts,
> The power of God will finally radiate through our wounds,
> We shall know that we are on the Way,
> and the whole of creation will sing for joy.

That will be the Day!

ANALYSIS OF HEALING IN THE GOSPELS

The numbers refer to chapters

Presenting symptom
Blindness 2, 9, 22
Leprosy 20, 21
Paralysis 1, 3, 19
Deaf/dumbness 8, 15, 18
Fever & unspecified illness 5, 7, 10
Death 23, 24, (? 10)
Injury (? 19), 28
Assorted illnesses: Dropsy 17, Haemorrhage 4
Congenital 2, (8?)
Neurotic element 1, 3, 29

Initiative
The initiative with the Lord 2, 3, 12, 17, 19
The initiative with patient 4, 9, 13, 14, 20, 21, 22
The initiative with others on behalf of patient 1, 5, 7, 8, 10, 11, 15, 24

Treatment
Touch (but not the 'laying-on of hands') 2, 7, 8, 9, 17, 20, 23, 25
Laying-on of hands referred to 6, 11, 12, 25.
The laying-on of hands requested 8, 10, 11,
Healings which mention anointing with spit 2, 8, 11
Healings which mention Jesus' Word of Authority 1, 2, 3, 4, 5, 7, 8, 9, 10, 11, 12, 13, 14, 15, 16, 17, 18, 19, 20, 21, 22, 23, 24, 28
Distant healing 5, 16
Exorcism 15, 16, 17, 18, 25
Inner healing 1, 3, 12

Environment
Hostile environment 1, 6, 10, 12, 13, 16, 17, 19
Positive environment 7, 10, 24 (the rest are either mixed or doubtful).

References to:
Faith 1, 4, 5, 6, 9, 10, 15, 18, 24 (lack of faith: 6)
Sin 1, 2, 3
Follow-up 2, 3, 21, 22 (supposed), 24 (Also Mary of Magdala)

Analysis of healing in Acts

The numbers refer to chapters

Presenting symptom
Congenital problems 30, 36
Paralysis 31
Blindness 35
Demonic 33, 34, 37
Injury 34, 38, 39
Illness 34, 39
Death 32, (? 38)
Inner healing 35

Initiative
Initiative with apostles 30, 31, 36, 38
    with disciples 32
    with others 37, 39
    with the Lord himself 35

Treatment
Laying-on of hands 35
Laying-on of hands with prayer 39
Hands used 30, 31, 32, 39
Word of Authority 29, 30, 31, 33, 34, 35

Who ministered?
One to one 33, (? 36)
'Two or three together' 34, 35, 36, 37, 39
As part of the *koinonia* 31, 32, (? 34 part 2), 36, (? 37), 38

Environment
Public 29, 32, 34, 35, 36 (second half)
In the setting of the *koinonia* 30, 31, (? 37)
In private 33, 36

Other books on **HEALING** *from Wild Goose Publications*

PRAYERS AND IDEAS
FOR HEALING SERVICES
Ian Cowie

The author of *Jesus' Healing Works and Ours* draws on his decades of experience to provide a complete guide to healing ministry which combines sound practical advice with conviction, refreshing realism and compassion. Among other topics he discusses:

The Iona Community and healing ● Should we have healing services?
Are healing services biblical? ● The individualistic or corporate approach?
Healing or blessing? ● The form of service ● Patterns of ministry
Preparation for those taking part ● The gift of 'discernment'
Physical healing gifts ● The 'gift of knowledge' ● The 'touching place'
People who come forward for healing ● Anointing
Those who have been healed ● Those who have not been healed
Counselling and follow-up ● A welcoming family or 'spiritual scalp-hunting'?

Resources include:

A possible order of service ● Prayers for blessing and for healing
Prayers based on the Celtic pattern and prayers of guided silence for:
approach ● confession ● intercession ● invocation
the healing of relationships ● thanksgiving and homegoing

1995 · 0 947988 72 6 · £6.99

Other books on **HEALING** *from Wild Goose Publications*

PRAYING FOR THE DAWN
A Resource Book for
the Ministry of Healing
Ruth Burgess & Kathy Galloway (eds)

A compilation of material from several writers, with a strong emphasis on liturgies and resources for healing services. Many aspects of healing are addressed, including

*The Church's healing ministry ● The Iona Community service of prayers for healing
Justice as healing ● The National Health Service and the health of the nation
The healing of Northern Ireland ● The memory of brokenness
To die healed ● The laying on of hands*

Some of the liturgies featured:
*A service of prayers for healing and the laying on of hands ● Keeping the Earth
beautiful: a service of creation and healing for all ages ● An order of prayer for
people with chronic illness ● For those facing serious illness ● Service for all souls
Liturgy for carers*

Includes a section on how to introduce healing services to those who may not be familiar with them, and suggestions for starting group discussions about healing. The book is rounded off by a section of worship resources – prayers, responses, litanies, poems, meditations and blessings.

2000 · 1 901557 26 X · £9.99 approx.

*If you would like to be added to the Wild Goose Publications mailing list to receive
our catalogue, please contact us at*

Wild Goose Publications
Unit 16, Six Harmony Row
Glasgow G51 3BA
Tel 0141 440 0985   Fax 0141 440 2338
e-mail: admin@wgp.iona.org.uk

Wild Goose Publications is part of

The Iona Community

The Iona Community is an ecumenical Christian community, founded in 1938 by the late Lord MacLeod of Fuinary (the Revd George MacLeod DD) and committed to seeking new ways of living the Gospel in today's world. Gathered around the rebuilding of the ancient monastic buildings of Iona Abbey, but with its original inspiration in the poorest areas of Glasgow during the Depression, the Community has sought ever since the 'rebuilding of the common life', bringing together work and worship, prayer and politics, the sacred and the secular in ways that reflect its strongly incarnational theology.

The Community today is a movement of over 230 Members, around 1,500 Associate Members and about 700 Friends. The Members – women and men from many backgrounds and denominations, most in Britain, but some overseas – are committed to a rule of daily prayer and Bible reading, sharing and accounting for their use of time and money, regular meeting and action for justice and peace.

The Iona Community maintains three centres on Iona and Mull: Iona Abbey and the MacLeod Centre on Iona, and Camas Adventure Camp on the Ross of Mull. Its base is in Community House, Glasgow, where it also supports work with young people, the Wild Goose Resource and Worship Groups, a bimonthly magazine (*Coracle*) and a publishing house (Wild Goose Publications).

For further information on the Iona Community please contact:

The Iona Community
Pearce Institute,
840 Govan Road
Glasgow G51 3UU
T. 0141 445 4561; F. 0141 445 4295
e-mail: ionacomm@gla.iona.org.uk